"If you are looking for inspiration to go on an epic, rollercoaster of an adventure, read this book. Kristen does a charismatic job of making a grueling bikepack trip seem like a casual walk in the park. The kind of park that is beautiful yet has torrential downpours, sickeningly steep hills and goes from one end of the globe to the other. It is in between these cyclical episodes that Kristen shares her and Ville's optimistic interactions with humanity."

—TOMMY FORD, U.S. Ski Team, Three-time Olympian, Nine-time National Champion, Team World Champion

"Full of hijinks and heartbreak, *Joy Ride* is a celebration of the human spirit, an entertaining journey about the lengths we can and will go to live our lives fully, deeply, triumphantly. It takes a special kind of person to drop everything to ride your bike thousands of miles. It takes an extra special kind of person to then write about that journey with such humor, honesty, and humility."

—AMANDA KNOX, *Waiting to Be Heard: A Memoir*

"Fasten your seatbelts, you are in for a ride of a lifetime. What is most remarkable about Kristen and Ville Jokinen's bike trip from the top of Alaska to the tip of Argentina is not only the two years on the road, 20,000 miles ridden, the salt deserts, or the many mountain passes over 16,000 feet, but how the couples' wide open hearts led them into homes, cafes, schools from big and small towns up and down the Americas. Beginning their travels during 2016 when relations between the US and its southern neighbors were strained, readers will quickly see past the news headlines into the best human kind has to offer. The Jokinen's commitment to a life of adventure traveling the world on bicycles is a gift to all. And lucky us, I suspect the Americas are just the beginning. "

—LEE MONTGOMERY, *The Things Between Us: A Memoir*

"You could be forgiven for thinking that *Joy Ride* is a novel. The characters, Kristen and Ville, are improbable. And their journey is the kind of tale of adventure that you might invent from your breakfast nook while remaining safe and warm and stationary. But this is no novel. It just might be the inspiration for you to drop everything and live the kind of life you've only dreamed of. *Joy Ride* is warm, vivid, and unforgettable."

—CHRISTOPHER ROBINSON, *Deliver Us: A Novel*

"To read this spectacular book is to feel lucky that we, too, get to be propelled along with Kristen and Ville—two wild and kindred spirits, and what a joyous ride it is."

—CHERYL STRAYED, *Wild: From Lost to Found on the Pacific Crest Trail*

JOY RIDE

A Bike Odyssey from Alaska to Argentina

KRISTEN JOKINEN

Introduction by CHERYL STRAYED

HAWTHORNE
BOOKS & LITERARY ARTS

Copyright ©2023 Kristen Jokinen
Introduction ©2023 Cheryl Strayed

All rights reserved. No part of this book may be reproduced in any form
or by any electronic or mechanical means, including information stor-
age and retrieval systems, without prior permission in writing from the
Publisher, except for brief quotations embodied in critical articles and
reviews. For information, contact Hawthorne Books & Literary Arts,
3636 NE 45th Avenue, Portland, Oregon 97213, hawthornebooks.com

Published by Hawthorne Books & Literary Arts
Distributed by Publishers Group West

Library of Congress Cataloging-in-Publication Data is available
Library of Congress Control Number: 2023932947

First US Edition 2023
ISBN 978-0-9988257-5-5 (paperback)
ISBN 978-0-9988257-6-2 (ebook)
Printed in the USA

Interior design: Diane Chonette
Map illustrations: Paul Evers

Cover illustrations: Rawpixel, iStock

Author's Note

To write this book, I relied upon my personal journals, notes, blog, and Ville's memory when mine was foggy. Dates, roads, and border crossings tend to fade into one another after so many hours on a bike seat. I have changed the names of most but not all the individuals in this book. Many people and events have been omitted due to book length.

For all the people who helped, supported, followed, and loved us along the way. Without you we would never have made it.

And for my companjera, Ville. Minä rakastan sinua.

TABLE OF CONTENTS

Introduction

There was so much working against Kristen and Ville Jokinen when they decided to travel 18,215 miles from Alaska to Argentina on bicycles that were neither fancy nor particularly fitting. The weather. The terrain. The staggering distance. The grim realization that they didn't know how to adjust something called a derailleur, which apparently you need to know if you intend to pedal from the Arctic Ocean to the Antarctic Ocean while going up and over an endless number of mountain ranges in between.

Oh, and there's also the fact that they'd barely ridden their bikes twenty miles before they set out on a journey that would take them two years.

Despite all of this, set out, they did. Into the cold and the heat, the mud and the snow, the scorching sun and unrelenting wind and endless unknown. They biked through remote landscapes where they encountered black bears and wild pigs and too many dogs bent on attacking them to count. They rode through vast cities where the traffic and exhaust fumes and blaring clammer of human existence rattled them to their bones and sometimes off their bicycles.

And all along the way, wherever they went, they met people who helped them. Cops and children and truck drivers. Farmers and priests and women who made sweets they sold on the street. As Kristen and Ville pedaled their way along the fathomless length of two continents, they were offered food and shelter and rides and conversations that showed them that the true clammer of human existence isn't traffic jams, but generosity and connection.

There is so much that is epic about *Joy Ride*—the enormous distance and the difficult terrain the Jokinens traversed—but the truly epic story at the center of this book is about the kindness of strangers. They never stopped being surprised by it, though it happened again and again. The ease with which they connected with people across divides of language, class, culture, religion, and lifestyle became like a steady wind at their backs. It propelled them as powerfully onward as their own strong bodies did.

To read this book is to feel lucky that we, too, get to be propelled along with Kristen and Ville—two wild and kindred spirits, who are astonishingly well-matched travel companions.

The best travel memoirs reveal to readers the ever-shifting landscape of the outer world the protagonists pass through and the inner world of the ever-deepening ways the journey changes them and Kristen Jokinen delivers beautifully on that in *Joy Ride*. With candor and humor, writes not only about the spectacular landscapes and amazing people she and Ville met on their grand adventure, but also about the ways the trip enlightened, challenged, and transformed her ideas about herself and the world. In her quietly heroic dedication to keep going even when she struggled, even when she suffered, even when she thought she couldn't do it because it was just too hard, Kristen showed us the power of the most humble sort of perseverance—the kind that happens step by step, pedal by pedal, breath by breath.

On their bicycle trip, the Jokinens had to grapple with many of the hardest things that every one of us must grapple with in life at one point or another, whether we ever get on a bike or not. How to find the strength and courage to endure the tough times. How to muster the stamina to do what needs to be done even when it hurts. How to trust ourselves to find the way eventually. How to laugh when there's nothing else to do but trust the universe.

In that way, the story of this trip becomes not only about something grand a couple of free spirits rather bravely did, but something all of us can learn from, be inspired by, take to heart. Even if we never find ourselves pedaling the distance of North and South America. This spectacular book is the story about them and us. And what a joyous ride it is.

—CHERYL STRAYED

JOY RIDE

A Bike Odyssey from Alaska to Argentina

THE ROUTE

Prudhoe
Bay

ALASKA   CANADA

UNITED STATES

MEXICO

COLOMBIA

ECUADOR

PERU   BRAZIL

CHILE

ARGENTINA

Bahía
Lapataia

PART 1

Alaska, Canada, United States

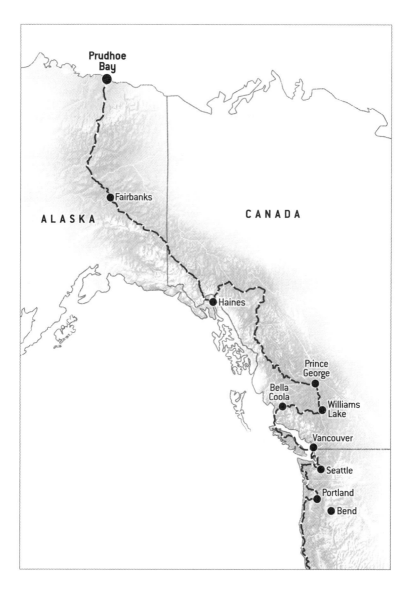

1

The Top of the World

I stepped back to survey our shiny new bikes at a bike shop in my hometown of Bend, Oregon. The bike shop manager, my friend James, had told Ville and me to tape foam, cardboard, and an assortment of hard pieces of plastic to our bikes to protect them once they were in cardboard boxes and checked as luggage on the plane that would take us to Alaska. Neither of us had any idea what parts were important enough to tape, so we were haphazardly taping almost everything. We'd picked simple bikes with very few moving parts, keeping my dad's words in mind: "The fewer moving parts a machine has, the fewer things there are to break." But now it looked like the bikes might not have enough moving parts to get us across town, not to mention from Alaska to Argentina. There weren't motors, only pedals, chains, and gears to be driven by strength and willpower. No cushioned seats, only rock-hard leather saddles that were not yet broken in. No steering wheels, just metal handlebars without handwarmers, cushioning, or an autopilot button. And there were certainly no warm cabins to climb into out of the weather. Our bicycles didn't look like modes of transport. They looked like children's toys.

We'd chosen the bikes because of the price break, forgoing bikes that had matching wheel sizes or that may have fit us better. The wheels had been hand built with extra heavy-duty parts capable of lasting the miles we planned to ride, a suggestion from an adventuring friend who knew far more about bicycles than we did. Before packing them into bicycle boxes, the racks, fenders, panniers, and bicycles themselves had to be assembled by us—two soon-to-be-cyclists who had absolutely no idea how to put together a bicycle. We implored James to help us with this task less than a week before flying to Alaska.

"How exactly do you adjust a derailleur?" Ville asked, hunched over James, watching his every move as he assembled his bike.

James stood up, lifted his baseball cap, scratched his short brown hair, and set the cap back onto his head with a deadpan stare. "You don't know how to adjust a derailleur?"

"Um . . . nope. Is it hard?"

"Okay, well, let's have a crash course in bicycle maintenance, shall we?"

James cracked a beer and launched into an impromptu crash course, describing which parts go together with what grease at such-and-such torque. ("Never—and I mean never—overtighten that thing, just hand tight.") When he finished, he grinned, self-assured we were ready. He thought wrong. I'd followed almost none of it. When I glanced at Ville, his nose was scrunched, forehead creased in deep thought, pretending to follow, but I knew him better than that. I would've bet money he remembered even less than I did. Luckily, James had ordered us a small hand-tool set to take on the ride. After watching the assembly, I was pretty sure we were going to need it when things started falling off. It wasn't that either of us would know how to put anything back on, but we would have the comfort of knowing that at least we had the tool for the job.

2

Bear Floss

Prudhoe Bay, or Deadhorse, is an unincorporated town about ten miles south of the Arctic Ocean with several thousand transient workers to support the Prudhoe Bay Oil Field. It is also the northernmost town in the Americas with road access. I stared out the frosty window of the plane and looked down over the gigantic snow-capped peaks and wide-open tundra that stretched below us, imagining it would be days upon days to travel this stretch on bicycle. The realization of what we were about to embark on finally started setting in. We started to get butterflies-in-our-stomachs excited. We were going to be biking down there for weeks and possibly even months. Down there among the trees and across the tundra was The Next Adventure. And we were almost there.

As the commuter plane bounced down the lone airstrip, coming to a quick halt, all the passengers began to stand and gather their things. We emerged from the plane and bounded down the steps, the biting cold slapping us in the face. Until that very moment, it hadn't occurred to me that the Arctic might actually be frigid, hostile, and unpredictable. It was still afternoon, and the air hovered barely above freezing, lacking the fragrance of trees or blossoms. The wind whipped my hair ferociously. Two days earlier, a foot of snow had covered northern Alaska, and patches of it remained in the shadows. I wanted to get out of this weather and realized that we would be biking, living, and sleeping in it for at least ten days on the way to Fairbanks with only a gas station halfway. If we couldn't maintain fifty miles a day we would run out of food. We hadn't ridden bikes fully loaded with gear one mile, let alone fifty miles. There was no turning back now.

We filed into the single-room airport with the scientists and oil-field workers, watched through the windows as two neon-clad baggage handlers carted bags to the roll-up door, and rejoiced when we saw our boxes had arrived with minimal scuffs and tears. We now had to put them together with our nifty little hand tool. I felt as ill prepared as new parents being handed their baby as they leave the hospital. Once the passengers filed out, we were given permission to assemble the bikes in the airport—a tighten here and pump of air there, and we were ready to set off—leaving the boxes for hunters to mail home their game racks (or, in layman's terms, *wild animal horns*).

Our plan was to begin The Next Adventure with our new bicycle tires right at, possibly even dipped in, the Arctic surf, then pedal south to the Antarctic Ocean—where we would dip in our worn-by-then tires. However, upon our arrival, we were informed that the oil companies required us to wait for a mandatory twenty-four-hours security clearance before taking a mini-bus shuttle—minus our bikes—that would leave the following day for the Arctic Ocean. Best-laid plans changed. We'd still go, but our tires wouldn't touch the water.

Many of the workers we met and befriended came from the southern states, but the majority came from Texas. After a night at the Prudhoe Bay Hotel, we meet two fast-talking Texan helicopter pilots at breakfast who work in Prudhoe Bay flying scientists and oil workers all over. They showed us their Bell 412 helicopters, let us sit in them and man the controls before taking us in their car to the Prudhoe Bay General Store. We bought bear spray and fuel for our stove, and we promised to call them for a helicopter rescue if the need arose out on the Dalton Highway. "You guys are carrying a gun, right?" one of the pilots asked.

"Nope. Who needs a gun when you have these big guns right here?" Ville said with a big smile, pointing to his biceps and trying to make light that we preferred to be mauled by bears.

"No gun?" he gasped. "You know this is polar bear country. And past that is grizzly and black bear country. No weapon? Shit!" He took a long pause and inhaled deeply. "You'd better call us if anything happens. We will be there. No, but seriously. We will be there."

Our tiny shuttle bus to the Arctic Ocean was exorbitantly over-priced and packed with loud-mouthed tourists from all over the world. Although the temps were hardly above freezing, the sun was shining. I felt energized and ready to take on the world. With my pants rolled up to my knees and my feet submerged, I reached down into the ocean and picked up a small black stone. I slipped it into my pocket, a talisman I was determined to carry all the way to Ushuaia, Argentina.

The frigid Arctic Ocean made it feel more real that we were about to embark on something big. Bigger than anything we'd ever done. Bigger than ourselves. We returned to our bikes locked outside the Prudhoe Bay Hotel and climbed aboard. At the beginning of something so monumental there should at least have been a large gathering of people screaming, cheering, posters flying, banners waving, horns blaring, a gun shot into the air to start us off. But there was nothing. The wilds of Alaska were quiet. Just me and Ville. Large white thunderheads gathered overhead, the breeze was light, the gravel road stretched out miles on the flat tundra before us, and the bears were nowhere to be seen. We hugged, we high-fived, and we did the only thing we could do. We pedaled south.

3

Blind Luck

The precise distance from Prudhoe Bay, Alaska, to Ushuaia, Argentina, is quite hard to calculate, as it is dependent on the mode of transport and the route taken, any of which will be fraught with obstacles. The distance as the crow flies from one to the other is 9,484 miles. A vehicle or bicycle on the most direct route would roughly take 17,488 miles. The Pan-American Highway is calculated around 19,000 miles linking all the roads through the Pacific coastal countries of the Americas. According to the *Guinness Book of World Records*, it is the world's longest "motorable road." But because of the Darién Gap (a seventy-mile roadless section of rain forest in Panama and Colombia), it is not possible to cross between South America and Central America except by sea or plane or illegally by foot because there is no immigration office to stamp out of or into either country. The only foot traffic between Panama and Colombia is Narcos and drug trafficking. I did not know this until we got there.

By car, driving an average of eight hours a day, it would take about three months to get from Prudhoe to Ushuaia. Motorcyclists driving the Pan-American Highway can take from four to six months. But what if you don't take the most direct route? Or if you ride a bicycle? How long and how many miles would that take?

Without researching routes and never having looked up miles, Ville guessed we could cycle it in two years. Biking the length of two continents we would pass through diverse climates and ecosystems from barren polar tundra through water-soaked rain forests, boreal forests, arid deserts, expansive grasslands, dense jungles, high-altitude plains and, if taking a less direct route, zigzagging over the second-highest mountain range on earth, the Andes. The timing of the route around seasons, particularly through the polar climates, is of utmost importance. The optimal weather window for northern Alaska is in mid to late July, after the snow has melted and before the fall flurries begin. We hoped flying up at the end of June and getting a jump on summer would give us more time. This was the main reason we began our ride June 25, 2016.

Never forgetting for a moment that we had to carry every ounce in the panniers, a frame bag, and a front handlebar bag, our gear included a tent, sleeping pads, a sleeping quilt, a gravity filter for water, a cooking pot, a fuel can, a stove, sporks, headlamps, spare batteries, toiletries, first-aid supplies, a food knife, a cell phone, a bug net, a tent stake for digging poop holes, food bags, clothing bags, sleeping gear, puffy jackets, rain jackets, and rain pants.

We had some room to add a little bit of weight, right? And this was where we became a little reckless. Planning to blog along the way, I threw in a laptop, a full-frame camera, and two lenses. Having already pared our gear to the essentials, the additional weight seemed minimal. We were confident we had the right gear and were ready to go.

Our excitement at the beginning of our adventure eroded ten minutes from Prudhoe Bay on the muddy gravel of the Dalton Highway after the heavens poured on us. The James W. Dalton Highway was built as a supply road to support the Trans-Alaska Pipeline System back in 1974 and runs 414 grueling miles. Of those miles, only about one hundred of them have some form of pavement. The remaining miles are anything from dirt to loose gravel to packed, hard clay, clay that when wet, which was often, packed itself into our bicycle fenders stopping us dead in our tracks and requiring us to dismount and dig it out with our tire levers. This same highway was included in an episode of an American television series called *Americas Toughest Jobs* and an episode in BBC's *World's Most Dangerous Roads*. It's no cakewalk to drive and essentially a death wish to bike; of course, we knew none of this before we set off.

"Weather up here changes every ten minutes," the fast-talking helicopter pilots had warned us. They said they are paid to sit at the ready, for flight orders came at a moment's notice. Cutting through the open tundra, the road—a dirt-packed berm, two lanes, no shoulder—became a sloppy slip and slide, and my knees could barely rotate the pedals. Temperatures hovered just above freezing, I knew this not because I carried a thermometer with me, but because the water in my drinking tube began to freeze, and I could barely feel my fingers through my waterproof gloves.

I thought back to the previous week in the glove aisle at a gear shop back home, deciding between basic gloves or waterproof/windproof ones. At the time, Ville and I had both agreed the extra ten dollars must be worth the added comfort, but as I pushed through icy and freezing Arctic winds, I would have given my right arm for my weighty snowboarding gloves. At least my hands would remain dry if the rest of me were sopping wet.

Ten long and grueling miles from Prudhoe Bay we arrived at an abandoned construction site with no shuttle to carry us over the unpacked gravel. We had no other option, but to push on. My legs felt like lead. I was cursing my laptop for making my load even heavier and the loose gravel for swallowing my tires. Before this trip I had not biked twenty-five miles on flat pavement for at least a decade, let alone in deep gravel. Did riding a bicycle always feel this bad? We cursed through every single mile. It was pure hell.

Our brand-spanking-new bikes had arrived only a week before our flight to Alaska, so we rode them ten miles up the road from my parents' house to make sure no parts fell off before packing them up and getting on the plane. The bike box on the airport scale read just under a hundred pounds before adding the laptop, camera, two lenses, and my filled water bladder. What did the laptop, camera, and lenses weigh? They might as well be bricks. Water, I remembered from trail days, weighs 8.3 pounds a gallon. I had just over a gallon in my frame bag. My bike was heavy, the miles on my odometer were barely ticking by, my knees were hurting, my brand-new leather bicycle seat felt like I was sitting on a rock, and I hated the ice-cold rain running down my spine. *What the HELL was I thinking when I signed up for this? Great! Just great.*

I was angry for getting myself into this mess. The only thing I could do was keep pedaling as the rain continued to fall and my anger continued to grow. I could hardly see because the rain blurred my vision. I could only make out the gravel road right in front of me. Anger turned to sadness with the reality that *I* chose this. *I* wanted this. And *I* was stuck in it. There was no backing out now. There was nowhere to go. So, I kept repeating to myself, "Just keep pedaling."

Sometime around midnight, the sun low on the horizon and the rain still coming down in sheets, Ville turned to me, water dripping off the tip of his nose and asked, "Hey, KG, are you ready to camp? I can't feel my toes." I had quit feeling from the waist down an hour ago. We had covered only forty-two miles after riding for nine hours, and although we were exhausted the sun's light had kept us going. In the northern latitudes this close to the summer solstice, the sun wouldn't drop below the horizon. We dismounted resembling drowning cats frantically looking for a place to hide as we searched for a campsite. Ville, who had grown up in the tundra of Finland, was keenly aware that we couldn't pitch our tent just anywhere on the marshy sponge of tundra. This was news to me. We would need to find packed dirt with minimal puddles in the pouring rain. The best option was a tiny side road between the highway and the oil pipeline, mainly used, and only occasionally, for maintenance.

A bit rusty from our days of well-oiled tent erecting, we set up our two-person tent, managing to keep it mostly dry, and shoved all our gear from our panniers into it. We peeled off our rain clothes and, with nowhere to hang them, piled them in a wet heap at our feet. We Twistered around each other in our cramped tent, trying to blow up our sleeping pads and zip together our sleeping quilt. There was no cover from the rain to cook, and we were too tired to boil water, so we ate a Snickers and called it dinner. Long johns and sleep shirts in place, we donned our snazzy sleeping masks to block out the light, inserted our ear plugs to block out the pounding rain, kissed each other goodnight, spooned for added warmth, and crashed hard.

I slept surprisingly well. In the early morning, we awoke to a drizzle and a gray haze. It would follow us the entire day. My handlebars had enough room for my hands in two positions: on top or on the dropdown bars. My body was forced into a forward lean that put so much pressure on my hands and wrists that every so often a couple of my fingers would go numb, and I would have to shake them back to life. I could feel the steel bar through the one-and-a-half millimeters of thinly wrapped handlebar tape. I insisted we stop every couple hours so I could stretch myself upright. Our bicycles had steel frames without shocks, recommended for long distances; however, I could feel every bump in my wrists all the way into my teeth. My dashboard had a speedometer on the right—reading speed, time, and distance—and on the left a little squeaky-toy sumo wrestler to use as a horn, a parting gift from my friend Marc. I stared at the sumo's butt crack for about nine hours a day.

Atop the black canvas handlebar bag strapped to the front and center of the handlebar, I counted eighteen mosquitoes hitching a ride, waiting for me to let my guard down and expose some skin. I slapped at them out of boredom, squished two, and watched the rest buzz off only to re-land moments later. I listened to their ear-piercing whine as they clung to the mosquito net I had to wear over my head, their tiny bodies blurring my vision. My speedometer read 8 mph, not fast enough to lose them. I had only gone 1.2 miles since I last checked. This would be a long day.

About every half hour, a semi thundered past, moving into the oncoming lane to give us plenty of airspace, and we watched it hang on the horizon for over fifteen minutes before disappearing. This far north temperatures are cold enough to prevent tree growth, making the skyline seem infinite. By lunchtime we passed a shipping container in an abandoned parking lot that read Happy Valley Camp and stopped to inquire about a dry place to eat lunch. Although it looked like a dump, the staff informed us that it was a hunters' resort and that without a reservation we had to stay outside. The rejection stung. While shivering, we stood in the parking lot in the pouring rain without as much as a tree to stand under and tried our best to make sandwiches. *If a foot of snow were to fall on us now, what would we do? There was nowhere to hide and riding through it would be impossible.*

By day three, ninety-four miles in, the cold I picked up set deep in my chest and created a sinus infection. I learned exactly what saddle sores were. My knees felt the strain of the extra ounces I was carrying, my monthly friend showed up to join the party, and my brand-new sleeping pad decided to quit holding air, leaving me to sleep on the hard ground. Needless to say, it was not my best week. I had never been so miserable and so ill-prepared to manage everything. All day I yo-yoed between thoughts of *Why the hell am I doing this again?* to *Wait, I chose to do this?* before settling on *Why am I not sitting on a beach with a margarita right now?*

It was not all misery and misfortune. Occasionally the sun would pop out from behind the clouds, the rain would take a breather, and expansive Alaska would appear. The scenery was stunning even when viewed through the haze of our mosquito nets. The blue sky was wide open with pale green and orange shrubs; grasses and mosses stretched as far as we could see, interspersed with small icy streams meandering to the ocean. We saw very few birds or animals, only swarms of mosquitos en masse. Limiting the exposure of skin to the bugs during bathroom breaks became feats of survival. We ran at full speed while wrestling down our pants, trying desperately to stay in front of the swarm before screeching to a halt in time to go, swatting with ninja hands all the while. This method was not foolproof, and we were left covered with itchy bites, but it was the best defense we had.

We set out with a target and hope of being able to cycle around fifty miles a day and came miraculously close to staying on track. Fifty miles a day may seem reasonable, but after years of sporadic physical negligence, pedaling two heavy bicycles in the Arctic becomes way less practical, perhaps even ludicrous. The first ten miles can be done in a full-bellied daze after a bland oatmeal breakfast. The next twenty need more snack breaks. By thirty, I found myself asking, "Is it lunch yet?" every other mile. Forty was just painful, especially if we did stop for lunch and entered food comas. And fifty miles was just torture. Every single mile that ticked by on my odometer got noticed. Every single one.

4

Bumble Bee and Vole

At 10 p.m., after covering fifty miles in just over nine hours of riding, we approached the Brooks Range and Atigun Pass looming out of the flats with a staggering 4,700 feet of elevation. Until this point, northern Alaska had been as flat as a pancake, with a fluctuation of a hundred feet here or there, allowing almost no training for serious climbing. This looked to be a serious climb. I had yet to summit a mountain on a bicycle, let alone on a fully loaded bicycle, and I felt as ill equipped to summit this mountain as I would have been heading off to summit Everest. The skies were ominous and we paused, unsure whether to camp and tackle it early in the morning or take a chance and try to climb it quickly.

"Better go now while it's not raining!" a trucker yelled out the window of his semi as he swooshed past, noticing our hesitation. Casting aside doubts and what possibly remained of our sanity, we clicked down to our lowest granny gears, removed some layers, and began climbing, offering our blood to the mosquito gods. *Could this mountain get any larger?* Each pedal stroke took an eternity, each switchback forever, and when I was sure I could not pedal anymore or climb any higher, the mountain grew larger and we continued. We could not quit in the middle because there was nowhere to camp. After quitting in my mind a hundred times, then telling myself I would quit after just the next switchback, then the next, and just one more, we reached the summit a little before midnight. We stood in howling wind on the ridge of the pass, jackets flapping loud snaps, looked back over all the switchbacks, and breathed sighs of relief that we had managed to dodge the rain. A few drops beaded onto my jacket like warning shots. We realized we needed to get down off this mountain and camp before the rain. Downhill on the backside felt steeper than the road up, but we eventually found a flat spot to camp and went to sleep feeling elated that the worst of the climbing was now behind us.

When I rolled over on my sleeping pad early the next morning, Ville was already gone, likely starting breakfast. I fantasized about bacon, eggs, veggies, toast, although I know we are having oatmeal. The loud *ZIIIIIP* of the tent alerted Ville that I was awake, and he turned to look at me as he sat on a rock hunched over the stove. "Good morning, Bumble Bee," he smiled. Ville loves nicknames. He calls me Pocket Tornado, Pocket Rocket, Armadillo, Bumble Bee, and my least favorite, Stink Bug. He developed that one when we thru-hiked the Pacific Crest Trail and before I discovered I was lactose intolerant.

"Good morning, Vole," I retorted. Although it's only five letters, most Americans completely butcher the pronunciation of his foreign name, and I like to do the same. It makes him feel special.

The sun shone without a cloud in sight. I took a deep breath, tasting the early morning sweetness. Atigun Pass was safely in the distance behind us. The road ahead descended into a shadowy chasm cut wide open by the Atigun River. After breakfast we rode down the canyon detouring to a crystal-clear river beckoning us to come for a swim and necessary scrub down. It had been five days without a bath, and I stunk. The water was so cold it burned my skin and left it tingling long after I climbed out. It was on this decline that the first tree appeared since the beginning of the ride, and the desolate alpine turned into boreal forests. The intoxicating smell of pine, spruce, and aspen trees grew around us. The sun was shining, birds were chirping, we had not yet been eaten by a bear, and we were on track with our calculated miles to land us early at Coldfoot.

Coldfoot—population ten, according to the 2010 census—primarily serves as a truck stop on the Dalton Highway with its combination gas station–post office–motel–tiny restaurant. It was the first place we'd seen with services in the 240 miles and six days since leaving Deadhorse. We were ecstatic. I would order one of everything on the menu with salty fries and finish it with a hot-fudge brownie with caramel sauce and vanilla ice cream. Ville was going to order three icy-cold India Pale Ales. We were giddy and ravenous and could not make it inside fast enough.

The silver-haired, gum-snapping waitress and postal worker handed us our large box, which we had mailed to ourselves before leaving Bend, knowing it would greatly lessen the amount we would have to carry from Deadhorse. Ville cut it open with his Leatherman and divvied up the dehydrated meals as we hunkered down in wooden chairs at one of the four tables in the restaurant. We made fast friends over the next few hours with the young women waitressing and living there for the season, exchanged contact info with a couple of diners from Fairbanks who offered us a place to stay if the need arose, ate like a bunch of truckers, washed our faces in the bathroom sink, fixed things on the bikes that needed fixing, and recharged our batteries. It was glorious, and I never wanted to leave. Prying ourselves out of the restaurant after three hours was brutal, but having hit pavement on the way in, we were jonesing to make up some miles. The sun was still shining, and I inhaled the clean mountain air. I did not have cell service or a care in the world because I was in the great outdoors with my husband heading south, ready for more adventure. It felt damn good to be alive.

More adventure was just around the corner because the pavement ended after leaving Coldfoot. Oil Spill Hill was graded so steeply we had to dismount and push our bikes to the top. But that was not all. No, no. Then there was Beaver Slide, Oh Shit Corner, and The Roller Coaster. All aptly named by the truckers who drove them. We grew accustomed to dismounting and pushing our burdensome bikes up long, steep hills followed by kamikaze descents in loose gravel or slippery clay trying to keep our speed up so we could fly up the next hill.

The Dalton Highway was a roller coaster. Our moods ebbed and flowed with the terrain from epic highs to abysmal lows. At times the sun was shining, the road was dry, my wheels were spinning, and I was amazed at the mountains rising out of pine forests that surrounded us. At other times the thought of more uphill took the fun out of the downhill.

We heard piercing screams from circling red-tailed hawks. We saw thousand-pound moose as tall as buses wading in lakes and grazing with calves, zippy squirrels dodging our path, a caribou running mad past our tent, wild horses and cattle, a barn owl so close I felt as if I could reach out and pet it, and a herd of hairy musk oxen grazing on an open plain.

The sun shined as we snapped a quick picture in front of the sign marking the Arctic Circle. A moment later, the skies opened, torrential rains soaked us cold to the bone, and cascading rivers of water flooded the road, making it almost unpassable. The animals scattered, and the birds quit chirping. I was still out of shape. My bike seemed to weigh more than the semitrucks that flew past, my knees aching enough for me to have ditched the idea of cliping into my pedals long ago. My stomach was always growling. And still there was another hill to climb. I was miserable and at the same time the happiest I'd ever been. Before this trip life had become too easy, we had become complacent and stagnant. Discomfort was a catalyst for growth, and it forced us to adapt and change.

Why would anyone in their right mind do this? Punish oneself when they could be sitting on a warm sofa, flipping channels? Because when life is at its most challenging and you hit your lowest lows some of the most beautiful things happen. Early on as the rain pelted us in the face a truck pulled up, an older man reached out the window, handed us snack bars, and said, "Looks like you could use these." Another time, while sick, battling headwinds and hill climbs, a dump truck driver pulled over and handed us pizza, sandwiches, and cake in a brown paper bag. He even drove back to collect the garbage so we didn't have to pack it out. The heavy rains had muddied the rivers, which clogged our water filter. So when a trucker slowed to hand us bottles of water, his gift was a lifesaver. Simple acts of kindness when least expected were sacred aspects of this adventure.

We were just forty miles from the end of the Dalton, where it joined the Elliot Highway for the last sixty paved miles before coming to the second-largest city in Alaska, Fairbanks. We rode through horrendous mud in merciless rain with storm clouds following us. We had to push our bikes up steep hills that climbed to the sky. After ascending one such hill, we were met by a gigantic water truck spraying the highway and three grading machines completely unearthing it. The descent was a deathtrap mudslide with nothing but "thoughts and prayers" to keep us alive.

When we finally arrived at the end of the Dalton Highway ten days and 420 miles after leaving Prudhoe Bay, tears cascaded down my face. We dropped out of the mountains onto the Elliot Highway, where the rain let up. The thunder that cracked behind us in the distance seemed like an announcement that we had been spit out of the bowels of the beast called the Dalton Highway and that we had survived. Unless I am sitting in a chopper flying overhead with two loud-mouthed Texans from Prudhoe Bay, I am forever done with that cursed stretch of road.

When we hit the pavement of the Elliot Highway, a couple gave us water after watching us struggle to purify water from the river. At an overlook the sun popped out for an hour, giving us enough time to drag out our soaking wet clothes and gear and spread it out everywhere to dry. I can't imagine how bad I must've smelled from days without bathing. I looked over at Ville. He had stripped down to a filthy pair of shorts, boney from caloric depletion, caked in days of sweat and mud, with his shoulder-length dirty-blond hair half in a hair band, the rest flying in every direction, wild-eyed like a rabid beast. I know I looked the same. We attracted the attention of a passerby in a rusty one-ton pickup, who pulled over for a chat.

"What are you kids doing out here?" Leroy asked. He was a third-generation gold miner on his way back to his homestead after resupplying in town. He was my height, scruffy, wearing a worn baseball cap, and with wide-open spaces between his teeth. His truck was loaded with large, rusty oil drums of fuel, coolers of food, and cases upon cases of Milwaukee's Best.

"You want a 'Beast?' Or I have some Mountain Dew," he asked, reaching into a cooler in the back seat. We each took a Mountain Dew, and he cracked a "Beast." We chitchatted awhile about life off the grid, his VHS collection, his mangy mutt who is his roommate, and his gun collection. He whistled a bit when he talked. Excited about our adventure, Leroy reached into the back of his rig, dug out cans of spaghetti and two fruit cocktail cups, and handed them to us for dinner. Hungry enough to eat the soles off our shoes we gladly accepted. He grabbed himself another "Beast."

After more jabbering, he asked Ville, "Can I give your wife something?" I stood there a bit stunned. *Well,* I thought, *I just don't know, Leroy. Will I get an itchy rash or require a doctor's visit after you give it to me?*

He walked over to the bushes, picked some flowers, and handed them to me. I smiled and thanked him. He cracked yet another beer, then pulled a large gold nugget out of his pocket and let us hold it. I had never held a real gold nugget before. He claimed it was worth about $700. A hundred bucks shy of our combined monthly budget for the trip. He walked to the other side of the truck, peed into the tire well, ripped a big, boisterous fart, zipped up, cracked another beer, wished us well, climbed in his truck, roared back onto the highway heading for the hills, waving at us as he thundered past. Ville turned to me and said, eyebrows raised and chuckling, "What a character." I had to completely agree.

Just ten miles outside Fairbanks— after dining on large portions of truck stop food and chewing the fat with the truckers—we inquired at the Hilltop Truckstop in Fox about a place to camp. We were given permission to pitch our tent out back in the weeds and granted access to the restroom. In the morning, we texted the diners we had met at Coldfoot who had been gracious (or crazy) enough to give us their numbers. Donald picked us up off the road wearing only our rain pants and jackets, the only things not completely soaked and filthy. Our bikes were covered in mud and clay; rotors squealing, shifters not shifting properly, brakes barely working. We had tried to wash the bikes in a muddy creek, but it only seemed to compound the problems. It was a miracle we had made it this far.

At Donald's house, we were given a bedroom, clean towels, a hot shower, laundry room, and even a car to run errands. It was as if we had just been handed keys to the Taj Mahal and a Maserati. We were stunned. I would have hugged the guts out of Donald right there if I did not smell like dead animal carcass. I hugged him anyway, and he hugged me back. Normal day-to-day necessities had become novelties to us now. I shed the rain clothes and stared into a full-length mirror in the bathroom, not having seen myself, save for the tiny mirror in the Coldfoot restroom, in 500 miles. It was still me, but bonier, tanned, and filthier. My skin had turned an olive bronze in stark contrast to the whiteness of what my socks, shorts, and T-shirt covered. My knees still ached, but my legs felt stronger, sturdier. The lower half of my hair that poked out from my helmet was lighter, and more freckles dotted my cheeks. I looked exhausted and euphoric at the same time.

I took the greatest hot shower of my life, watching the water run brown down the drain, and scrubbed everything twice. Ville and I lounged in a fragrance of clean, ate at a buffet in town like two ravenous hyenas, called home, and hosed and scrubbed down our bikes. I struggled to walk up stairs without bracing my hand on my thigh. I felt like I had aged thirty years in ten days, but there was a spring in my step.

That evening, Donald and his wife, Marie, made a salmon dinner with heaps of side dishes, salad that tasted of the earth's sweetness, a stark contrast to ten days of salty, dry prepackaged food. We pored over their maps, making general plans for the next stretch. We planned to leave the next morning, but Donald and Marie insisted otherwise. I was hazardously sore. Ville resembled a skeleton, and we were obliged not to fight them. If they were insistent we stay, well, we would stay, dammit. With a day off, we gorged on more food while draped in clean towels. Through more friends-of-friends connections, we had help getting our bicycles road ready, as we had discovered that one of the brake pads on my bike had malfunctioned, the wire holding them in place becoming mangled and wearing the brake pad down completely. Luckily, I carried a set of spare brake pads and we learned how to change them out. With a little tweak here and there, we were ready to set forth.

We were told the Alcan Highway heading southeast out of Fairbanks would be paved with a shoulder big enough to land a 747 on. After the Dalton Highway, anything would be better. Beginning a bicycle tour while simultaneously getting in shape for it on the Dalton

Highway would be the equivalent of being helicoptered into the High Sierra Wilderness on the Pacific Crest Trail to get in shape for the rest of the hike. We could have flown to Fairbanks or Anchorage. Ville had suggested it early on. However, neither of those places was the northernmost point of the Americas, and I was insistent we begin at the very top. What a naive little girl I was. The remote Dalton Highway was not made for bicycles and was one of the most difficult places we could have begun. It would be smooth sailing from here on, I told myself, knowing it could not possibly be true. After all, this was an adventure.

5

Floating Shorts

Ville and I met on a scuba diving boat in Nah Trang, Vietnam, eight years prior to beginning our bicycle adventure of the Americas. I had been teaching abroad, living in an orphanage in Chiang Mai, Thailand, for half a year through a college internship, and I was backpacking with a girlfriend after completing my studies. Ville, on the other hand, had been working long hours as a finance guy for a giant company. When he needed a break from the prison of the office he booked a three-month backpacking trip through southeast Asia.

I had noticed him immediately outside the dive shop the morning I arrived. He sat at a small table with a boisterous, pale Brit. My friend Lori and I sat down with them for a chat. Ville had shoulder-length, dirty-blond hair, piercing blue–green eyes, sun-kissed skin, a noticeably crooked smile, and a body that was sculpted by years of sport. His muscles tightened when he lifted his hand to tuck the stray hairs behind his ear. When he smiled I felt a tightening in my stomach. His Finnish accent was icing on the cake. He was what we ladies call *hot as hell*.

As my diving class broke for lunch, I made my way over to the side of the two-story boat away from the others and dove from the top deck, plunging deep into the clear, blue water, and surfaced near the side of the boat. I was about to climb out when Ville came swan-diving over my head, plunging into the water only a few feet away from where I bobbed, treading water. At the moment of impact, the drawstring on his shorts gave way, and they shot up out of the water and slapped flat on the surface, where they floated quietly. Now Ville likes to think that it was surely at that moment, viewing him in the nude, that I had fallen for him. It wasn't the only reason, but it didn't hurt his case.

We traveled for ten glorious days together from the south to the north of Vietnam, falling deeper and deeper in love before we were forced to part ways. My visa was up. I had an airline ticket to my home in the United States, and Ville was heading through Laos before his return in a few weeks' time to Finland. He promised we would see each other again as we said our goodbyes. My eyes filled with tears while kissing the softness of his lips, desperately clinging to the memory of every caress. I was not as sure. After all, we lived on opposite sides of the globe. We stayed in touch through emails and occasional phone calls, and after six weeks of missing each other deeply I bought a plane ticket to Finland to see if it was real. I planned to stay three months. From the moment he picked me up at the airport with a bunch of flowers, we fell back into step. I moved into his 300-square-foot apartment for a summer of blissful romance. I had found my mate.

A few years and adventures later, we had packed our bags and flown to southern California to start the Pacific Crest Trail, having never even slept overnight in a tent together. We made all the rookie mistakes: no training, almost no research, no practice run, carrying way too much gear the first day on trail. But we learned quickly. We both knew how to walk, and what is hiking but lots and lots of walking?

We had one big fight very early in the hike. I am a night owl, and Ville is a morning person. You are more likely to survive waking a sleeping bear than me in the morning. This created quite the dilemma when sharing a tent and a day-to-day routine on a five-month hiking sojourn. The fight happened somewhere in the Tehachapi wilderness after we had walked roughly 600 miles in a month. "I think we just need to hike this separately at our own paces," Ville said angrily, crossing his arms across his chest. "I think we should just meet back up at the end or something."

"Well, if we are going to hike this separately, we are not ending this hike together," I rationalized, knowing that separating on trail would be a separation of us. "I just think we need to compromise. I promise to do my best to get up early and get going as quickly as I can, but you need to be patient. And I will do my best to be patient with you when we need to hike late when you're tired."

After talking things through we agreed to that compromise and never fought like that again. Sure, we had disagreements and quarrels, but we learned the importance of communication, of getting things out, of saying words that would hurt but that needed to be said, of listening when the other spoke, and, most importantly, of giving each other time to process once words were spoken. On a five-month hike there was an abundance of words. We shared our hopes, dreams, nightmares, regrets, sufferings, grievances, every trivial thing until there was nothing more to talk about and then we talked about nothing. And just kept walking.

6

Gargantuan Burgers

The Alcan Highway—or Alaska Highway, as it is officially known—is 1,387 miles long, beginning in Fairbanks and ending in Dawson Creek, British Columbia. Only 285 miles are in Alaska; the remaining 1,102 are in Yukon and British Columbia. The road opened to the public after WWII but was quickly closed again due to the number of vehicles that were continually breaking down. Until the 1980s, much of the Canadian portion was gravel, but today it is a paved, two-lane highway. Road crews working during the short summer months can be found tearing apart large sections for replacement after the long harsh winters take their toll. There are few motels, grocery stops, or gas stations along the route, and the distances between them are substantial when traveling by bicycle. If the Dalton Highway had been our nightmare, the Alcan was sure to be a dream.

After fattening up at buffets and resting in Fairbanks, it was time to get back in the saddles and pedal southeast on the Alcan. We were clean and refreshed, our bikes had been repaired, and their chains oiled. Our panniers were loaded with as much food as we could carry. I was beginning to resemble someone who could be mistaken for a cyclist. Where twigs once stood as legs, I now had tree trunks. Where my muffin top had rested I now had abdominal muscles. Where sanity may have lingered, there was none. I had battled the Dalton and won. I was strong and brave. I learned to ride this bike on the fly.

We planned to pedal for about two weeks, covering 850 miles on the Alcan, passing through Alaska and Yukon before we would head south on the Cassier Highway through British Columbia. We pedaled up mountains and through expansive valleys and dense spruce forests, along ridges with views of more ridges, skirted pristine lakes with surfaces like glass, and down hair-raising descents on the shoulder of a road never wider than a human is tall. Pedal is what we did.

Our first stopover after three days from Fairbanks was an overnight stay in a roadside motel in Tok to get out of the rain and hit up a hot shower. The room was more of a hovel than a room. Sandpaper towels, a window only a baby could pass through, and a kaleidoscope of stains that resembled a carpet were pure heaven to us. We showered and ran across the street to the only diner. The place was packed with people wearing plaid, camo, and trucker hats with the weary RVer here and there. The waitresses called us "honey" and "sweetheart," and over half the menu listed burgers with names like Gargantuan, Colossal, and Heart Attack. We ate every last crumb and had to refrain ourselves from licking the plates. When Ville handed over the money to pay our bill, we felt violated. Alaska is expensive, like vacationing in Hawai'i is expensive. Everything must be shipped up from the lower forty-eight, so the price really ticks up on food items. A plain hamburger never cost less than twenty bucks, so for both of us to eat just one meal took five percent of our entire budget for the month. Multiply that by a few stops and we would have no money left. And all I wanted was food. It consumed my mind all day as I rode. If my mind wandered, my stomach growled. Money was a constant stress, and a couple times we had to repress our urge to eat a greasy, expensive burger at a roadside stop and opt for our cold sandwiches instead. It pained us. Luckily, there were not many stops on the Alcan.

As we rode, the terrain slowly changed as the Saint Elias Mountains and Alaskan Range came into view, glacial-covered mountains towering around us, the scene changing hourly. Trees grew taller, streambeds more swollen with snowmelt, and the meadows were a prism of color. We rode past a small wooden cross on a grassy knoll weathered and long forgotten. MOTHER had been carved into it. The largest crow I'd ever seen perched atop the cross and turned its head to watch us as we rode past. I remember reading that the Hopi Native Americans believe the crow is Mother of All Things. I thought of my mother and Ville's mom. I would see mine in Bend in a month and a half, but Ville would not see his until the ride ended in two years. It must have pained him, but I dared not ask if he missed her, because it would just bring on heartache.

Eighty-three miles past Tok, in relatively warm weather, we crossed over into Yukon and received a stamp in each of our passports, the first of many. We felt the weight of ending one chapter while simultaneously beginning another. *One state finished, three more to go*, I thought as we entered Canada. Puffy white thunderheads ballooned in the sky; a wall of rain was rapidly approaching. We pulled over, rummaged through panniers, and dug out our rain gear moments before the deluge was upon us. As quickly as it had come, it was gone. We stopped, stripped off the wet gear, strapped it to the exterior of our panniers, and continued, the sun hot on our skin.

Beyond the town of Beaver Creek we dropped into a valley of lakes, a necessary stop for thousands of migratory birds, nestled between the Kluane Ranges and the Nisling Range. We watched an eagle pluck a fish from the lake next to where we were swimming. Kindness from strangers accompanied us: roadside snacks, sodas, cooked meals, even a couple who paid our dinner bill on their way out. It touched us how genuinely kind people were. It brightened the darkest hours and made every painful mile worth it.

We camped in the yard of a roadside maintenance crew worker in Destruction Bay and had a long sit and feast at the Village Bakery in Haines Junction. On the advice of a friendly couple, we decided to detour off the Alcan onto the Haines Highway, which promised spectacular snow-capped mountain views and far less traffic. The Haines Highway runs 152 miles and connects the towns of Haines Junction in Yukon with the coastal town of Haines, Alaska, losing two thousand feet of elevation on its descent. Originally a trail used by traders and prospectors during the Klondike Gold Rush, the highway was built by the U.S. Army in 1943 but remained unpaved and plagued by blizzards and mudslides until the 1980s.

The Haines Highway did not disappoint. Robust mountains dwarfed the clouds. We rode past a peaceful lake and agreed on a swim. We leaned our bikes next to the road and scrambled down an embankment of scree to the lake. Cursing and swatting at the biting horse flies, Ville stripped down naked and shimmied his radiantly white butt out waist deep where there were two small white birds. I sat on the shore with only my toes in the water, thinking that if I sat there long enough the water might warm up a bit. I noticed a large white bird circling overhead. Suddenly the bird tucked its wings and dove straight down at Ville and clocked him in the back of the head.

I sat stunned, mystified by what had just happened.

Ville grabbed his head, spun around to face me, and yelled, "KG! Why the hell did you—" Just in time for the bird to regain its composure and take another dive at his head. This time, as agile as a boxer, he ducked, and the bird narrowly missed. It began screeching loudly, obviously enraged. It dawned on us that the little birds in the lake were her babies and this protective momma was pissed.

Ville ran for it, as fast as he could waist deep in water, arms draped up over his head like a helmet, back to the shore, with the bird dive-bombing his head and squawking. We both dressed quickly, scrambled back up the scree, climbed onto the bikes, and pedaled fiercely south in the direction of Haines. So much for our refreshing soak in the lake.

Dusk was setting when we dropped through multiple climates and crossed the Yukon–Alaska border and collected another stamp in our passport. We arrived in the coastal town of Haines nestled on the Chilkat Peninsula that has a population around two thousand. It was bustling with summer tourists. A campground on the seafront with laundry facilities and a shower put us in a warm-and-fuzzy euphoria, and we went to sleep with smiles. In the morning mist we boarded the half-hour ferry to Skagway, where we were inundated with cruise passengers.

Skagway has over a million tourists each year, almost all arriving by cruise ship, and the town looks like Disneyland. We immediately felt out of place but managed to find a bicycle shop, where we met Phil and April, fellow touring cyclists, who spend summers working in Skagway to fill their coffers and pay for their winter travels. We joined them for a game of soccer and slept on a fold-out couch in the living room of their rented trailer to get out of the rain. The next morning, we boarded a train headed for White Pass Summit and the Yukon border. The White Pass and Yukon Route Railroad was built in 1898 during the Klondike Gold Rush and was steam operated until 1954, when it transitioned to diesel-electric power. In 1988 it became a tourist attraction, operating as a narrow-gauge railroad between Skagway and White Pass Summit. We disembarked at White Pass Summit, received more stamps in our passports as we reentered Canada, and biked up the Klondike Highway until we joined the Alcan Highway again.

We fell into a simple routine on the bikes. Each morning we rose at first light, having stealth-camped somewhere in the forest with our food bag slung high up in a tree away from the tent. Ville cooked oatmeal while I rolled up sleeping pads and stuffed the quilt into separate stuff sacks. We broke down camp, pooped in the woods, and then pedaled south. We would ride from about seven or eight to six or seven, stopping for pee and snack breaks and a good-sized lunch break when it wasn't raining. Through almost all of Alaska, Yukon, and British Columbia, it rained. When it was not raining, there were headwinds to battle. Very occasionally there was sunshine, and then thunderheads creating lightning storms with winds and more rain. We kept our rain gear on top of the panniers close at hand.

We always biked together. Ville chose to bike behind me because my wheels were smaller than his and I was slower. He preferred me to set the pace so we could always stay together. He insisted on carrying more weight than I did, taking the tent, cookstove, pot, water filter, and spare parts. I just carried my things. He also prepared our meals, allowing me to rest longer during stops. He did all this without complaint. Ville is a saint, and I married way out of my league.

We saw things differently on our bikes than we had any other way we had previously traveled. On a road trip in my truck, we would be thrilled for the first hour or so until the scenery began to feel like watching a TV, separate and removed. On our Pacific Crest Trail thru-hike, we were part of the scenery. However, shrouded in trees, we had to stare at the ground to avoid tripping. Our bicycles allowed us to cover distance faster and experience more. The pace was slow enough to take in the details yet fast enough to keep us alert. The energy required to propel us forward kept us in a constant state of self-awareness and consciousness.

We found ourselves aware of everything: wind on our faces, tasting the rain, seeing colors found only in nature, hearing the wild animal calls, and smelling the wildflowers. As the scenery unfolded before us, we meditated on time and place and replayed memories while creating new ones. We kept track of miles until it became of no importance to do so. We were not in a hurry, not wasting anyone's precious time.

In all my time biking I never got used to the shrill of a motorist flying past. We always opted for the road less traveled when possible. The in-between were the places we enjoyed the most: The winding mountain roads, country roads, and forgotten routes where the grass grew tall, cattle grazed in fields close enough to smell the sweetness of their sweaty hides, wild animals outnumbered domesticated, kids ran alongside us, and farmers waved from astride tractors as we passed by.

Town stops were for resupplying: shower, sex, food. In that order. We grew so grimy from days without showers that even *I* wouldn't have sex with myself. We refrained until we became so desperate that we either climbed into frigid lakes to sponge off or coughed up the cash to get an overpriced shit-box for a shower and a shag. Food was usually on the backburner but always a necessity. We needed towns to resupply food, but once we reached a town the shoulder or bike lane often disappeared, traffic increased, and drivers became less aware of us. Towns or cities had amenities we dreamt about, but we often regretted the labor it took to reach them.

We rarely talked to each other while riding, having to stay single file in the shoulder, but we did carry iPods and listened to music and podcasts to pass time. We took every opportunity to swim and bathe in streams and lakes and filtered drinking water when we could. At least five miles before it was time to camp, we stopped to cook our dinner, never eating where we camped for fear of being a bear's dinner.

Around six or seven, we would find a flat spot hidden in the woods for camp, making it our number-one rule that no one should ever see where we camped. We set up the tent, changed into sleeping clothes, and played fierce games of cards or dice before bed. Both being competitive by nature, whoever lost would roll over and threaten never to speak to the other again. Sometimes, we would read books on our Kindles, and other times we lay awake in darkness listening to the sounds of the wind in the trees and the rustling of things that scurry until we fell into deep sleep. I often woke to pee in the middle of the night, always stumbling about in the brush to find an open spot to squat, trying not to wake myself up too much but enough to find my way back to the tent.

I had imagined Alaska and Canada to be wild, desolate places untouched by man, reachable only by bike. As we rode on paved roads we were no longer alone. At the beginning I hated anything motorized, despised every motorcyclist who zipped past, throttling up every hill with ease. My legs ached, my crotch hurt, and I was barely moving. Ville and I would spend the next ten minutes grumbling about "how nice it must be to be so lazy." That is, until we pulled over at a lookout and shared snacks and small talk with the motorcyclist, begrudgingly admitting that, after all, he was not such a bad guy.

By the time we reached Yukon we hated RVs. Nine out of every ten cars that passed were RVs, mostly occupied by elderly people, little white heads, mouths agape, just above the window line, narrowly missing us as they flew by. I was sure if we had been sucked into their tire well or under their bus they wouldn't know it until they pulled over for gas miles down the road. But at every pullout, every rest area and lookout, we encountered the kindest RVers stopping to chat about what we were up to, sharing their icy-cold sodas, frosty beers, candy bars, and snacks.

On one of our wettest, coldest, and windiest mornings, the chip seal pavement chattering our steel-framed bikes so badly I was sure our teeth would be littering the roadside, we stopped for a snack after making only twenty miles in three hours. Up until that point we had been averaging sixty to seventy miles a day after getting off the Dalton Highway. We began shivering so badly we were forced to pitch our water-logged tent under a large tree to climb into and try to warm up. Deep into an aggressive hand of cards, an RV pulled up, and a man yelled out the window, "Cooking some hot food in about a half an hour if anyone wants some!"

This was how we came to know Dan and Carol from Montana. Once inside the RV, we sat down to an enormous pot of spaghetti, salad, bread, and copious amounts of beer. And not crappy, cheap beer—as if it mattered by now—but the good stuff. We shared travel stories and hours of laughs, leaving my sides aching. Dan was a soy and corn farmer who recently retired, and he and Carol loved to travel the world. Kindred souls. The following morning was frosty, and while Ville was trying to fire up the stove for oatmeal, Dan walked by our tent, eyes a twinkle, and hollered, "I wouldn't eat that slop if there was bacon and eggs available." They packed up all the leftovers and sent them with us when we rode away, with full hearts and bellies.

By British Columbia we had time to relax. My shoulders dropped just a little. I sat deeper in my saddle that had finally begun to soften. I released my death grip on the handlebars, and my breath fell into pace with every pedal stroke. I was no longer needed in my former life as Kristen, the teacher, the real estate broker, the city dweller who walked the same route to work every day and shuffled through the same paperwork by night. I no longer had duties, obligations, or commitments. I subsisted on only my basic wants and needs. My only responsibility was to pedal. I was now Kristen on the Bicycle Journey. Where Ville and I were headed was a place I had only seen on a map and knew nothing about called Ushuaia.

7

Wild Country

After five days and 290 miles since crossing into Yukon, the Alcan Highway had become boring. I was ready for a new road. My crotch had been numb for an hour, even though I changed my positions by sitting back in the saddle, balancing on one sit bone and then the other. There was not much room on a six-inch hard Brooks saddle. I was ready for a break. As I rode in the front, I usually decided on the stops. This time I lucked out with a gravel pullout, as opposed to a roadside sit, complete with informative signposts to read. The Alaska Highway: Wild Country. We were alone with our bikes and a view of surrounding green, thick brush and not much else. We dismounted, rested the bikes against the signs, touched our toes, stretched our arms behind our backs to open up our shoulders, stiff and sore after hunching over handlebars for four hours.

If we were concerned about missing the turn onto the Stewart–Cassiar Highway, we need not have worried. It was the only paved road exiting the Alcan Highway. The shoulder disappeared, the less-well-maintained road narrowed, and the forest engulfed the road. The upside of a road less traveled was less traffic. We passed a half-dozen roadside trailers with cars on blocks in the yards. We saw a hand-painted sign reading Watch Out for Horse nailed to a tree. And we noticed a quickie-mart stickered with Lotto signs, loitering vagrants outside, complete with blank stares and mouths agape.

As dusk set in we started to look for a place to make camp, scanning the roadside for a level place to hide deep in a thicket of trees. As we came down a steep, small hill about to rollercoaster into the next small uphill, a large black bear popped up from the shoulder of the road directly in front of us. I braked hard, jolting Ville to a stop right behind. "Oh, shit." I held my breath. I had given it no thought until this very moment how brazenly vulnerable we were to the elements on a bicycle. We couldn't lock a car door or roll up a window. We quickly dismounted and moved the bicycles between us and the bear, watching its every move. The bear was on all fours about waist high, dark brown wild eyes, nose twitching, searching for our smell. Its claws clicked on the pavement as it stepped closer. I felt my pulse quicken, my breath catch, and my senses become acutely aware. Two adorable black balls of fur jumped onto the road behind mama, bounding behind her for protection.

"OH SHIT," we both stammered in unison as we moved closer together, Ville protectively moving in front of me with his bike. "Oh shit, shit, SHIT!" The mother bear, sensing danger, pinned her ears, made quick, loud snorting noises, and started waddling toward us. I don't know about you, but neither Ville nor I grew up in bear country, where one might be instructed on what to do in this situation. Nothing I was told in school—"Stop, drop and roll"; "Line up single file and quickly exit the building"; or "Dive under your desk for cover"—would help during a bear mauling. And did you know a bear can reach speeds of up to thirty-five miles per hour? I sure did, because we had startled one while hiking the Pacific Crest Trail and watched it take off like a rocket, flattening every bush, tree, and blade of grass like a bulldozer. Bears were not to be underestimated; they were beautiful creatures and killing machines.

I scanned my bike for the bear spray we had bought at the Prudhoe Bay Store, alarmed to realize it must be buried deep in one of the four panniers. Now was not the time to search for it, to be unstrapping bags and rooting around inside. I was frustrated with myself for not being prepared. "Ville, where is your bear spray?" I asked shakily, hoping he had been more prepared than I.

"I think mine is buried in my front bag. You?" He looked at me.

"Same. What do we do? I don't know what to do." I felt I was shrinking in size with every step the bear took toward us. She kept moving closer, each step pounding in my ears. Her snorting and grunting getting louder.

We were in really deep shit.

A bear is a wild animal, and regardless of what you do it will decide what it wants to do with you. You could either run, play dead, or hold your ground and beat your chest like a gorilla. Whichever one you do might be the thing that saves your life. Or it could be the thing that gets you killed. And let's say you played dead in your previous bear standoff, there's no guarantee that the next bear will buy that ploy. It's a complete gamble. The only thing that is certain is that you will need to do *something* because you can't just do nothing.

I snapped to attention. I raised my hands over my head, stretched them wide, and started yelling as loudly as I could. Ville quickly followed suit. We were not just yelling, but angrily snarling and grunting more loudly than the bear. We were smaller than she, but now we became larger, angrier, wilder. Mid-waddle, about ten feet from us, close enough we could almost smell the berries on her breath, the bear paused, stopped, sniffed in the air, and bounded back down into the wash and straight into the thickness of woods, her tiny, little balls of fluff bounding right behind. The sea of green swallowed them, leaving the branches shaking in their wake, then a return to stillness.

We stood there looking after them in shock and realizing that a moment before we had almost been mauled by a protective mother bear with paws the size of shovels and large, gleaming, white canines. If she had chosen to stand her ground and charge, we would have been goners. We stood rooted next to our bikes, unsure if she had really gone or if she might leap back out from the trees and charge. Our fight-or-flight response—adrenaline coursing through our veins—was a human, behavioral response adapted perfectly and fine-tuned over thousands of years, passed down from our ancestors for this exact moment: to run from a bear. It was working. My hands were shaking, and I felt like I could sprint a mile.

We climbed back on the bikes and rode with gusto up the next hill, checking over our shoulder every so often to make sure we were not being followed. We agreed to put five more miles between her and us before making camp, lessening the possibility of seeing her again tonight. We found an area with dead and downed trees, which would allow us to see farther into the distance and give us more time to react to a surprise attack, checked our pants to make sure we hadn't defecated from fear, and then hung our food bag an extra hundred yards away from the tent. Ville went around violently hitting every tree with a loud stick just for good measure. He couldn't be too careful. As luck would have it, she didn't return.

8

Afraid of Nothing

After fighting nasty headwinds and more rain on the Cassiar Highway, we blew into Meziadin Junction, a mere gas station, and decided to thumb a ride to the fishing villages of Hyder, Alaska, and Stewart, B.C. Once there, we hoped to catch a glimpse of grizzly bears feeding on salmon at the Fish Creek Wildlife Observation Site and view the massive Salmon Glacier.

We stood next to our bicycles, mustering the most pathetic, poor-starving-kids-just-needing-a-break looks on our faces. Having hitchhiked many times while hiking the PCT to get into towns for resupply, we were not newbies to what it took to get a ride: look clean, respectable, angelic, and desperate. However, we hadn't seen any cars pass while eating breakfast at the gas station, and as we had two large, loaded-down bicycles, we needed a truck or a large vehicle to stop. There was no way we were getting a ride.

Not fifteen minutes had ticked by before a little white Ford pickup passed, braked quickly, slammed into reverse, and backed up. Surprised, we looked at each other. The driver stepped out, a behemoth of a man, covered head to toe in tattoos, with a shiny bald head, glasses that hid his eyes, and a sleeveless shirt, even though it was cold enough to see your breath in the air. He must have left his Hells Angels jacket in the truck. His hands were big enough to choke both of us at the same time. "Wurd ya doin' out here, eh?"

The female passenger bounded out of the car, all four feet nothing, wild curly hair, glasses, looking like a middle-school librarian. "Eh there guys, you want a ride? Where ya headin'?"

"We would love a ride! We are on a bike tour down the Cassiar but are hoping to do a side trip to go see the Salmon Glacier and Bear Glacier. We don't have enough food or time to get out there by bike and thought maybe we could find a ride." The Hells Angel opened the tailgate and climbed into the bed to help load our bikes. I began removing the panniers as Ville started handing up the bikes.

The Hells Angel slammed the bed of the truck closed and quipped, "Op' in." We were happy to be squished on the bench seat in the back of the pickup, knees at our chins, and not pedaling for a change. The little lady introduced herself as Janine, and her husband was Rod. Janine translated because Rod fired sentences at us in a local dialect (many immigrants in the area are of Irish decent) that we struggled to understand.

They toured us around the glaciers before dropping us off back where we started, hugging us tightly before heading on their way.

The next day, after a full day's ride with blue skies and rocketing tailwinds, Ville and I came to where the Cassiar ended, dumping us east on the Yellowhead Highway, also known as the "Highway of Tears," which we planned to ride to Prince George. The section we would be traveling on is bordered by twenty-three First Nations. Since the early 1970s there have been seventy-one cases of women, disproportionately indigenous or of First Nation, who have been murdered or gone missing along this stretch of highway. Systemic racism, drug abuse, domestic violence, disconnection from traditional culture, foster care, Canada's Indian residential school system, and poverty contribute to these cases. Those in poverty are less likely to own a car, so hitchhiking is used to get to work, school, and medical and family services. The special task force formed to solve the cases of missing and murdered women have not made much progress, at least not publicly.

We passed many towering billboards with the faces of those missing, reminding those who travel "Never to hitchhike." A sadness filled my chest as I looked into the eyes of each girl. *How many more will follow them?* It was a dark cloud that followed us. Pedaling just in front of Ville, I was grateful that I was not alone on this highway.

I ran over a three-inch screw and heard a *psssssst* as the rear tube deflated. I pulled to the shoulder, got off the bike, and walked it up a long driveway to inspect the damage. The screw was still lodged deep in the tire. I looked down at my odometer and said to Ville, "Well, we made it just under two thousand miles before getting a puncture. Not bad!"

"Not too shabby," Ville responded, bending down to inspect the tire. He pulled out his hand tools and used the plyers to extract the screw, then pulled out the patch kit and tire lever. He paused. "Geez, it's been years since I've patched a tire. Let's see if I remember how to do it."

It had been years since I had done one either. I flipped my bike upside down, resting it on the seat and handlebars, and removed the rear tire, being careful to remove the chain from the cassette so the tire would come off easily. Unfortunately, the tire fit snuggly onto the rim and removing it with the tire lever proved to be far more difficult than either of us expected. We were sweating profusely by the time the tube was removed. With the help of instructions, we sanded, glued, and patched up the tube and had it back inside the tire in no time. Getting the tire back on the rim was a different story.

"How the hell can this be so difficult!" I yelled, taking my turn at the tire. I straddled the wheel, jammed the tire lever inside, and attempted to guide the tire inside the edge of the rim, with limited progress. Sweat poured into my eyes. *Is it going to be this hard every time I get a flat?* I wondered. *Damn, I hope not.*

Of course, I knew it would be.

"My turn," Ville said. I handed him the tire. Twenty minutes passed before we managed to wrestle the tire back inside the rim. Ville used a small hand pump to reinflate the tube, and I slipped the tire back into place, being careful to drape the chain back onto the teeth of the cassette and tighten the lever on my thru axle. I flipped the bike back upright, climbed back on the saddle, and we headed toward Smithers.

Smithers was a decent-sized town with a population just over five thousand a couple days' ride on the Yellowhead Highway. It was also home to Jim, an older brother of Martin, who I had been a nanny to for over ten years in Bend. Jim was a lawyer, towering, solid as an ox, with hair and a beard flying in all directions. His wife and two kids were out of town for the weekend, and getting fully dressed seemed optional, as was cleaning up after oneself. He welcomed us with a large bottle of Wild Turkey. Drinking whiskey felt like swallowing fire and went straight to my head. Within minutes, I was floating happily at the kitchen table. In addition to a shower, laundry, and resupply, Ville and I craved conversation with friends. Preparing food in a fully stocked kitchen and dining at a table with ice-cold beverages was a novelty. We purposely didn't plan our entire trip route; instead, we asked those we met along the way for recommendations. We spread out Jim's maps across his dining room table while sipping on whiskey and snacking on wild boar sausages.

After a few days' rest, we headed east through the Bulkley Valley and rode for a couple days through beautiful rolling hills of farmland littered with giant rolls of haybales, as overhead thunderheads threatened rain and the weather remained unbelievably hot. We stripped off our rain jackets and then our sleeves. The four-lane highway was congested, but the shoulder was big enough to retain our senses of space, safety, and sanity.

Ville's tooth started aching. When I questioned him about it, he admitted to having cracked it somewhere on the Dalton Highway, about eight days into the ride, due in part to the excessive dirt and gravel that got into every nook and cranny, including his mouth. When we arrived in Prince George, Ville was in excruciating pain and in dire need of a dentist. By the time we tracked one down who was willing to see him, Ville was nearly rabid and scared shitless. He had told me he was afraid of dentists, but I thought it was a joke, since he is not afraid of anything. It turned out that he had suffered trauma as a child, knocking out his front tooth on some poor little girl's forehead, and has been deathly afraid of dentists ever since. He must have been in sheer agony to be begging to see one.

Late that afternoon, after an hour in a dental chair, he charged out of the dental office like he had been violated in there. They told him he needed a crown, a procedure that would take a month or more to complete, but without the time or money for that, he asked them to fix it as best they could. They filled it and sent him on his way. We found one of those cheap Mongolian buffet places and stuffed our faces. Our bike-building friend, James, had told us to change our chains every two- to three-thousand miles, and since we had traveled 2,200 miles since leaving Prudhoe Bay we decided to look for chains. A bicycle shop around the corner had the right chain size for our bikes, 116-link ten-speed chain, so we switched them out and poked our way through the sprawling city of Prince George until we reached Highway 97 and headed south.

Traffic choked the highway as the shoulder disappeared, making climbs and blind corners a nightmare. About 20 percent of traffic cared enough to move over and give us room. Since there were multiple, large, lumber mills along this stretch of highway, most of the passing traffic were giant log-loaded semis. If you have been in a car when one of these passed, loaded as high as a two-story building, you know that the vortex nearly blows you off the road. Imagine what it would feel like to be on an itty-bitty bicycle when one of these monsters thundered past about a foot from your body at sixty miles per hour. It was pure, repeating hell.

Prince George to Williams Lake was a logging truck nightmare. We rode silently and slowly through hot, sweaty, sandy, windy forests of quaking aspens, lodgepole pines, and white spruce. We were now in the central interior of British Columbia, more desert-like than the pine forests at the coast. As we traveled south, we were catching up to hot deep green summer. The noise from this large arterial road scared off anything not rooted. By the time we arrived at Williams Lake we agreed to take the adventurous Highway 20 route back to the coast.

Ville had no sooner fixed my rear tire, digging out multiple metal, needle-like shards that had been lodged in the rubber when, not five minutes later, it was flat again. For those who have not toured by bicycle—at least not long enough to wear down some tire tread—these metal shards are a total nightmare. They are left behind when an old semitruck or car tire explodes, leaving fragments of the interior radial of the tire, the width of a needle and no longer than a quarter of an inch littered about the road and undetectable to a cyclist. They lodged themselves deep into our tires, punctured tiny holes in our tubes, and frequently required pliers to dig out, which took up vast amounts of time while roadside, often without a shoulder, traffic whizzing by. A total joy. The last of the day's light was flickering through the trees, and we were both at our wits' end. "We just need to camp; we can deal with it in the morning," Ville reasoned as we searched the surrounding forest for a flat spot to camp. Only a three-strand barbed-wire fence for cattle lay in our way, so we removed and hefted the panniers, one by one, over it, followed by our bikes, and pitched the tent.

The 800-foot climb out of Williams Lake had been treacherous. We spun in our lowest granny gears, plugging away hour after hour, up and up and up into the hillside, until we summitted and quickly descended into a deep canyon cut by a river. The canyon grew wider as lush, green sprinklered pastures filled its breadth. As we descended deeper into the canyon, walls the color of fire rose up around us on either side, Rocky Mountain juniper and sage dotting the hillside. We crossed an old stone bridge over the wide Fraser River on the canyon floor and began a thousand-foot climb—more up and up and up—to an expansive plateau.

We pulled over to the side of the road to catch our breath and caught the attention of two women passing by in a Blazer, who stopped to see if we were alright. Suzanne and her daughter Lisa lived 115 miles west on Highway 20 in a small community called Tatla Lake. Suzanne had silver hair and thick glasses and was very direct. She and her husband had an extra cabin on their farm that we were welcome to stay in if we were riding that far down the road. These details were emphatically confirmed by Lisa, who told us she lived on the same farm in a separate house with her husband and two small kids. Suzanne gave us her phone number, and they left. We followed an undulating road through rolling pasturelands and lodgepole pine forests. That pleasure lasted until my tire deflated, leaving us stranded on the side of the road.

9

Chris Pratt

We reached Suzanne's farm at Tatla Lake and were sitting at the kitchen table in her house gorging on home-cooked food. She said, "You know, you guys are about to bike down the infamous Freedom Road (or some call it "The Hill") coming up in about fifty miles or so, eh?"

"We haven't heard of it. What is it?" I asked.

"Well, it's where the Highway 20 used to end, you see. Right at Anahim Lake, where the highway crosses the Coast Range. And back in the fifties, the government said they wasn't going to finish it, eh. A local man from down in the valley, well, he, and an engineer got some equipment and told the government they was going to finish the road. There was already a trail, but they found a better route and took to working their way up, digging the road in. And a man from up here on the plateau, he got fired up, too, and said he was going to build that road on down and meet them. And so's they both started to working on it, see, digging that road with machines and dynamite, and of course this took a year or more. One going down the hill, the other working his way up. And as they started going, the government, seeing as they was getting it done, started giving them money. And wouldn't you know? They finished it. And where they met, there is now a sign. Look for it, you'll see it. Where the machines met, they hit their buckets of those machines together like this," she demonstrated, her two fists coming together in the air. "And they had a big party, with all the townsfolk from up here and down there. A real big party, mind you."

I looked over at Ville, his face still slathered in barbecue sauce from the chicken Suzanne and Lisa had made. I wonder, *Should I be concerned my husband appears to not have any feeling in his face?* After meals, I go behind him and mop his face with a napkin to collect the scraps. He was already reaching for the warm apple strudel and ladling scoops of vanilla ice cream on top. He looked up at me with his cockeyed grin I love so much and said, "Well, sounds like an adventure!" And loaded his grin with the dessert.

Freedom Road is a gravel rock-pit of a narrow double, sometimes single, lane adventure descending from an altitude of 4,879 feet to the Pacific Ocean over twenty-seven miles of wildly steep road with hairpin turns and two major switchbacks.

Without the congestion of cars or noise, we saw a plethora of wildlife: eagles, falcons, tons of fleeting little birds and deer. Coming around a turn, I even startled a baby black bear that shot straight up into the air and then ran up the side of the cliff. We enjoyed every minute the whole way down. We saw the hand-scrawled Freedom Road sign nailed to a tree and even a blue metal sign—hand-drawn silhouettes of two backhoes, buckets hoisted in the air facing each other and touching above a single boulder, as Suzanne promised, at the very spot the road was completed.

Riding through cattle pastures and large-scale produce gardens, we passed over creeks and small rivers flowing out of the mountains to be swallowed up by the Bella Coola River. Ancient ponderosa pines towered with hairy green moss from the sea winds, while sprinklers ticked in circles over field after field. Summer enveloped us, and the sun felt warm on my arms. We stopped in Hagensborg to pick up groceries for the ferry and again in Bella Coola to eat some cheeseburgers and fries. We then found a little dirt patch near the dock to camp and wait for the early morning ferry that would take us from Bella Coola to Port Hardy.

I acknowledge that I am insufferable every time I must rise before the sun, and Ville already knew to give me a wide berth. "Are those birds chirping? I hate birds," I muttered in the early hours of morn. We were to check in for the ferry by 5:30 a.m., and I was not happy about it. We boarded the small ferry with seven cars and their drivers. I warmed up after a couple hours and made my way to watch an enormous pod of porpoises. Dall's porpoises, with black-and-white markings resembling those found on orca whales, entertained us with aerial acrobatics. I'd never seen so many porpoises. Three of them jumped, crisscrossed, and played in the wake of the ferry. I wondered, *Why don't we adults do that more? Somewhere along the way we lose our uninhibited playfulness.* A couple of humpback whales surfaced, their large tails gliding in and out of the water with ease, followed by a glimpse of a large black bear swimming across the strait. We disembarked at Bella Bella at dusk and boarded another ferry the size of a cruise ship headed for Vancouver Island. We stowed our bikes down below, sandwiched between vehicles, carried our panniers to an upper level, where we discovered a buffet.

The dining room had chandeliers, fancy paintings, white table linens, and even wine glasses. We had not bathed in four days since Suzanne's place. I wore a salt-stained shirt and pants and had no business in that buffet. We were the second ones in line when it opened. We practically sprinted to the trays heaped with steaming food. There was prime rib, salmon, curries, four different salads, rolls, soup, and six different desserts. We tried them all. And then licked our fingers. We even loaded our pockets with after-dinner mints on the way out.

We ate as if we had not seen food in years. I was not proud of what happened in there, but I felt sublimely gratified. With Ville's arms keeping me warm from the night air, we watched the sun set over Calvert Island from the top deck. He whispered in my ear just as the sun was disappearing, "We are so lucky we get to do this. And I am so grateful I get to do this with you. I love you."

"Yes, we are. And I love you too," I replied, turning up to kiss him.

It was a fiasco getting off the ferry with thousands of cars, trucks, and semitrailers, and due to the late hour and our fatigue we stopped and camped at a roadside pullout. In daylight the next morning, we realized what a weird spot we had chosen, next to a roadside information board that read Welcome to Port Hardy and Activities, Attractions and Wildlife with a picture of a bunch of giant grizzly bears. The weather was a bit overcast and misty, but around us was thick, beautiful forest. It smelled of wet dirt and decaying vegetation. Throughout the day, the kind people we had met and chatted with on the ferry drove past us, slowing down, honking, and waving fiercely out their windows. It felt like we were part of a traveling community.

On Vancouver Island we used the website called warmshowers. org—a resource hub for touring cyclists. It seemed like another great way to meet people along the way. The first host we found was Tom, a soft-spoken, gray-bearded rocker, who rode a motorcycle with a sidecar. He did not ride a bicycle but loved to host and had the skills of a master chef. He was a touring cyclist's dream. He cooked a multitude of homemade dishes: pizzas, spaghetti, and ice cream with grilled pineapple on top. We listened to his rock tunes, rants about politics, and wild tales of travel abroad. Upon leaving Tom's house, we rode south through days of hilly, thick green forests of towering pines, cedar, fir, aspens, and hemlock, with crabapple, oak, dogwood, and maple trees mixed in. So diverse and healthy were the trees that lumber companies wanted a piece of the action. The hillsides were checkered with large swaths of clear-cut baldness and snarled stumps.

We tried to find a place to camp near Nanaimo not realizing until we arrived that it was a sprawling city. We took a few wrong turns off the freeway, down what we assumed were country roads, arriving in thick brush with an abnormal amount of paper and plastic bags and such flittering about. We pitched the tent, cooked some spaghetti, ate, played a mean game of rummy, and went to sleep. In the morning, we discovered the sign we had missed on the way in: Nanaimo Garbage & Recycling. We camped in a real-life garbage dump. Maybe in my next life I will be born a princess who sleeps in castles and rides in chariots, but until then I am a vagabond who lives in a tent, rides a bicycle, and sleeps in garbage dumps.

Life on a bicycle, free from the constraints of our former lives, made the world feel both bigger and smaller. When we had been riding the Dalton Highway, a single mile had sometimes felt insurmountable, and now after two months we had completed almost 3,000 of them. At the start of the ride, a day in the seat felt like an eternity. I don't remember the moment I stopped counting the miles, but I know I noticed them less. My internal voice had been silenced. I was able to still my mind. Thoughts would come and go as I passed through ever-changing landscapes. I felt more peaceful, quiet, and calm. The chaos that had existed in my life before the ride felt far away. I wondered how it would feel to go back to Bend, for we would be riding through it in a couple weeks' time. *Would the chaos envelope me as soon as I returned, or would it take time to seep back in?* I told Ville we should not stay too long.

In Vancouver our friends Jussi and Maurine had a downtown high-rise apartment, and they welcomed us for four days to get off our bikes and the busy streets. An affluent businessman and entrepreneur, Jussi insisted on paying for everything, politely declining Ville's request to pay our share. He and Maurine showered us with luxuries. We exchanged our tattered cycling scrubs for borrowed dresses, collared shirts, slacks, and sandals. We dined at French bistros, sushi houses, and five-star hotels—restaurants we couldn't afford but were grateful to visit. We had cocktail hours in robes and toured the city in a Jaguar. It was decadent and gloriously over the top. We reveled in every minute of it and cherished the memories. When we said our goodbyes on the last day and rode away, I was genuinely excited to get back on my bike, albeit much heavier than when I had dismounted. My new world was on a bicycle. That was where I belonged and where I felt comfortable.

We hopped on another ferry, to Victoria, and rode through the heart of the vibrant downtown and then through tall, canopied trees, rolling pastureland, along country roads, along ocean vista bluffs and to the next ferry, easily stamped out of Canada and into the U.S. all at once.

On San Juan Island we disembarked at the pint-sized, pretentious town of Friday Harbor and after circling the island, we wrapped up our day with fish and chips at the Bait Shop. While standing at the front counter, the room no larger than a bedroom, a man and his son walked in and stood in line behind us. Ville leaned over and whispered to me, "KG, is that Chris Pratt behind us?" I glanced behind to check. It looked like the most famous Hollywood action film star of the moment to me, but I wasn't about to ask.

"Excuse me, are you Chris Pratt?" Ville asked, a little starstruck.

"Yes, I am," he answered, matter of factly.

Ville told him we enjoyed watching one of his TV shows and films, flitting around like a nervous teenager, stargazing his man crush.

"Do you guys live here?" Chris asked.

"No, no. We are on a long bicycle tour, and we are just passing through. We started up in Alaska and so far have made it to here," I said.

"Bicycles? You rode bicycles here from Alaska?"

"Yeah. I know! It sounds really crazy now, hearing it out loud. We are planning to ride all the way down to Argentina."

"That is crazy! How do you do that? Do you carry everything on your bikes?"

"Yep," and after Chris Pratt finished placing his order, we proceeded to explain our gear, panniers, bikes, how and where we camp, and all the details of our journey. He asked loads of questions and seemed to be as awestruck as we were to be telling all this to some giant Hollywood star. After our meals arrived, Ville and I set them on the counter directly under two big windows overlooking the street. Chris gathered his order, wished us well, walked out the front door, and waved at us through the windows before ducking out of sight down an alley. He had no sooner disappeared than a throng of squealing, sprinting, hyperventilating teens streaked past the windows and down the same alley. I was immediately overcome with gratitude that I was a nobody on a bicycle tour and not a Hollywood movie star. Thinking about it, nobody but family and some friends knew where we were right then or what we were in the middle of—and it felt perfect. Weightless. And free.

10

Looney Tunes

On Orcas Island, Ville and I finished the long climb to the top of Mount Constitution sweating like pigs, bicycles fully loaded with gear. Mount Constitution rises 2,399 feet above sea level, the second-highest island mountain in the lower forty-eight states. We had ridden a narrow, two-lane road full of hairpin turns to the stone observation tower on the summit. The tower—modelled after a medieval watch tower—was crawling with tourists. We made quite the statement, arriving like racehorses thundering across the finish line—snorting, panting, muscles gorged, and shiny sweat glistening in the sun. We leaned our bikes against a fence and took the stone steps to the top of the tower, taking great care as to avoid exposing anyone to potential contact with our sweaty, smelly bodies.

The 360-degree view on that beautiful clear summer day revealed Mount Baker and Mount Rainier, as well as Vancouver, Victoria, and the surrounding islands. The high vantage point underscored how far we had come and how far we still had to go. Ushuaia was as mysterious to us as the journey to come. Our life was living in the moment, our path forgotten, our future on the horizon. My heartbeat was all I felt, my breath all I heard, the beauty of the world all I saw.

Late that afternoon, after a zippy, winding descent down Mount Constitution, we found ourselves rifling through the leaflets at the front of the Orcas Island Public Library while we waited for all our electronics to charge. "Hey, KG, get a load of this guy outside looking at our bikes," Ville said. He stood and looked through the floor-to-ceiling windows at a man standing in front of our bikes, which were locked to a post. Pudgy with a scraggly beard, the man was draped in eclectic clothing and moved in an exaggerated fashion, throwing his hands in the air and repositioning them in a *Thinker* pose, crossing and uncrossing his legs, bouncing around the bikes as if they were a campfire and he were performing a wild dance. I rose out of my chair and joined Ville at the window.

"KG, that was the guy I opened the door for when we walked in," Ville laughed. "The guy who said to me, 'Why thank you, kind sir,' and bowed like a circus performer—remember?" Then it rang a bell.

As quickly as the guy began his wild antics, he changed course and stormed toward the front door of the library. He ripped open the front door and questioned loudly, "Are those your guys' bikes out there?" He gestured toward our bikes with wild eyes.

"Yep, those are ours," Ville said.

"Are those your frame bags on those bikes?" he asked.

The scene from *Dumb and Dumber* popped into my mind, the one where Lloyd asks a girl if the skis on top of her car are hers. When she replies, "Yes," he then asks, "Both of them?"

"Yep, frame bags are ours, too," Ville responded politely, telling him the brand and details about all the compartments. Ville's frame bag had the Finnish flag sewn across the outside, and mine had a bright yellow beaver that came from the Oregon state flag. "Actually, I have a card from the company," Ville said, then rifled through his front handlebar bag for a business card and handed it to the man.

"Wow, gee, thanks so much. This is great, really great. I need to get one of these for my bike." He rolled the card over in his hand like we had just given him a hundred-dollar bill and stuffed it into a shirt pocket. "Is there anything I can help you kind folks with?" he asked, bowing like a hotel concierge. He reminded me of Jack Black.

"Actually," Ville responded, "we are looking for a safe place to stealth camp. Not in a campground, but somewhere in the forest or something." Ville turned, and out of the handlebar bag he pulled a small map we had of the San Juan Islands.

Our character drew us around him and said, "No need for a map. Check this out," as he raised his left hand, revealing a massive pinkie ring, about the size of a nickel and made of shiny gold, with a map of Orcas Island on it. "See, what you want to do is head here. We are here. Head down here and when you get to this cross section, there is a gas station . . ." he said, pointing to the ring, then pausing to stand up straight for full emphasis, hair flying about wildly, " . . . where you can get really good weed. Don't forget to stop there. And then head down here," more finger pointing at the ring, "where you want to turn across from a dirt road. You want to go up, not down, the road, up there into the trees and there you can camp. But don't forget to turn uphill from the road. Did I already mention to stop at the gas station? They have really great weed."

Completely puzzled by the directions given on a pinkie ring, Ville pointed at the map, and said, "Do you mind showing us on our map, so I make sure—"

"It's super easy, turn here, across from here. Here is the gas station, and here is where you want to camp." More random pointing at the ring.

"Got it. Thanks so much," Ville exhaled, smiling politely.

"Really appreciate your help," I chimed in.

He bowed gracefully, almost completely to the floor. "Well, folks, I bid you adieu!" And just like that, as flamboyantly as he had arrived, he flung the door open and headed back out with exaggerated, bouncing steps, his heels hardly touching the pavement. He flung open the door of a rusty brown and white eighties boat of a car that roared to life when he got in. As he passed, we noticed a rusty red bike, about as aged as the car, bungee-corded into the trunk, which rattled and bounced as he gunned it over the apron and out onto the main road, fan belt squealing as he rounded the corner. We both watched in awe as he sped out of sight, black smoke hanging in his wake.

We stood there in a moment of shock and awe until Ville broke the silence by asking, "Did you see what DVDs that guy was carrying?"

"No. What?"

"*Looney Tunes.*"

Of the 172 named islands and reefs in San Juan County only three are serviced by ferry: San Juan, Orcas, and Lopez. Like kids from the same family, each of them has its own personality, as well as unique terrain. San Juan is a patchwork of thick green canopied forests opening to expansive grasslands, intermediate hill climbs, and a glut of summer homes for the upper crust elites. Orcas, shaped like a horseshoe, is the hilliest, soddenly green, with farmers' markets and a wide assortment of locals. Lopez lies in the rain shadow of the other islands, making it the flattest and driest—covered in short, dry grasses, littered with farms and a population of friendly locals, who waved as we rolled past. It is home to Spencer Spit State Park, perched on the eastern shorefront, and where we spent Labor Day with an enormous group of Seattleites, camping out for the holiday weekend. They invited us to join their party for dinner and breakfast the next morning, adopting us immediately as friends. It felt warm and inclusive after seventy-two days on the move.

In the tepid sunshine, with full bellies and hearts, we pedaled back to the ferry and took it west of the small town of Anacortes on the north shore of Whidbey Island. As we pedaled farther south down the island, ever closer to the metropolis of Seattle, the houses grew larger and more opulent, and the traffic grew increasingly worse. After a long ride to the end of Whidbey Island, I looked down at the very moment my odometer clicked over to 3,000 miles.

Incredibly, we had done it, biked all that distance, and still my odometer clicked on. I had never thought to look at what the distance might be from Prudhoe Bay to Ushuaia, but having biked 3,000 miles we still had a daunting number of miles to ride before we reached the bottom of the next continent so far away. It really didn't matter because I was in a rhythm. My wrists hurt less; my seat had softened, as had the leather one I sat upon; my knees stopped aching long ago; my now-muscular legs felt stronger and sturdier, and they pedaled automatically. Somewhere along the way, I had become a cyclist, although I still did not feel like one. A cyclist wore a jersey and padded spandex while I wore a T-shirt and padding inside shorts. A cyclist set out to do miles on a bike, but I set out to see the world and it happened to be on a bike. Being a cyclist was not in my nature, but somehow I had become one.

Pedaling through the sprawling skyscrapers of Seattle, we passed many cyclists: bike messengers, bike commuters, touring cyclists, BMXers, those out for sport, cruising, racing, jumping, spinning, you name it. There were all ages on all types of bikes, mountain, tour, road, triathlon, BMX, fixed-gear, tandem, trike, folding, cruiser, recumbent, kid, and fat bikes. Our world was instantly inundated with cyclists and bikes. There were hordes of people and an overdose of lights and noise. I felt stressed and anxious, ready to leave the city immediately.

Let me start with this: If you are driving a car around the peninsula and make your way into the Olympic National Park to hike, climb, camp, soak in hot springs, wander through old-growth forests and the plethora of rain forests inside, then climb back into your cozy car out of the rain, turn on your windshield wipers, and drive yourself back to a warm shower somewhere, I imagine it to be an epic experience.

We circumnavigated the Olympic National Park on exposed bi-cycles on the overly trafficked and logged Highway 101—chip-seal pavement with mostly little to no shoulder—looping around the peninsula through beautiful forests hacked into a patchwork of clear cuts and recently replanted saplings with only a fifteen-mile stretch of peekaboo sea views and the remainder shrouded by forest. Apart from a brief stretch of road winding along the beautiful shoreline of Crescent Lake and the stunning, southern end of Bone River Natural River Preserve, the rest was painful.

After the Olympic Peninsula we pitched our tent just north of the Columbia River and hunkered down for the night. After a scrump-tious breakfast of oatmeal, nuts, and cocoa powder made in our lone titanium pot, we were beckoned to a roaring fire by a couple sitting next to their RV. Dalver and Sam were a sweet middle-aged couple, decked out in Oregon State University clothing, who invited us for coffee and eggs.

"Go, Beavers," I said, knowing the mascot of the school, because it was my alma mater.

"Huh?" they both chimed, looking puzzled.

"Your clothes. Oregon State. That's where I went to college. Well, I didn't go to the main campus, but the satellite campus in Bend. Where I'm from."

"Oh, honey, we bought these clothes at a garage sale the other day. Normally we don't wear clothes," Dalver replied, peeking over his spectacles while scrambling eggs in a pan. "We live most of the time in Arizona, where it's warm! We live in a nudist commune there."

I knew not to glance in Ville's direction, because if I were to see the look he had on his face I would start laughing uncontrollably. I was also trying not to picture these two seniors nude while they cooked, squatted, and tittered about.

"Honey, let me ask you this. Do you like wearing clothes?" Dalver asked me, staring above his spectacles while pointing at me with a spatula, as if it was the most normal thing to ask a stranger. I think back to the frigid temperatures out on the Dalton Highway wrapped in our puffy jackets, my cycling sleeves protecting my skin from the sun, and our rain gear keeping us dry in the rain forests of the Olympic Peninsula. *Yes, I feel that I can say with complete confidence that I genuinely love wearing clothes. I adore wearing clothes.*

Instead, I politely responded, "No, not really. Must be a really freeing experience to be naked all the time." I said this as I scanned their giant tour-bus-sized RV, decked out with all the creature comforts that we let go of so long ago.

"You better believe it, babe. It is wonderful, flinging off all your constraining clothing," he replied, while bending over to pull a tray out of the oven.

"Maybe I'll have to try it sometime," I said, imagining trying to ride a bicycle all day without padding on my butt, my breasts swaying to and fro. What a sight, Ville and me biking nude down the highway, shocking onlookers, and probably causing traffic accidents along the way.

We pedaled over the 4.1-mile Astoria–Megler Bridge connecting Washington and Oregon, dodging hundreds of flattened double-crested cormorants along the way that had been shot by the Army Corps of Engineers in an attempt to save endangered juvenile salmon, and jumped onto Highway 30, making a beeline for Portland, where we planned a short reprieve from bikes and some much-needed family and friend time. It was September 9. We had been on the road for seventy-six days, and we had ninety miles left to Portland. It was so close we could taste it. My skin felt electric. Having never driven the highway, I assumed it was flat, hugging the edge of the Columbia River the whole way into Portland. *It had to be flat just over the looming mountain pass I could see in front of us.* The four-lane traffic zoomed maddeningly close because the white-striped shoulder had all but disappeared. We came to the summit, our bicycles picking up speed on the rapid descent. I coasted and gripped the handlebars tightly. *That is behind us now,* I thought with gratefulness. *The city must be close because so many license plates that zoomed past us were from Oregon.* But I was mistaken.

We had two more mountain passes to climb over that afternoon, each one more grueling than the last. We questioned our safety around every blind curve, knowing the cars coming up behind us had no idea we were there being squeezed into the roadway. If we hadn't been so desperate to get to Portland by the end of the day we may have looked for an alternate route. We needed a break, to take hot showers, to eat homecooked food, and to be embraced by family. We had to get there that night.

Somewhere in the chaotic merging of the highway into the city, Ville was sucked off his bike by a vortex left by a passing bus. He overcorrected in the soft sand of the shoulder and cartwheeled into the bushes. Being in front, I saw none of it, and didn't know it happened until Ville caught back up to me, flagging me to pull over into the parking lot of a bicycle shop. I felt sickened that I'd left him behind. Now his knee was swollen, and his back was locking up. I hugged him and was relieved he was all right, sustaining only minor bumps and bruises. Bad things seemed to happen to us when we threw caution to the wind, and they were only compounded by exhaustion. We tended to pile on too many miles.

The two young mechanics went right to work, adjusting the fork and brakes on Ville's bike, finishing as my brother, Jordan, pulled into the parking lot. I was over the moon with excitement, tears welling in my eyes. We made it home. My brother leaned down and engulfed me. I inhaled deeply. He smelled like home. After he released me, he brought Ville into a big hug, too. There is nothing more gratifying, calming, and happiness-inducing than family. And here was my brother, eight years younger than I, tall and lanky, short brown hair and brown eyes with an electric smile. Jordan is an exceptional rock climber and computer programmer, and we had grown up together with the same adventurous spirit, although his is more calculated than mine. We saw each other often, and when apart spoke on the phone frequently, always supporting each other from wherever in the world we might be. And here he was, in the flesh, hugging us and telling us how much he had missed us. It felt good to be missed, and Ville and I were home. At least for now.

We went to Tualatin, a southern suburb of Portland, to see my sister, Lisa, her husband, Sean, and their little boy, Braydon. Lisa is beautiful with long, dirty-blond hair, shining blue eyes, and a picture-perfect smile; and she is a far better person than I am. She is calm, patient, nurturing, and kind, the middle child and family peacekeeper. She was born sixteen months after me, and as a child I had no intention of sharing the limelight. I treated her awfully. I picked all the games, told her I would play the princess and made her be the toad. When she wanted to switch, I did not want to play anymore. I regret that I was so unkind to her, but she just loved me back. Friends of our family promised us, "You will love each other when you're older," but we were sure it could not possibly be true. Luckily, as time and life passed, we grew to love each other and now have a sisterly bond I had not imagined possible as a child. Sean is her perfect match, as kindhearted as she.

When we had flown to Alaska two and a half months earlier, Braydon was crawling and babbling. Now, he was running and uttering basic words. Nothing had changed, and yet everything had changed. My mom joined us the following day, and the only one missing was my dad, who we planned to see when we drove back with her to Bend.

Mom is a spitfire, energetic and chatty. She is about as tall as I am, five-foot-six, with dark brown hair and brown eyes, quite klutzy despite her relentless exercise. She doesn't know the meaning of rest, and more than likely I get my infinite drive from her. With similar personality types, we butted heads often as I was growing up, but she has always been there for me to answer my calls and talk me through homesickness and travesties when I have felt helpless abroad. She is the glue that holds our family together.

The car ride over the Cascades to Bend was unnerving after traveling so long at an average of twelve miles per hour, but I've never been happier to watch the pavement fly past with my butt on a soft, cushioned seat. I calculated that if we had biked it, it would have taken us about three days. From the back seat, Ville pointed out all the flat spots in the trees where we could easily pitch a tent. As it rained, I watched the windshield wipers whisk the water off the glass and disappear in the wind.

I thought of all the times those rivers of cold water had run down my spine. With chills at the thought, I reached down and adjusted the heater. "Honey, are you cold? You can just push this," my mom said, reaching down and pushing a switch on the dash. "It's a seat warmer." Just like that with a flip of a switch, my butt began to warm. How comfortable and sheltered we humans have become, and how far removed from those comforts I had been. I sat thinking on it as the rain came down harder, for once, not on my face.

We turned into the driveway at Bear Creek Ranch, the farm where I had lived since I was twelve, and spotted my dad raking leaves under the orchard trees that lined the driveway. I asked my mom to pull over, too excited to wait until we reached the house. The car rolled to a stop. I unbuckled my belt, jumped out, and ran to throw my arms around my dad's waist. My dad is over six feet tall and towers over me, but he has always wrapped me in hugs. He has dark brown hair and brown eyes like my mom, and just like her he never stops working. He is a master craftsman carpenter, perfectionist, and overly dramatic. He is always joking around and teasing and is only serious when he is angry. He dropped the rake in the leaves and hugged me tightly back, my family complete. Now we were home.

11

Waterlogged

Outside my sister's house thunderstorms left everything sodden in their wake. It was not an encouraging morning, but Ville and I were itching to get back on the road. Two weeks off bikes in Portland and Bend had slipped into four; we were growing pudgy and soft. It was now October. Rain or shine, it was time to go. We hugged and kissed with promises to see each other again at the end of our ride, an estimated year and a half later. I did not want to look back over my shoulder as we pedaled away, did not want to see my baby nephew waving from my mom's arms, or see Lisa and Sean standing close by. The heartache and gloom cinched a tight knot in my chest. As we rounded the bend, I looked back over my shoulder anyway. They were still standing there waving. The knot moved to my throat and tears stung my eyes. I tried to brush them aside, but more fell.

We headed west toward the Oregon coast, the coastal mountain range in our path. Once we reached the coast, we intended to ride along the coastal highway through Oregon and California. A drizzle settled in the air as we climbed, and before long it turned into constant, merciless, punishing rain. There was a good chance it wouldn't lift until the following summer.

Rain is the cultivator of life, something I enjoyed singing and dancing in on the rare occasions it fell from the sky in the high desert where I grew up. But as I rode a bike in it, it became something I loathed. I found no pleasure riding in a jacket and rain pants; it was like wearing a tarp. Cold water pelting you in the face, running down the back of your neck, and cascading down your spine, was deeply unsettling. Rain gear never keeps you dry. I thought of the butt-warming seat and windshield wipers in my mom's car with a wry smile. By evening, the rain came down so violently we could hardly see ten feet ahead, but as luck would have it we happened upon a gazebo above a picnic bench in a gated park. We crammed our tent under the awning to get out of the rivers of water, now cascading down the mountainside. Ville refused to go out to pee, preferring instead to stay under the shelter of the awning and face the thick forest. I went to sleep with my family weighing heavily on my mind.

Early the next morning, we rode out in the continuing drizzle. Radiant fall leaves covered the ground, making squishing noises under our tires. The fall colors were an absolute spectacle of yellows, oranges, and reds of all shades. We coasted down the canyon toward Highway 101, hardly having to pedal at all, the road winding slowly as it hugged the mountainside. We made it ten miles before we were flagged to a stop by a road crew in bright orange vests. They told us a massive boulder the size of a pool table had hurtled down the side of the mountain, taking with it a large portion of the hillside and parts of the road. "You need to head back up the way you came to where there is a fork in the road, take that detour 'round to getcha to the 101," said nice Mr. Flag Man.

"Sorry, but how far back is that?" we asked, deflated. "Do you know how long the detour is?"

"Oh, I'd say about twenty-five extra miles round," he said, apparently disregarding the fact that we were sitting on bicycles in the freezing rain.

We sat there for a moment, contemplating what to do next. Mr. Flag Man explained the alternate route in greater detail, then asked where we had come from. His name was Richard, and he had been working on the job all morning. He had just recovered from a bout of Lyme disease and had a wife and three kids. After twenty minutes of talking, he told us to wait and he would get us through as soon as it was safe enough for us to pass. What a world of difference it made to smile, show kindness, and talk respectfully with someone. We had both made a new friend and shortened our day by twenty-five rainy miles on muddy, slippery roads. It took an hour and a half to get around the landslide, but pushing bikes over a bunch of fallen trees and loose dirt was far better than the alternative. He waved at us as he continued to turn around cars, their taillights disappearing back up the mountainside.

Our ride down the coast went downhill from there. We rode 638 miles in three weeks, chilled, gear sopping wet, and feeling miserable. There are variations of rain: drizzle, deluge, downpour, cloudburst, sun shower, and flooding. We rode through it all. We watched it fall as we huddled under trees, bus stops, a church, from inside the homes of kind strangers who allowed us shelter and grocery stores, where we sat with our gear draped over shopping carts to dry. We watched it from inside a rented yurt with our friend Marc, who drove over to the coast from Bend to cheer us up, listened to it pound on the roof while sleeping on a garage floor of a young guy in Port Orford. We were pounded by it every day of the 16,000 feet of elevation gain we pedaled in Oregon.

After we crossed into California the rain sprayed into our faces from speeding cars as they zoomed past. The posted speed had changed from fifty-five to sixty-five, but clearly that was only a "recommended speed" because everyone exceeded it. We watched rain fall from the soaring, branches of the ancient redwood trees in Humboldt Redwoods State Park as we pedaled the Avenue of the Giants through the park, half expecting unicorns or fairies to leap out from behind the trees or ferns. We purchased a large, heavy, camouflaged tarp, the kind used for covering lawn equipment and such, at a hardware store in Arcata so we could string it up over our tent when it became so waterlogged it no longer kept the rain out. And right there, in the unrelenting rain, was where Ville began to crack or, you could say, lose his mind.

"KG, I can't take this rain anymore. It's hell!" Ville yelled as it pelted the pavement so hard it seemed to bounce back up at us. We were stopped at a red light, and when I looked over my left shoulder so I could hear him shouting behind me I saw pity in the eyes of the female driver pulled up alongside us. I pitied us both. After all, I was miserable, but Ville was visually distressed. "We need to get down to L.A. We should get sunshine there at least. I just can't take this rain anymore."

But we had to take it, three more days of it. We shivered constantly and rode to stay warm. At the sleepy town of Leggett, we turned off Highway 101 onto Highway 1 and climbed two gargantuan mountain passes, shrouded in fog, on our way to the ocean, the rain stinging our faces like needle pricks on the speedy descents. When we dropped to the coastal road hugging the shoreline, we could barely make out the waves. It was so dreary. As we rode into the town of Fort Bragg, the clouds dissipated at last, and the blazing sun came out in full force, as if infuriated it had been obscured for so long. We stopped at a roadside café, took off our shoes to pour out the water, rung out our socks, peeled off all our layers down to shirts and shorts, and sat at a picnic table to let the sun warm our cheeks and dry our clothes. We ate greasy burgers with boatloads of fries and topped them off with milkshakes. Right then I couldn't think of a happier moment in my life. Time stood still. Because we had suffered, because we had endured, the sun that day was brighter, cheerier, more appreciated, and more undeniably real.

With ten miles left to get to our friends' place in Mendocino, we rode as if we had sprung giant sails and were carried on the breeze. It felt effortless. Every crash of a passing wave punctuated our excitement for the sudden turn of weather and a few planned days of rest. Karen and Jared lived in a white, dilapidated, Victorian doll house that clung to the cliffs just above town, and they came out to greet us at their picket fence when we arrived. Karen was an acquaintance from Bend, and Jared was her boyfriend with whom she had recently reconnected. Both active and spontaneous, they also lived in flux. By nightfall, the rain thundered on the roof, lulling us to sleep snuggled up in their cozy spare bed. Thankfully, the rain was gone by morning. We cooked the last of our oatmeal, mixing in dates and some maple syrup, and then set off for town. We poked about in little knickknack shops and wandered along the rocky shoreline. By lunchtime, I realized that something was wrong.

My face was tingling, swelling with red, splotchy patches that were becoming more noticeable by the minute. We walked back to the house, where I took an antihistamine and waited for it to get better, but it only worsened. I went to bed trying to push it from my mind, figuring it would be gone by morning. But when I woke up the rash covered more of my body. Jared offered to drive us back to the hospital in Fort Bragg, and we climbed into his truck, reaching the hospital in what felt like a minute. The doctor gave me an IV with a shot of epinephrine and a prescription for Prednisone to take for six days.

Ville took my hand in his, "I'm so happy you're okay, Bumble Bee," he said, squeezing my hand. Then he kissed my forehead and said with a smile, "Poor KG, you look like a botched plastic surgery patient. Man, you got butchered. But I still love you."

He always knows just the right thing to say. That's why I love him so much.

As we rode south from Mendocino the weather perked up, as did my health. It was now early November, and we were averaging about sixty miles a day. The sun came back out, the air grew lighter and breezier, birds chirped and twittered about, and the steroids, now in my system for a couple of days, diminished most of the swelling so only small patches of the rash remained. The sun sparkled in the clear blue sky as we rode over the Golden Gate Bridge into San Francisco. For the entire length of the bridge, we weaved in and out of surprised, spaced-out tourists. We took a rest day in San Francisco and then rode twenty-five miles the next day to Mavericks, the famous surf spot just north of Half Moon Bay, where we watched brave surfers get towed in on jet skis into thirty-to-forty-foot waves. The ride to Santa Cruz was what we'd dreamed the best part of bicycle touring to be, a gentle, undulating road hugging the coast, with crashing waves foaming on a perfect, breezy, mild, sunny day. I wanted to be nowhere else but right there, right then, in that moment, riding my bike with Ville.

We knocked on the door of Kayla and Ben's home in Santa Cruz a block from the cliffs overlooking the sea. The sun was setting, creating rivers of orange that danced on the water, and we felt euphoric. Kayla and Ben were the parents of a traveling friend, Holly, and we were welcomed into their home with open arms. We prepared and ate dinner and laughed together around a large table as friends, although we had met only hours ago. We were given Holly's studio above the garage all to ourselves and fell asleep cozily nestled in her bed.

When I awoke the next morning, my face was swollen, and the rashes had returned. The Prednisone, having run out the day before, had only staved off the symptoms, which were now coming back with vengeance. Ville and I were forced to stay put. By the next day the rash metastasized to a burning fire of hives that spread over my body, consuming my healthy, freckled skin on its path. Only my eyes were saved. I was miserable. I couldn't go outside because the sun aggravated the burning fire. Bedsheets scratched and irritated everything. Only cold showers eased my suffering, so I took as many as I could handle in a day. At my insistence, Ville borrowed a wetsuit and surfboard and went surfing, checking in on me frequently. It would do neither of us any good to both be stuck inside all day.

I refused to take more steroids. Aside from the list of possible side effects: irritability (*have it*), mood changes (*already there*), swelling (*check*), trouble thinking, speaking, or walking (*yes to all three*), trouble breathing at rest (*I would be doing the complete opposite of rest all day*), and possible death (*that did not sound good*), a sticker on the bottle also cautioned against prolonged or excessive exposure to direct and/ or artificial sunlight. Laughable, when I had been and would be on a bicycle all day, every day, in the blazing sun. Perfect.

While on my bike I sometimes wanted to be doing absolutely nothing—that is, until I had nothing to do. Then all I wanted was to be pedaling on my bike. Neither Ville nor I were very good at sitting still and doing nothing. It was killing me inside. I felt just shy of being bored out of my mind. I had flipped through all the magazines on Holly's coffee table three times over, hoping some new story or article might emerge. I turned on the TV and soon turned it off again after scanning all the channels, paced the room like a caged animal, took all the herbs the doctor had given me to take three times a day—a lifeline that promised to bring me back to health and end this boredom. I spent time with Holly's family and helped cook more dinners. By the third day, my skin was slightly better, and we needed to go. We hugged and kissed our friends goodbye, thankful this had happened with friends who, without hesitation, let us stay, and rode back out on Highway 101, once again pedaling south.

Ville and I pedaled on, passing through Monterey and Big Sur, a section of highway we'd been dreaming about since beginning the bike tour. The narrow, two-laned Route 1—known for its winding turns, rugged, seaside cliffs, and unsurpassed views of the often-misty coastline—teetered precariously between the Santa Lucia Mountains and the Pacific Ocean. The steep cliffs made for less encroachment of buildings and population growth; there were no strip malls, billboards, fast food chains, or even cities. Condors circled tranquilly overhead as we descended into canyons and cranked back up cliffs, the dramatic, stunning views beckoning us to pull over repeatedly to take it all in. I was thrilled to be back on my bike, and even though fire still burned my swollen skin, pedaling helped me forget. The weather couldn't have been better—warm sun with a cool breeze that swept up the cliffs by the churning of the waves. I tasted the salt in the air. The only obstacles we had were the long stretches of privately owned (and fenced) properties along the road that forced us to plan for stays at exorbitantly priced and crowded campgrounds.

San Luis Obispo is an old Spanish mission turned college town, and there we stayed with my aunt and uncle for the night. We left the next morning, but the crowded cities and towns made it more difficult to find secluded camping spots. A motel room was out of the question because we didn't have the money.

As we pedaled, I tried not to think about the fact that it was November 18 and we were running out of money to get us to the end of this month. Ville and I had dumped all our savings into our project house, getting it buttoned up and livable for our friends to rent before leaving. We left with a $1,526 cushion in our bank account and would receive, minus expenses, $800 each month in rent. As it turned out, $800 a month for all expenses was an unrealistic budget. We had two bicycles to maintain: a new chain and cassettes for each bicycle about every two months, plus tubes, tires, brake pads, cables, bar tape, oil and whatever else rattled. Additionally, we had to budget for medical expenses and all meals and snacks for two continually starving cyclists (after all, food was our fuel). If there was any money left over, we could get an occasional hotel for a shower and some time alone together.

But now we were almost out of money, which I tried not to think about. I pushed myself to think instead of those living on the street, those forced to live in tents not by choice, and it made me feel less sorry for myself and sorrier for those less fortunate. I'd chosen this ride and adventure, after all. We knew our $800 would go farther once we crossed into Mexico, in 415 miles. We just needed to get there. Besides, everything always worked itself out, maybe not in the way we imagined, but somehow. I told myself this, and deep down I believed it.

My uncle in San Luis Obispo, a fire chief, had called ahead and arranged for a weight room floor for us to sleep on at the Los Alamos Fire Department. Then my cousin gave us her bed in Santa Barbara for two nights, allowing us a day off our bikes to explore the city and pretend to window shop. In Ventura, we watched the surfers paddle furiously to catch waves next to the pier while we ate cold sandwiches sitting on a beach in the sun.

We rode through Malibu with spectacular ocean views to the right and towering desert hillsides to our left. For over thirty miles we rode past houses the size of hotels and cars worth more than our house. I understood the American Dream of a big house, fast car, and more toys, but I preferred to be a cyclist with less than $800 to her name. I had the one thing they did not. No responsibilities. And that made me happy.

Passing through small towns on bicycles had been challenging. When it was sprawling cities, it became a larger brain drain that weighed on our nerves, but when it was a monolithic metropolis, the size of Los Angeles, it was pure hell. After Malibu, according to Google Maps, we would be riding our bikes through the greater Los Angeles area for just under one hundred miles. We needed to endure one hundred miles of continuous urbanization, solid houses, businesses, highways, freeways, pedestrians, drivers, traffic, and chaos before we'd escape at the other end and arrive at Camp Pendleton. My stomach hurt just thinking about it. Navigating through Los Angeles would be a complete nightmare in a car, but on a bicycle it was a death wish. Our only map, displayed on a small cell phone screen clipped onto Ville's handlebars, made navigating intense. Google Maps's bike route often failed to update the route as quickly as we pedaled, and the necessity of keeping our wits about us to predict unexpected traffic maneuvers by drivers who should never have passed a driver's test was exhausting.

In Tustin, we pulled into my Aunt Lori and Uncle Steve's driveway, where we were greeted with smooches, squeezes, hair tussling, and "You kids are crazy," before being ushered into the car to get fattened up at a nearby restaurant. It was glorious. The following day, they took us to REI, where they replaced my tight cycling shoes with a bright green pair and bought us a new gravity filter. Then at my uncle's favorite bicycle shop, he paid to fix absolutely everything on our bikes, including replacing all cables and rotors. It hadn't occurred to me that we might need to change those parts out. Embarrassed that we couldn't pay to fix our own bikes, my uncle insisted that it was their way of being included in the journey. I knew I would think of them often when my bike wasn't spewing parts all over the road behind me. I imagined I would be able to repay my aunt and uncle someday, but more importantly I was reminded that paying the kindness forward was just as important as money.

We were feeling energized to take on this giant new chapter, Mexico. Of course, not everyone was as excited as us. Voiced concerns had started before we even left home. They'd say, "Where are you two headed?"

"Alaska to Argentina," we would answer.

"No way!" they would say. Or "On bicycles?" or "That's impossible!" but always "You're not biking through Mexico, are you?"

No, we planned to bike to the border, then levitate over that country and land in Guatemala and keep biking south from there. Of course, we were going to bike through Mexico. It happens to be a part of the Americas, a large part of it, actually. I would think all that, but instead I would say, "Yes, all the way through it to Guatemala and then through Central America and south."

We heard all their gruesome stories; however, none of them had actually been to Mexico.

"Oh, God, no! I would never go to Mexico. It's so dangerous!" they would say. What they knew of Mexico was hearsay or what they watched or read in the news. This would be our fourth time traveling in Mexico, but by the time we reached southern California we began to doubt even our own knowledge and experience in the country. *Were we being reckless? Had things changed so much since we were there before that we were now risking our lives just crossing over the border?* Heaps of Americans seemed to think so, or even swore as fact that we would surely die.

Perseverance had brought us here on bicycles to Los Angeles, and it's what would keep us pedaling to Argentina. If I'd wanted life to be easy I would have sat on the couch and eaten bonbons. But I wanted to live, really live, to travel the road less traveled, to see parts of the world not yet seen, and to live my life to the fullest. If I died along the way, I knew I would be doing what I loved with the partner I loved. The only two things we know for sure in life is that we are born and that we will die. Between the two lies the journey.

PART II

Mexico, Guatemala, El Salvador, Honduras, Nicaragua, Costa Rica

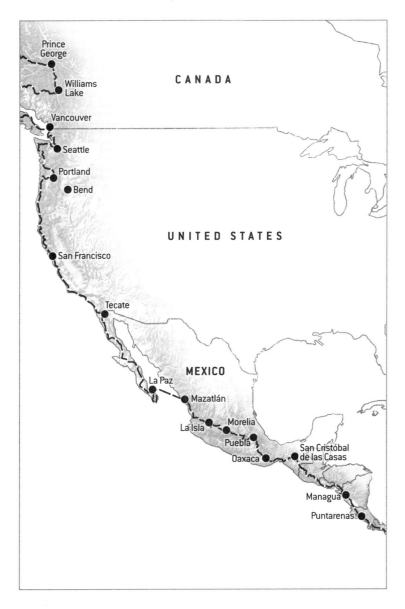

12

¡Hola, Gringo!

Ville and I pedaled out of Los Angeles as the sun was peeking over the palm trees and traffic choked the streets. Cars with drivers scowling, crying babies strapped inside, the arms of teenagers crossed tightly at their chests. I was grateful that I wasn't in one of those cars, was not late for a job, was in no rush to be somewhere, and that there was nowhere I had to be apart from exactly where I was. We went through the apocalyptic and eerily desolate military base of Camp Pendleton before entering the congested sprawl of San Diego, where we stopped off to visit friends before climbing the sandy mountains east of San Diego toward the town of Tecate. We planned to cross into Mexico from there instead of into Tijuana because the border crossing would be far less chaotic. The windy climb was tiring, but the congestion and traffic eased as we climbed toward the border.

Mexico would take us from everything familiar. Although we had traveled together through the Yucatan Peninsula in 2010, it felt as if we were traveling through uncharted territory. We knew this was where the real adventure would begin.

Crossing the border was a breeze. Officials waved us through with a pleasant "Welcome to Mexico!" as they pounded two more stamps into our passports. Immediately on the other side of the border wall was the small town of Tecate. The madness of Los Angeles and San Diego now behind us was replaced by expansive desert. We found a currency exchange in the tiny, dusty town, and after exchanging our dollars to pesos we continued southeast on the La Ruta del Vino Highway, which winds through parched, sandy hills covered in vineyards as it meanders its way toward the Pacific Ocean.

We camped in Guadalupe, where we found a campground that funded a school for the deaf and met another young bike touring couple, Riley and Lauren. Both in their early twenties, wiry with brown hair, Lauren was more soft-spoken, while Riley punctuated every story with a contagious giggle. Originally from the East Coast, they had worked jobs in Bend the previous year before setting off to bike Baja California. What a small world.

We hit it off instantly and decided to head south together for added safety in numbers and increased sanity with company. Although it was December, the weather was warm and breezy, "T-shirt and shorts weather," my mom called it. We were passed repeatedly by well-wishers; honking, waving, and yelling, "¡Hola, gringo!" and "¡Buen viaje!," faces pressed up against glass or hanging out windows. I smiled, uplifted.

The road dropped steeply out of the mountains onto the coastal Carretera Federal 1 Highway just north of the town of Ensenada, a touristy beach hub popular with American tourists and only seventy-two miles from the U.S. border. We were in Mexico, but everyone was speaking English. We stopped to eat fish, shrimp, and stingray tacos at an aromatic street cart loaded with an array of colorful homemade salsas. When I asked the husky, mustached Mexican man at the cart if one of the salsas was spicy, he replied, "No, no, no. Not spicy," with a little click of the tongue and finger wave. What he forgot to add was, "Eat it with caution, gringa," because it was spicy enough to take the paint off a car.

I imagined Baja to be a cyclist's dream; the road winding along the coastline, the sea breezes calm and cool, whales and dolphins surfacing on the water, and opportunities for a refreshing dip whenever the mood struck us. However, when we tried to take a back road out of Ensenada and our thick tires sunk into deep sand, my dream dissipated.

After returning to the 1 Highway heading south of Ensenada, we climbed back up the hot barren hillside and enjoyed views of the ocean. I took solace in the quiet and open space. Clouds were blown away by winds unchecked by tree windbreaks, only cacti lay scattered over sand upon endless sand. The landscape was so empty that the sky seemed to swallow me whole.

Our foursome quickly discovered the hospitality and kindness of Mexicans in Baja, and so often, when we inquired at restaurants for campsites, we were shown to the person's own backyard. We pitched the tent among the chickens, ducks, and mangy puppies out back. We played with kids, made friends with families and their neighbors, and forced ourselves to work on our rusty Spanish. They often switched to speaking English to make it less painful for everyone, but Ville forced the conversation back to Spanish. It would be the only way to learn and improve. And slowly, our Spanish improved.

The wind blew steadily for days. High pressure over the southern U.S. created strong northerly winds that howled down the Gulf of California. The roar of the wind in my ears was a constant all day every day and threatened to drown out my thoughts. From Punta Colonet to La Curva, we passed over fifty miles of massive greenhouses crowded with farmworkers growing food mainly exported to feed Americans. The work looked dirty, grueling, and backbreaking. The trucks that passed, loaded with produce, kicked up dust that hung in the air. I pulled my neck buff up over my nose and mouth to help keep the dust out. My sunglasses collected layers of dust, making it difficult to see.

On the seventh day, 350 miles since leaving Tecate, nearly half-way down Baja, we found ourselves exhausted from fighting fierce headwinds for over fifty miles. Our entourage agreed to camp in a field of towering sandstone boulders that sheltered us from the wind. After setting up tents, Ville and I sat on some stones, hunched over our little titanium pot set in the sand between our legs and cooked a decadent meal of goulash. Riley and Lauren sat cooking theirs, and we watched the sun set behind the sandscape together, the orange sky turning to a dull bronze before fading. Another day gone. Riley and Lauren climbed into their tent, and we into ours. We snuggled beneath our sleeping quilt, under the stars and drifted off to sleep.

"Good night, Lauren. Good night, Riley," I called out.

"Good night, Ville. Good night, Kristen," they both chimed in response. It felt good to have friends after months traveling alone.

Ville and I had spent almost six months together and we had meld-ed into one. I rarely found myself annoyed with him, only at times when he was so bouncy, fidgety, and anxious to get on the road in the morning when I was still sleepy, fragile, and moody. I loved the sight of him, the smell of him, the feel of his caress, and loved the feeling I had in my heart when we were together. He was predictably kind. He always knew when to listen and he had the best witty retorts to my sarcastic jokes. He loved me for who I was, but he exemplified what it was to be a better person. He was my wholehearted, perfect soulmate, and life without him seemed insurmountable. I kissed him and as I rolled over to face away from him so he could wrap his arm around me, spooning as we did every night, we each said, "*Hyvää yötä, kauniita unia oman kullan kuvia, nuku hyvin, mä rakastan sua.*" In Finnish it means, "Good night, beautiful dreams of your loved one, sleep well. I love you."

I awoke an hour later to the sound of wind thrashing our tents. When I rolled over, Ville was already awake, trying to hold the tent poles against the storm. He climbed outside, desperately attempting to stack additional rocks to give some protection to our little two-person tent, but it was no use. If we didn't take the tent down quickly, it would be shredded. There was no way for us to sleep outside either because we would be sandblasted. All four of us pulled on headlamps and scoured in the dark for anything that might offer up more protection. Our voices carried away in the wind as we called out to each other in the darkness. We opted for a gnarled scrub brush about head high, laid our tarp under its branches on the leeward side, and the four of us lay down on top. Riley and Lauren climbed into their sleeping bags and cocooned themselves inside, whereas Ville and I pulled our sleeping quilt over us and gripped the tarp against the wind as it tore it from our hands and flapped wildly in the air every time we drifted in and out of sleep.

As the morning sky turned pink, we emerged from our camp into the wind, having hardly slept. We packed up our gear, filled with gritty sand, as best we could and trudged back out to the highway, planning to ride until we could find some shelter out of the wind. The wind only grew fiercer throughout the day. Fatigue and backache from sleeping on sand for eight nights were getting to me. Ville insisted on riding out in front, trying to lean into the side wind, breaking the wind for me and the others who rode behind. It was grueling, and when the wind became too fierce, the gusts toppling us off the bikes, we were forced to dismount and walk them for long stretches. I tried to push aside bitter thoughts, replacing them with the suffering others were enduring.

I chose to be here. I could quit at any time. Go home. Be in the same place I was before. Or I could push on, see more, do more, be more.

Somewhere, the direction of the highway and wind turned and our luck with it. We were blown at thirty-five miles per hour into the next town, El Rosarito. We splurged for a shared hotel room to get hot showers to wash the sand out of our eyes.

The next day, my mind wandered. Time and place blurred. Out of the fog appeared a light-brown, mangy dog with dark, black eyes, no taller than my knees, boney and scruffy, wandering along the road. She was nosing through trash on the opposite side of the road looking for morsels. She sauntered onto the road, crossing without regard to the speeding car. I called out, and she darted to the shoulder just as the car sped past. My tire caught the shoulder, where the pavement dropped off to the sand. I pulled hard to correct, but it was too late. My bike went down, my hand extended to break my fall, and my knee braced against the jarring impact of the pavement. I hit the pavement hard, so stunned it took me a moment to realize I was now in a heap on the road.

Ville picked me up and pulled me from the road. Lauren asked me, "Are you okay?" Riley pulled my bike from the road. I looked down at my wrist, which was scraped and bleeding but not broken. I rubbed my knee, also bleeding, but not broken. "Yeah, yeah, I'm okay," I said, tears stinging my eyes.

"Are you sure you're okay, KG?" Ville wrapped his arms around me, deeply concerned.

"No, no, I'm okay. Wow, that really hurts . . . I thought that dog was going to get hit." I looked up to see where the dog was, but she was gone. "I'm fine. Really, I'm fine. Let's just go." I was in pain, maybe had a bruised ego, but I was not broken. "Thank you, guys. Thanks for getting my bike," I said, as I took my bicycle back from Riley, who held it, worried. "Thank you, really, I'm okay," I said as I climbed back on to prove it. Riley and Lauren also climbed back on theirs and pedaled back onto the road.

"KG. Are you sure you're, okay?" Ville repeated, still looking worried.

"Really, I'm sure," I said, even though I wasn't sure. I pulled back onto the road and fell in behind our friends, trying to prove to myself and the others that I was fine. Ville fell in behind. And just like that, a little bloody and battered, but thankfully not broken, the adventure continued.

The four of us rode into Santa Rosalia, a filthy coastal mining town on the Gulf of California, and crammed into the only available hovel of a hotel room for Christmas Eve. We passed around a bottle of tequila that had been gifted to us from a kind Mexican man at the grocery store with a smiling, "¡Feliz Navidad!" while the town resounded with festive, drunken revelry that rolled into the early hours of morning. We rose early and pedaled through the eerily, quiet streets heading south, hoping to find a quiet beach to camp the following night.

On Christmas we camped at Playa Santispac on the Bahia Concepcion. It would have been my worst nightmare at any other time, but now, packed with gigantic RVs and RVers, generators and boats, these boisterous Canadian and American retirees made room for our tents and kindly lent us a kayak, snorkeling gear, and a fishing pole. We spent Christmas Day watching dolphins feed in the bay and cooked a triggerfish that Ville caught for our Christmas feast. We then passed through Loreto and spent my birthday and the New Year climbing to the top of the large rock south of Playa Ligüí, where we made our resolutions to keep on traveling.

Rejuvenated on New Year's Day, we climbed back on our bikes and began the long, slow climb away from the Gulf of California toward Ciudad Insurgentes. The long climb was cake compared to the screaming sidewinds we encountered once back on the plateau and open desert. Headwinds and sidewinds felt like dragging a car tire behind the bike, lots of output with little reward. For two days we pushed through the windy desert until Riley, who had been struggling with a stomach bug, pulled over and decided he and Lauren would hitchhike to La Paz. We watched the van pull away, them waving out the back windows. Sadness crept into my chest. Goodbyes were always so hard.

Ville and I rode 147 miles from Cuidad Insurgentes to La Paz on some of the most dangerous and scary stretch of road yet. The shoulder disappeared, and drivers were in too much of a hurry to move over in the slightest. I counted six near-death experiences. My heart quit beating, and I held my breath waiting for the impact. By dark we found an open gate along the road and pitched our tents amid cacti. The open desert made for a fantastic night's sleep, the cool night air, no crowing roosters, no sewage, no barking dogs, no loud music, no engine brakes, or any of the chaos we found in the cities.

We rolled into La Paz and reunited with Riley and Lauren for a night in a hotel. They were headed back to jobs, school, and life without bikes. For a moment I was jealous that Riley and Lauren would be in normal life again with stocked grocery stores, restaurants, hot showers, flushing toilets, and soft beds, but I realized I preferred my bike and Ville. We had found our rhythm. My bicycle now had a name, Blue Bullet. Ville had called me Blue Bullet once, when I zoomed past him on a sled while wearing a bright blue jacket on the ski slopes in Oslo, Norway, but the name now seemed fitting for my zippy, blue speed racer. Ville called his bike Rufio after the Lost Boy in *Peter Pan*. He liked the part in the movie when they chant, "Rufio! Rufio! Rufio!" The kid had a bad-ass red mowhawk. Everything I needed for survival was on Blue Bullet. In La Paz we booked a cabin on the twelve-hour overnight ferry that would arrive in Mazatlán by morning.

13

Blue Agave

The blazing sun hurt my eyes. I slipped on my sunglasses and helmet, and we pedaled from the ferry into the searing Mazatlán heat and humidity. We rode under an umbrella of amapa trees, their plump, deep-green leaves shading us from the early morning sun, and wove through the narrow streets, surrounded by concrete buildings vibrantly colored in pinks, oranges, yellows, blues, and reds. The city was just beginning to wake up. Stray dogs snoozed on sidewalks, children dressed in white and navy school uniforms were walking to school, business doors were being unlocked and opened as shopkeepers hosed or swept the sidewalks out front. It was still delectable Mexico but a vastly different one than that of Baja Sur. Far fewer tourists, less sand, and no more desert.

As we rode, our eyes scanned for a hotel or motel sign. We never planned ahead or made reservations. We kept our expectations low. "Inexpensive, clean, and safe" were our only requirements. We spotted a sign, and I stayed with our bikes while Ville entered to assess the situation. He returned moments later with a thumbs up, and we rolled our bicycles into a small, tidy, sparse room with a bed, bright blue walls, and a large, vaulted ceiling. Our voices echoed off concrete walls that kept in the coolness. After settling in, we ventured out to get breakfast and check out the town. Mazatlán is perched on a rocky coastline with a vibrant "old town" in contrast to the touristy "new town" to the north. The city was alive with music, theater, and almost everyone had a bright smile or gave us a "Buenos dias" as we passed. After exploring the city for a couple of days it was time to keep on keepin' on, so we rode south, zigzagging through the chaotic streets headed for the town of Tepic 172 miles away.

We rode along the coastline, relatively easy miles, as the highway cut through marshes and mangroves, filled with the singsong of birds everywhere around us. Although the days were long, riding by eight and camping by seven, we averaged fifty miles per day, and time passed quickly. My mind wandered for hours that felt like minutes. Without the Baja Sur winds, the sun baked my skin, and with fewer towns to ride through, we struggled to find enough water and stay hydrated on our way to Tepic.

George and Lynn, a couple we had met earlier on the road and who offered to host us, welcomed us into their modest, concrete, two-room, rented casa, let us shower and do laundry, and drove us around the sprawling concrete city. It was heavenly. Tepic had numerous drive-thru shops serving boozy drinks and snacks, immensely popular with the locals. We each ordered a liter-sized spicy and refreshing michelada—beer with lime and tomato juices, spices, and chili peppers. Apart from the main square, the city was cigarette factories, manufacturing and textile plants, and food processors. It was the first Mexican city where we did not see any other non-Hispanics. With a population of over half million, that is an impressive feat. Much later, we learned that Tepic was plagued by gangs and regularly ranked high on the list for most dangerous cities in the world. We were glad we didn't find this out until after we left.

Upon leaving Tepic we encountered long, grueling hill climbs in brutal heat on the way to Tequila. We added electrolyte packets to our water to help stay hydrated, but it was a losing battle. Drip . . . drip . . . drip. In contrast to the cool windy deserts of Baja, we found ourselves in hot humid mountains perpetually climbing. Since leaving Oregon, we had averaged around sixty to eighty miles a day with relative ease, but since our climb up to Tepic, forty to forty-five completely wiped us out. I began getting migraines and heavy nose bleeds every day. Anyone in their right mind would quit, throw up their hands, and say, "I've had enough! I just can't take it anymore!" However, neither of us were in our right mind. I suffered migraines and stuffed toilet paper up my nose to stop the bleeding and I continued to pedal, heading southeast in the direction of Guadalajara. The toilet paper flapped in the wind, and my sweat continued to drip. Drip . . . drip . . . drip.

I stood next to our bikes outside a tiny tienda while Ville was inside buying water. A scrawny teenager rode past on his bicycle and looked at me with a broad smile. I smiled back and said, "Buenos tardes." As Ville joined me, the kid asked, "¿A donde van?"

"Argentina," I replied.

Angel was his name, and he was anxious to chat with us about our ride. He showed us pictures of his bicycle group on his cell phone, there in Ixtlán del Rio. Ville asked for recommendations for affordable accommodations and a place to buy lunch, and Angel had us follow him home. We walked our bikes through the concrete house to the backyard with the chickens. We sat at the table in his one-room house with a dirt floor, sheets hanging from the ceiling separating bedrooms, and a single bulb casting a weak light. His mother served us tomato soup at a small metal table while Angel proudly showed us his few cycling jerseys and spoke highly of his bicycle group. Ville felt compelled to offer him money for lunch, and Angel brushed him off, offended, saying, "You are my guests."

After the meal, we followed him to a hotel on the second story of an old wooden building on the main square downtown. Ville paid for the night, and Angel helped us carry our bags and bikes upstairs. The room was plain, yet tidy, and the old, wooden floorboards creaked under our weight. He took us on a walking tour and introduced us to his friend, a woman in his bicycle group, who made sweets she sold from a small cart. She loaded us up with a couple paper bags of goodies and then also refused our payment, saying, "It was a gift." I pulled a mazapan from the bag, popped it in my mouth, and let it melt on my tongue. It tasted like sweetened peanut butter. Next, I tried a tamarindo candy, made from tamarind fruit, chili powder, corn starch, and sugar. It is one of the most popular candies in Mexico because of its mix of sweet and spicy. I sucked the chili powder residue from my fingers. I was in dire need of a shower, so we made our way back to the hotel with our goodie bags, showered, washed our dirty clothes with a bar of soap in the bathroom sink, and hung them all over the room to dry.

We walked back to the Central Square, where we met Angel and his friend. As we stood there, families with young kids, teens, adults, all with matching Ixtlán en Bici bicycle jerseys gathered around us. They came from all areas of the city and with an eclectic array of different bikes. One of the group leaders had bungee-corded a giant speaker to the back of his bicycle and used a microphone to introduce us to the crowd. Ville spoke about our bicycle journey, which got cheers from the crowd. Afterward, we took a group photo with everyone. Ville was presented with an Ixtlán en Bici jersey, and everyone set off for a night ride. It was beautiful, everyone brought together by riding bikes. I felt happy and included.

Early the next morning, the elderly hotel night watchman asked us what direction we planned to ride. Ville told him Guadalajara. Worry lines creased his face as he begged us to be careful, while holding up his small hand-held radio. He told us the president of Mexico was speaking, saying that President Trump, who had just taken office, had announced plans to build a wall between Mexico and the U.S. and that Mexico would be paying for it. I felt sick to my stomach. The kind old man helped us carry the bags downstairs to the street. I sat with the bags as Ville fetched the bikes. While I stood there in a daze watching people walk by, a man asked me, "American?"

"Finland," I lied.

"Oh," he said, and walked away. He probably meant no harm, but I was at a complete loss for words. I felt terrible having to lie about my own nationality. We rode in a heavy fog of sadness back to the highway and headed forty-five miles southeast toward the town of Tequila. I couldn't reconcile the toxic racist politics back home with our wonderful experiences in Mexico.

My mind was swirling. When we took a break that afternoon I talked to Ville about it, choked up and teary. Ville and I tried extremely hard to respect others and their opinions and stay out of politics, especially while traveling as a guest abroad. We were both white, from the United States, and the president of my country was starting a conflict with Mexico. It was all over the news and we could not avoid the situation.

We had spent a month and a half bicycling in Mexico, and we had had nothing but kind, welcoming, positive experiences with the people. We were at a complete loss as to how to handle the situation. *Were we now in danger? Could we now be possibly killed?* I didn't want to let myself become afraid. We spoke Finnish in public and told people we were from Finland or Canada if they asked. We refused to give up and go home. All we could do was keep pedaling.

Near the foot of Tequila Volcano, surrounded by fields of blue agave, lies the town of Tequila, known for its production of the famous spirit. After touring a distillery, on our walk back to the hotel, Ville and I were ambushed by a group of partying Mexicans standing next to a car, windows open, with loud, pulsating music. They pushed beers in our hands and insisted we dance with them. I could not stop laughing as three different people passed me around for a dance. We posed for pictures, hugged them all, and headed to our hotel.

Standing next to the bed, I kissed Ville's lips. The taste of tequila still lingered there. Then I kissed his flushed cheeks. Ran my fingers through the softness of his hair. I love his hair. It had naturally lightened in the sun, blond highlights mixed into the brown. Girls pay lots of money to have their hair look like that. We walked into the bathroom, brushed our teeth, and pulled on T-shirts and underwear. The room was hot, and only a thin sheet was necessary for sleeping. I grabbed his hand and led him to bed. He lay down below the top sheet, and I lay next to him and rested my head on his chest. I could hear his heart beating, boom, boom, boom, his chest rising and falling with each breath. He fell asleep quickly, stroking my hair.

We left Tequila on a Sunday and had seventy miles before we reached our friend's house on Lake Chapala, just south of Guadalajara. In Mexico, Sunday was the day reserved for family. Most people spent the day together in parks, on beaches, in backyards, or such, resulting in far fewer drivers being on the roads. The other days, the roads bustled with activity. I had been fascinated to discover that the colectivos and city buses were retired yellow American school buses, painted an assortment of colors. They almost always left us in a cloud of black smoke as they flew past. Flames or murals on the exterior were popular, scantily clad ladies or roaring animals seemed to be favorites, while inside they were outfitted with everything from dingle balls and flashing disco lights to televisions. But always, and I mean always, they had a sound system with a pounding bass so powerful we could feel it in our chests as they passed. Surely it left ringing in the ears of its passengers. The buses were driven by locals, usually hormonal teens, with more confidence than skill. The buses were throughout the cities, driving the roads between towns and picking up passengers by merely slowing, not stopping, forcing people to run to jump aboard. The driver usually had a companion who hung out the door calling out the direction the bus was heading and collecting payment as people jumped aboard. Nothing was turned away, not even animals, making it common to share a seat with a goat or a bag of potatoes.

Many of the pickup trucks transported piles haphazardly roped and stacked far above the cab of any conceivable thing, including garbage, recycling, boxes, bags, hazardous materials, even living creatures. Truck beds were packed with people, farm workers, or hitchhikers, who always waved at us. We passed wooden carts pulled by donkeys and horses loaded with farm-grown goods headed for town, sometimes stacked so high they seemed to buck the laws of physics. I pitied the donkeys peeking out from below.

We passed people walking, biking, waiting for buses, hitchhiking, and playing on the roadside. We passed a dirt field full of young kids playing fútbol and pulled over to watch them play. They ran over to check us out, and Ville asked them to throw him the ball. Ville headed the ball back at the crowd of kids, a young boy headed it back, and they proceeded to play a game heading the ball back and forth around the group of kids, everyone laughing and cheering. Fútbol, the universal language. Ville pulled our camera from the handlebar bag and tried to capture them chatting with me and playing with my squeaky sumo wrestler toy, but every time he raised his camera to his eye, the group of kids turned and gave a thumbs up. Their smiles were beautiful, their laughter infectious. When we climbed back into our saddles and continued up the road, a large group chased us, talking, questioning, laughing, and cheering. They made it almost a half mile up the road before falling behind and waving goodbyes. It warmed my heart, and the smile on my face lingered for hours.

We spent the night in Santa Cruz de Las Flores and the next morning, as Ville and I sat at a roadside taco cart, eating carne asada tacos for breakfast, we met a group of cheery, boisterous construction workers polishing off plates of food. They asked us questions about how we had arrived there, about the bikes, and about the two of us. They couldn't believe we'd ridden bicycles over such a great distance. I regarded the bikes leaning against a nearby tree, covered in dust and a collection of peeling and faded stickers from along the way that we had plastered all over the frames and panniers, the seats beyond broken in, and the handlebar tape almost worn through in places. It sounded like an impossibility for someone to ride a bicycle 6,600 miles from Alaska to Mexico. It felt as though I'd watched someone else do it, yet here we sat chatting with construction workers.

"¿Todavía se gustan?" (You both still like each other?) one portly guy asked with a toothy grin. We all laughed, full belly laughs, the ones that hurt your stomach for a while afterward.

"She hasn't killed me yet!" Ville replied in Spanish, provoking another round of laughter.

"¡Buen viaje, amigos!" they said, as we stood, cleared our plates, and paid for our tacos. We shared waves and smiles as we climbed back on our bikes and rode away. It was a positive and joyful start to our day.

Via a patchwork of bumpy dirt roads, we rode to a tiny village in the hills surrounded by farmlands called La Isla. After a long ninety-mile day we were happy to meet Samuel, a friend from Bend who was there visiting his family. Samuel was short, portly, and soft-spoken, with a thick black mustache. The moment we dismounted from our bikes we were pulled into bear hugs by Samuel and given a bedroom and cold shower. We were introduced to everyone in town and fed copious amounts of tacos from a cart in the town square. Samuel cut a pile of fresh fruit sprinkled with chili powder for breakfast and took us to meet his extended family. It turned out his extended family made up a large majority of the town, so it was a busy day. Our intention was to stay a day, but each morning we planned to pack and leave he had another party, potluck, get-together, fiesta, sightseeing trip, and tequila fest planned.

Samuel's friend, a cowboy named Oscar, and his wife, Sol, invited us to their farm to taste our first pajarete. Oscar mixed coffee, sugar, chocolate, and a splash of alcohol in two large cups, walked over to one of their white cows locked in a chute, and added warm milk from its udder. It was delicious. We drank two each and decided it'd be a better idea if we didn't bike that day. Instead, still tipsy, we were driven to see a popular pilgrimage site, San Juan de Los Lagos, then on to Arandas, ending with us being showered with gifts for the road.

When it became apparent that we'd need to pull the plug and leave because no one would ever kick us out, we loaded our gear into our panniers and hugged everyone goodbye. Samuel, a man of few words, pulled us into his arms. He made us promise to be careful and to visit often, and then he stood at the roadside as we rode away.

14

Sleeping in Sex Motels

"Morelia? Is it a big city?" I turned around to ask Ville. We had ridden 200 miles since leaving Ajijic at Lake Chapala.

"I read something about it. It's a UNESCO World Heritage Site and supposed to be a beautiful, colonial city. I don't know . . . Do you want to go? We can skip it," Ville replied with a hint of indecisiveness.

It was late in the evening, with the sun waning and around the time we needed to be searching for a safe camping spot or motel. The heat from the sun radiating up from the pavement was still making me sweat, and I was exhausted. I looked up the road toward Morelia again, the steepness of the climb looming ahead. I didn't want to climb a hill. I was spent. But I didn't want to miss anything either. After all, this was our adventure, and so I sighed and said, "Fine. No. We should go. I don't think we should skip it if it's worth seeing."

"KG, you sure? We can just keep going," he said, pushing me to be honest.

"No, we should go. At least stay one night and see the town. Sounds like something we shouldn't miss."

And with that, I climbed back on my saddle and started pedaling up the hill, clicking my gears down to my small chain ring to spin more easily uphill. After an eternity of riding uphill, the road crested and became a giant thoroughfare. Buildings lined the road, and traffic became more aggressive as the shoulder disappeared. It was only sixteen miles from the cuota into Morelia, but it was much farther than expected, and there was not much sunlight left. Searching for a campsite or a motel in the dark is both unpleasant and dangerous, and we usually tried to avoid it at all costs. The speeding traffic unraveled my nerves and forced me to pedal faster. *Just get there, just get there, just get there* became my mantra.

"KG, it's getting dark. Let's just stop somewhere at a motel. We can ride the rest of the way in the morning," Ville yelled up to me over the roar of traffic. "Here! Let me see if this motel has room!"

I pulled into the driveway of a bright pink motel set back from the road behind a large concrete wall. Ville rode up to the glass window of a kiosk at the entrance, where a man sitting in the office spoke to us through a speaker in the glass. After a short negotiation, Ville waved me forward. We secured our bicycles, unclipped our panniers, and carried them inside.

As our eyes adjusted to the darkness of the room, we noticed the curvaceous paintings of ladies on the walls, poorly painted ladies at that. We set down our bags, and I began rummaging for clean clothes to put on after my shower. Ville picked up the remote from the bedside table and turned on the TV, flipped a few channels and said, "Oh, football!"

He watched for a moment, then flipped to another channel and said, "Oh, porn!"

I spun around to catch a gynecological exam being performed by a well-endowed lumberjack. "What. The Hell?" I stuttered, giggling at the hilarity of the channel.

"I wondered why he asked us how many hours we wanted to stay," Ville said, laughing hysterically. "Babe, this is a sex motel! Are you excited? Your husband takes you all the way to Mexico and brings you to a sex motel." He stepped across the room, wrapped his arms around me and began kissing me seductively. "Bet you can't wait to tell all your girlfriends about this. You lucky girl."

"Yeah, who'd want to go to one of those boring resorts when you can go to a sex motel?" I agreed sarcastically, still laughing, and returning his kisses. Then I gently pushed him away from my stench cloud.

In the shower, I thought about how drastically different our lives had become to be thrilled to have a room in a sex motel, but there we were, thrilled. Sex motel or not, the room was cheap, clean, had soap, shampoo, and even clean towels. And let's not forget, free porn. This "lucky girl" drifted off to sleep on the stiff, plastic-covered mattress, looking up at the reflection of us lying in bed in the giant mirror on the ceiling.

Ville and I ventured back onto the highway for the remaining few miles' ride to the heart of downtown Morelia. While pulled over on the shoulder of the road, checking the phone for directions, a cyclist rode up and asked if we needed help. Ville asked the local where we might find a cheap motel (preferably one without a free porn channel on the TV) and he told us to follow him.

His name was Piter. He was a jolly hyper fellow, and he took us to a few places before we found a hostel in the heart of the city center. We dropped our bags in the room and followed him on our bikes to his restaurant for breakfast. Piter was the owner of a cute Italian café, Restaurante Palermo. When we arrived, he unlocked the doors and personally made us a breakfast of fruit, yogurt, eggs in garlic olive oil, and toast. While we were beaming with gratitude, he insisted he was so happy to meet us.

"I was supposed to arrive earlier to open the restaurant. But I overslept, and then I was nearly stopped by the train but passed before it. Just in time to meet you both! Destiny!" he clasped his hands.

I'm amazed how we met so many incredibly special people, always in the right place at the right moment we were meant to meet. Destiny. I'm grateful we were able to be there on this adventure and that we had the time in that moment to share our lives together. That is what life is about, people. Bicycles were only cheap transportation to get us to Destiny!

After breakfast, Piter took us to a bike shop to replace our chains. The owners of the shop, thrilled to hear about our adventure, gave us a discount and even threw in a free patch kit. We spent the day walking around the historic city and Plaza de Armas and ate gazpacho, an extremely popular cup of chopped fruit mixed with cheese, hot sauce, salt, and pepper, the perfect blend of sweet and spicy. We discovered bathrooms around the city to be small business opportunities, manned and cleaned by people who took your money on the way in and handed you a small, perfectly folded handful of toilet paper, an overabundance for a pee, but not quite adequate for a poop.

Morelia was founded in 1541, and the federal government lists 1,113 buildings, built from the sixteenth to the twentieth centuries, as having historical value. Nearly all of them were built with pink Cantera stone in the colonial architectural style. Various plaza fountains and the city's aqueduct were built in the eighteenth century. It was really a sight to behold, and we were surprised to see so few tourists.

For dinner, Piter made us cilantro sauce on jicama, pesto pasta with bread, sangria, and a fruit, nut, and cheese desert. Afterward, he took us on a wild night ride through the city. We passed lit football fields, boisterous groups of walkers, lovers necking on park benches, stray dogs nosing through garbage, and people drinking and laughing loudly. The city pulse was pounding. We stopped at a food cart and tried tacos de cabeza, steamed and shredded meat that comes from a cow's head, on warmed, corn tortillas, tasting of onion and coriander. We were welcomed into Morelia as friends. I hoped they knew how much it meant to us to be so accepted.

On our way out of town, fattened and happy, we fell back into the cadence of the ride and began to climb. And climb and climb. The terrain slowly shifted from dry agave fields to muggy grasslands to coniferous forests. The trees grew taller and lusher, streambeds swelled with water, the meadows were dense with wildflowers, and everywhere bright, orange butterflies fluttered.

It was exciting to be enveloped in surroundings that felt familiar, like Oregon pine forests. I inhaled deeply. It even smelled like home. Sunlight filtered through the branches overhead, throwing rays of light on the road ahead, and the crisp, coolness of high altitude returned to the air. Extreme climbing had put our bodies into new positions on the saddles, and suddenly new saddle sores were born. Hallelujah! After reaching the summit we had a glorious descent in shaded woods, the road graded so perfectly we could coast sitting back on the seat, arms outstretched in front of us enjoying the scenery.

At dusk, we asked a man working in his yard if he knew of a safe place we might camp and were given space on his front porch. We bought candies from his children's small tienda out front. In the morning chill, we found ourselves zipped into our puffy jackets, not having used them since Alaska, and cupped our hands around our stove to catch the warmth while cooking oatmeal.

Back on the road, we spotted an OXXO, similar to an American 7–Eleven, and stopped for Ville, the coffee addict, to get his fix. There we met Javier, a motorcyclist, who bought us coffee while we chatted about our ride and his motorcycle. He gave us directions on how to get to the Monarch Butterfly Biosphere Reserve, which becomes home to billions of migrating butterflies every October to March. We exchanged contact info before he headed to work. We continued southeast, climbing up into more mountains. By the time we reached Ocampo that evening, Javier rode up and met us in the town square, helped us secure a cheap motel, and hung out with us for the evening.

He had ridden over thirty miles out of his way to see us, an act of kindness that had become customary in Mexico.

Early the next morning, we left our bikes at the motel and caught a minibus up a steep, winding road high into the cloud forest. From where the bus left us, we hiked two hours for five miles up a steep, forested trail into the reserve, which sits at 9,400 feet in elevation. This may seem like an easy task relative to how much we were exercising daily, but on rusty, hiking legs, it was a feat of monumental proportion. I stopped regularly to ask, "Are we there yet?" while sucking wind, leaning heavily against the nearest tree. Deep in the dense woods, we came upon a roped-off area where large pods of butterflies hung in bunches swaying in the branches of towering oyamel fir trees. These rare fir trees provided a microclimate, helping to protect the butterflies by keeping the temperatures consistently cool. We reflected on the fact that these delicate butterflies had originated in the northeastern United States and Canada and had flown, albeit much faster than we had ridden, the same distance we had biked. These beautiful, flying arthropods, making use of the air currents, left their summer feeding and breeding grounds in the north and winged it over 3,000 miles south to winter here in one of only a few suitable places, high in the mountains of central Mexico. Kindred souls with adventurous spirits.

While we biked down out of the mountains headed east toward Mexico City we were surrounded by thousands of butterflies suspended in air. It was surreal. Like being submerged in the ocean and watching fish swim by. After waiting out winter, it will take these monarchs four to five generations to make it back north, while Ville and I continued our migration south. May the winds be at all our backs.

Highway 15 climbed up out of Cerrito de la Independencia for over seventeen butt-kicking miles, the road graded steeply along hills that grew into mountains. The sun had set deep into the canyon at our back, and darkness was settling in.

"Hey, Ville, we really need to find a place to camp. It's getting dark," I yelled back over my shoulder. For over an hour, we'd been looking for a farmer to ask permission to camp in his yard and were running out of daylight. "What about here?" I asked, pointing to the right, where there was a small break in the guardrail and steeply, terraced fields beyond. There were tire tracks that led from the break in the fence, uphill through the over-head-high scrub brush. "What about up that road? Maybe we can find a spot in the trees?" I suggested. There was no farmer in sight.

"I wish there was a farmer to ask, but it's getting dark. Let's go scope it out," Ville said as he pulled to a stop just before the break in the guardrail. We looked both ways up and down the highway. When the coast was clear, we pedaled up the dirt road and laid our bikes down in the brush and headed off in different directions in search of a flat spot big enough for our tent. While out scavenging, we heard the downshift of a noisy truck, which sounded as if it was turning up the dirt road. We ran back to our bikes and discovered a farmer and his family in a rusty truck turning up the road followed by a tractor. What luck!

Ville and I picked up our bikes and flagged down the farmer, asking him permission to camp, which he happily granted, telling us to camp near the fence. We pushed our bikes out onto the open terraced, grassy field, discovering a small patch flat enough for our tent out in the open, laid down our bikes, and cooked dinner. After eating, we set up our tent, changed into sleeping clothes, and climbed in to play cards before bed.

Out of the darkness, two men appeared outside the tent. They spoke rapidly in Spanish, which we struggled to follow, but from what we understood, we were camped in a dangerous spot out in the open. There were bad hombres around, and we should move up by them next to a tractor because they had guns. *Guns.* I felt sick to my stomach, confused, and uprooted. Telling someone in the darkness you have guns is never settling. *Oh, you have guns? Well, good for you guys, we have pocketknives.* We crawled from the tent, and it was so dark I couldn't see their faces. We packed up our stuff haphazardly in the glow of our headlamps, took down the tent, all while in our pajamas, and struggled to push the bikes up the hill through the thick grass. *I think if they were going to kill us, they would've done it already, right? I mean, they wouldn't drag us up by the tractor and then kill us, right?* I felt terrified. My hands were shaking, and my legs felt weak.

One of the men walked behind me and began pushing my bike from behind, helping me get up the hill. The other man fell in behind Ville, helping him push while Ville pulled. *They wouldn't help us and then kill us, right?* The sickness in my stomach eased slightly. We came to the fence, then had to drag the bikes straight up a wash before coming to where the tractor was parked.

"¡Gracias, amigos!" we both said, thanking them for the help pushing our bikes. *I think we are safe.* Ville and I unpacked our things and re-established our tent while the two men went and started a small fire near the tractor. I climbed back into the tent, uneasy, while Ville disappeared to talk to the men at the fire. When he returned, he told me he felt fairly sure they weren't going to kill us, but his Spanish was just not good enough to follow everything they were saying. We slept fitfully, waking often, listening for footsteps, drifting in and out of sleep.

At first light, Ville crawled out to go find somewhere to poop (At least we now know that in near-death situations Ville's bowels work swimmingly.) when someone fired up the tractor. It appeared they had waited for us to stir before making noise. I dressed and packed our stuff while Ville was gone. When he returned, we took down the tent and made oatmeal. One of the men was out grading the field with the tractor. We packed up, pulled out all our snacks for the day, a few Snickers bars, dried fruit, and nuts, and approached the man. He turned off the tractor, climbed down, and walked up to us with a toothy grin, hand outstretched for us to shake, and introduced himself as Enrique. His shoes were so worn his foot and toes hung out in multiple places, his shirt was full of holes, and the nicest thing he wore was a baseball cap. Nevertheless, his smile said everything.

We thanked him for watching out for us and asked him where the other man was. He said his cousin, Antonio, had already left for work. He told us Antonio had come to spend the night with him to help guard the tractor and farm equipment. They were paid by the farmer to sit up all night on watch. He told us we were near the state border, and this was a bad place for shady activities. We handed him all our snacks, so broke it was all we could offer, and thanked him profusely for watching out for us. He smiled as if we had handed him a hundred-dollar bill. I choked back tears, having feared for our lives and then discovering this man, who had next to nothing, had kept us safe. We thanked him again and walked back to our bikes. As we pushed them back through the grassy field toward the highway, Enrique yelled, "¡Bien viaje, amigos!" He jumped back on the tractor for a long day's work, still waving and with a smile on his face.

15

Dancing with the Devil

High in the forested hills east of Toluca, twenty miles west of Mexico City, Ville and I found ourselves on a narrow seldom-traveled road, coasting quietly under ponderosa pines. It was February 24. We had been traveling in Mexico for eleven weeks and were headed toward the city of Puebla 150 miles away. It had taken us over an hour to make our way outside the chaos of the city limits. Mist gathered on branches, and drops fell on my rain jacket with loud thumps, but it was not raining. Thank Mother Nature for that. It had taken over a year, but I had found peace in the quiet places. Being an extrovert who thrived on friends, gatherings, and noise, I was surprised to find that I had grown to crave the quiet. I had traded listening to friends' stories and opinions for my own thoughts. It felt as if it were the first time I was listening to myself and who I was.

I realized I was not really listening before, only thinking about what I wanted to say. But with only Ville on the road, I found myself listening to the world opening, living, breathing, growing, and dying around me. I watched time pass with every pedal stroke and inhalation, looking only as far ahead as I could see and rarely looking behind me. Memories flashed into my mind. Before this adventure, I was so busy I didn't have the opportunity to dive deep. Now, on long stretches of highway, my mind wandered into depths I had not known existed.

While I was deep in reflection, we rounded a bend in the road and passed a walker, who smiled broadly and continued the charge up the road in the opposite direction. A moment passed before a large, boisterous group with matching T-shirts appeared, also heading uphill, followed by another large group with matching T-shirts, a few villagers carrying Virgin Mary statues, a man struggling to walk under the weight of a large cross with Jesus nailed to it, another massive group, and, finally, a giant farm truck blasting mariachi music, the back decorated in hand-scrawled signage and flowers. I looked back at Ville, giggling, a big smile on my face. It felt as random as watching an elephant riding a tricycle zoom past. Five minutes later, another large group was laughing and singing together, followed by a couple of elderly ladies dressed in Escaramuza dresses and carrying walking sticks. Behind them was another truck piled high with belongings, behind it another large group of students, and so on.

Our curiosity piqued, we pulled over to ask a couple where they were going. They told us they were on a pilgrimage, walking to the Sanctuary of Chalma, the second-most-visited pilgrimage site in Mexico. (The first is the Basilica de Guadalupe in Mexico City.) Because Ville and I lived in a peaceful delirium, we hadn't noticed it was Lent, which made this pilgramage quite a surprise. The toll of the pain and suffering from all those miles was on their faces. I saw it in their eyes. I knew it was in mine.

Over the next two days, we passed thousands of people, mainly from Mexico but also from around the world. The people we passed followed the same steep paths their ancestors, the Aztecs, once used over 500 years before them. This particular pilgrimage was to a cave wedged deep in a canyon near the town of Chalma. The Aztecs would have carried offerings of flowers and incense to their stone idol, Oxtoteotl, otherwise known as God of the Caves. In the early 1600s, during the Spanish conquest of Mexico and the spread of Christianity, Oxtoteotl was replaced by a cross, and then later a statue, of the Señor de Chalma, or Black Jesus. In 1683, Black Jesus, painted black by the Spaniards to look more like the natives, was moved into a church built near the cave, while the path the Aztecs had walked was now under the pavement we all were traveling upon.

"¡Buenos dias!" we called out, nodding, smiling, and waving at everyone we passed. By afternoon it became, "¡Buenos tardes!" I had made it a personal goal to smile, acknowledge, nod to, or wave at as many people as I could. At the very least, it made me feel better, but when I received a smile or "buenos dias" in return, I knew it made that person feel better, too. Although the people we passed didn't know about our bicycle pilgrimage, it was a special feeling to know we all shared a common goal: to learn more about ourselves while on an arduous journey.

What goes up must come down and, unfortunately for us, go up again. Ville and I encountered a butt-sculpting, long, slow climb on our way into the sprawling city of Puebla. The climb felt as if it would never end. We had no intention of riding through Puebla, because it was eighty-five miles southeast of Mexico City and far out of our way, but our good friend Piter from Morelia had a friend, Luis, he wanted us to connect with. We thought, *Why not?* We'd been pleasantly surprised by towns where we lease expected it. Puebla would be no exception.

On the outskirts of the city, we called Luis and waited for him on a bench in the town square, the afternoon commotion of Pueblans scurrying, playing, and selling their wares all around us. We understandably drew attention as two filthy, smelly gringos sitting near two bicycles. Luis came running up to us, and without knowing us from

Adam, gave us big hugs. In either Ville's or my home countries, it would've been considered rude to show up unannounced.

After carrying the bikes up three flights of stairs, we arrived inside Luis's modest apartment, where he frantically moved boxes, bike frames, and junk out of the back bedroom to make room for us. Colorful masks hung on the walls, terracotta figurines covered the shelves, and the furniture was a dining room set and a couch. We crossed the street and devoured plates of tacos al pastor, marinated pork shoulder with Middle Eastern spices and sliced pineapple, at an open-air restaurant. Later, back at the house, we met his wife, Ari, her sister, Sele, and Sele's boyfriend, Elvis. We planned to stay a day or two but were having such a good time we ended up staying a week.

Luis, Ari, and their friends worked six days a week, and when not at work they showed us around the city. We drank pulque (fermented maguey plant) at a bar where a kid walked in off the street with a guitar and had the entire place on their feet singing Mexican pop songs. We ate fried grasshoppers, mole, cemita poblana sandwiches, and all kinds of local eats. I "danced with the devil" in the streets on Good Friday for Bailando con el Diablo, a festival rooted in a folktale about a girl who disobeys her parents and goes out dancing, without a chaperone, with a man she does not know, who turns out to be the Devil himself. This folktale had obviously been created to remind children not to disobey parents nor to stray from the Catholic Church.

They persuaded us to join the gang for the quinceañera party for their cousin, Carinda, and the party did not end until sunrise, around 6 a.m.

We'd slept only a few hours before we were up for breakfast at the nearby indoor marketplace, and after their long day of work Luis, Ari, Sele, and Elvis took us to a lucha libre (Mexican Professional Wrestling or "freestyle fighting") match, where we purposefully paid for the cheaper, nosebleed seats to sit with the old ladies and boisterous fans. Lucha libre, known for its acrobatic-like, rapid sequences of holds and high-flying maneuvers, is performed inside, and sometimes outside, a roped-in ring by colorful, masked luchadors and can be seen in only three large arenas in Mexico. The crowd chanted, sang, and even hurled things at the ring. The worst of the hecklers by far were the old ladies, spewing obscenities so raunchy it would've made a trucker blush.

When the show ended, I ate a cemita sandwich outside the stadium from a street vendor that didn't sit well. By the next morning, when we'd planned to get our butts back out on our bikes and keep the party train riding south, I had a case of dysentery. This laid us up for another week at their house.

Did Luis and Ari roll their eyes, stomp their feet, and kick us to the curb, as I would've done? Nope. They took turns making me breakfasts and lunches mild enough for me to stomach before they left for work early every morning. They harassed us both with text messages during the day to make sure I was still breathing and to nag Ville to force me to eat. Luis tracked down a naturopathic doctor to take me to on his day off. I was insistent on not pumping my body full of antibiotics. After some acupuncture and herbs, I was able to walk more upright and find some much-needed relief. And *still* they were sad when we left. After we rode away, after all of us hugged and cried as we said our goodbyes, I couldn't believe that there were people so selfless and kind. I wouldn't have been so kind. No one I knew would've been either. I realized I wanted to do better, be better, more like them and less like me.

Ville and I rode through hundreds of miles of desert hills and mountains covered in gnarled scrub brush, cacti, and empty washes with the sky wide open. The unrelenting sun cracked my lips and browned my skin. We camped by night under starry skies with planets and galaxies exposed. About twenty-five miles outside the city of Oaxaca, the highway turned into an awful mess. Broken glass lay everywhere. Scattered garbage and graffiti covered every retaining wall, building, and pavement. One of the graffiti read: *En México, la educación no es gratuita . . . Se paga con la vida y la libertad.* (In Mexico, education is not free . . . You pay for it with your life and your freedom.) Thanks to the broken glass, we had to patch multiple flats on the shoulder as cars flew past disconcertingly close. I felt frustrated and angry.

Fighting our way through chaotic traffic, we rode into Oaxaca. Up ahead, a commotion of four giant, white colectivos stretched out across the four lanes of highway. Cars were turning right onto a side street to go around, but as we rode closer, it appeared I would have enough room to squeeze between buses. I slowed down, squeezed through, and kept pedaling. The highly anticipated quiet highway stretched in front of us but lasted for only a moment before I realized the reason for the blockade was a giant crowd of protesters. I slowed my pedal strokes, coasting past a large sea of chanting people with signs and banners. The chanting was loud, the voices filled with rage and anger, a knot formed in the pit of my stomach as I began to second guess my decision to squeeze through the barricade. I turned back to look at Ville.

"KG, maybe we should turn around," he said, his voice shaky. He too had begun to scan the crowd. My senses heightened. I scanned the crowd. Some eyes caught mine, but no movement came in our direction. The people who noticed us didn't seem to care we were riding through the crowd. My confidence grew and I kept riding, sitting up taller, straighter. I smiled and waved at a group of people walking toward the protest. No one had stopped us, and no one seemed concerned we were there. Ville rode up alongside me then and said, "That sign over there says 'Total Support for Oaxaca.'" He pointed in the direction of a large, white banner stretched between three people. He continued, "It's a teacher's protest. You know what's crazy? I saw that graffitied all over the city when I was here back in 2006. Police opened fire on peaceful protesters, and something like seventeen people were killed. I can't believe they are still protesting! Poor Mexico."

As a former teacher, I felt sympathy for the teachers, children, and people of Oaxaca still marching in the streets. Why is it that the poorest and most vulnerable of the world always suffer the most? Those at the top, in positions of power, cut funding for education, music, the arts, social services, and everything important to the health and well-being of a community before ever taking a hit on their own salaries. I had experienced it firsthand in my own country and watched it happen in many others. Mexico was no different. It saddened me, and I carried it with me past the brightly painted stone buildings.

We found a reasonably priced hostel in downtown Oaxaca and walked around the central square looking at all the colorful embroidery and woven textiles made by indigenous tribes. Most of the signs and shop names were in English for the tourists, while foreign languages were spoken around us. It was crowded, and I was uncomfortable. Tourists brought money along with higher prices, and loads of cash was something we were greatly lacking. Even with most hotels costing around ten dollars per night and food around five dollars per meal, our monthly budget did not stretch far. Being on such a tight budget felt awful and stressful, but when those around us had far less than we did, it put everything into perspective.

From Oaxaca, we rode south to Santiago Matatlan, the birthplace of mescal, where I bought some locally made chocolate and we ate beef tongue tacos. We found a basic hotel room for the night, then in the morning we started riding south through the dry, windy hills on Highway 190, dropping from the mountains to the flatter, hotter Pacific coastline, although we never saw the water. It was a brutal four days of ups and downs over and through barren hills in wind gusts as violent as those we'd experienced in Baja Sur, headwinds so strong we had to pedal even on our descents. We passed whirring wind turbines capitalizing on nature's energy gift.

Ville and I had two rules we never deviated from on the adventure: always stealth camp where no one knows where you are; and, never ride in the dark. Up to that point, we had stuck to both of those rules.

That morning we ventured out early, but soon the heat began to boil us alive. It would be an utter miracle if I could feel from the waist down after the ride. I was cranky. I hate the heat. We had a long, steep, twenty-mile climb back over the coastal mountains, headed toward the interior of Chiapas and, surprisingly, it went pretty well, considering the heat and lack of shoulder. We summited by midday and ate lunch in a small village, sharing some leftover beans with hungry street dogs. With the wind at our backs, we managed just over sixty miles and made a vague plan to push on another ten miles or so and find camping. We had both just gotten over bad colds and were still slightly weak but felt strong enough to push farther. We rode over a sea of rolling hills with a beautiful backdrop of towering, green mountains and started looking for a spot to camp, Ville stopping us repeatedly to walk to the barbed-wire fence to see if he could find a hole we could climb through. Every stop yielded disappointment. Not only was there a solid fence, but the thorny brush beyond was impossible to climb into.

I looked down at my odometer as the miles ticked by. Every stop became more disheartening than the last. We were both worried. The last of the sun's glow waned and darkness was swallowing us. After a couple more tries, we were becoming anxious, as it was far too dark to be out on such a busy highway with semis and vehicles flying past. We still had another fifteen miles to the next town. Any strength I had at lunch had been drained from me. I didn't want to push that far, especially in the dark. The noise from the passing trucks grew so loud it was deafening, and the vortex of wind left in their wakes was terrifying. Then it was dark. So dark I could see nothing. Nothing but the fence in the headlights of the passing trucks.

Ville yelled, "KG, I think I saw a break in the fence. I'm going to go check it out!" But I didn't hear him. I was pedaling furiously, trying to reach the next town. This was our rule: no biking at night. And we were out on a dangerous highway with nowhere to go but forward. I just kept pedaling. HONK! Semis were laying on their horns and flashing their lights, reminding us we shouldn't be out there in darkness. Every horn made my blood run cold and the hair stand up on the back of my neck. Suddenly, Ville was yelling my name, but from somewhere far in the distance. I slowed and looked back, but I couldn't see him. His bike light was off, and I could only hear his voice. Hoarse and screaming.

"KG! KG! STOP!" I squeezed my brakes and stopped, my heart pounding in my chest. Ville appeared in the light cast by a passing car. "KG! OH, MY GOD!" he braked hard and pulled to a stop alongside me. "Dammit, KG! Why didn't you stop?! Why didn't you stop?"

"I'm sorry! I'm sorry! I didn't know you stopped!" I stuttered as tears started welling in my eyes. He threw his arms around me, squeezing me so tight.

"I was so worried. I was screaming and screaming," he said, his voice hoarse. "Your taillight isn't working." I looked down to the place my taillight sat, strapped around the stem of my bike seat, facing backward, unblinking. "I saw a break in the fence, and I yelled to you. I thought you stopped. I found a place we can camp in a cow pasture. But it's at least a couple miles back now. God, I was so worried. I came back to the bike and you were gone! Holy shit, I am so glad you're okay." And he hugged me again.

"We need to get off this highway, KG. This is unsafe. I don't think we can make it back. I think we have to keep going and try and make it to that town. We don't have another choice. Can you make it?"

"We have to make it," I said, shaking.

"Let's go." And with that, we sat back on the seats and kept riding. The only direction we could go. I sang to myself. *You'll make it. Just keep pedaling.* The semis continued to honk and flash their lights, the noise deafening. I kept telling myself, *you'll make it.* It was the longest fifteen miles of my life to get to the outskirts of Tuxtla Gutiérrez. When the city lights came into view, rising out of the darkness ahead of me, I wanted to scream, yell, and cry all at once. My legs hurt so bad they throbbed. My back was so locked up I couldn't sit upright. When we exited into the town we looked frantically for a hotel sign. As soon as we found one, I sat holding Ville's bike in the glow of the porch light while he went inside to pay. When he emerged, he said with a big grin, "The guy asked me how many hours we needed. It's another one of those sex motels. I said twelve, and I could tell he was really impressed." My anxiety melted away, and I laughed. At least he still had his sense of humor.

After cold showers, we lay down on the plastic-wrapped mattress and hugged each other. I was so grateful this night ended safely. We fell asleep to the noise of two lovebirds, pounding against every piece of furniture in the room next door.

We started at five the next morning, hoping to beat the heat to San Cristobal de las Casas, but the heat found us again. Sweat was pouring down my face, running into my eyes, coating my hands, and making it slippery when I gripped the handlebars. There was nowhere to hide from it in the desert.

Suddenly, a large, white box truck pulled over into the shoulder right in front of me. *What the hell is that guy doing?* I wondered. I was moving at a snail's pace, listening to a podcast on my headphones in one ear, the other exposed for safety. I looked back to check for cars and passed him on the left, pulling briefly into the right lane of traffic. Ville followed closely behind. As I pulled back onto the shoulder, I heard a man yell from behind us, "¡Hola, gringos! ¡Gringos! You want some oranges?" We both stopped and looked back. There was a middle-aged Mexican man standing in the doorframe of his semi, its door wide open, yelling to us with a huge grin on his face.

"¡Hola, chicos locos! ¿Qué hacen aqui?" he asked, laughing.

"Biking to Argentina!" Ville yelled back.

"What?! No! You're totally crazy amigos! ¿Quieren naranjas? Do you want some oranges?" he yelled back.

"Really?" Ville asked, laying his bike down against the berm. "Yeah, we would love some oranges! ¡Gracias, amigo!"

The man climbed into the cab of the truck, reached under the netting stretched over the top of the cargo, pulled out a handful of oranges, and began tossing them down to Ville as if he were a baseball player. One, two, three, four. Orange after orange. Ville set a few on the ground and caught a few more. "¡No mas, no mas! ¡Gracias, amigo!" Ville said, laughing as the man kept tossing. "You need them for the road!" He tossed two more and stopped. "You crazy kids be careful out there. ¡Suerte!" He climbed back into the cab, fired up the truck, and away he chugged, passing us as we waved, yelling to us, "¡Suerte amigos, suerte!" and gave us a thumbs up.

When we reached San Cristobal de las Casas we were greeted by an incredibly kind and generous host from warmshowers.org, Edu, who welcomed us into his apartment and let us stay for five days while we waited for new bike tubes to arrive. As luck would have it, they arrived on our last day in town. We thanked Edu for his hospitality, leaving five pounds of oranges on his dining room table.

16

Ville Rides Naked

I stood on the side of the two-lane highway just before the border crossing into Guatemala with camera in hand trying to capture a video of Ville riding naked but for a luchador mask, a gift from Luis in Puebla. I had concocted this brilliant idea that Ville should perform in a video clip to post on our website to thank everyone for their kindness riding through Mexico. It wasn't the busiest stretch of highway, but it would be awkward if a car passed by while Ville was riding a bike in nothing but a mask. As I started the video, Ville rolled past the frame, pointing at the camera, mask on, and it was then that I realized his legs were positioned in a way that his manliness was out, exposed and flapping in the breeze.

"Cut!" I yelled at him, folded over in hysterical laughter. "Ville, I can see your junk. Did you want to expose yourself to all our friends?"

"Well, I guess that would be a real ice breaker," Ville laughed, pedaling his naked, white butt back uphill to reposition himself for another take. It took a few more tries before we captured the shot perfectly, Ville's "junk" hidden by his leg, while the rest of him was exposed perfectly. Luckily, only a few truckers and a couple other carloads of people were pleasantly surprised by a gringo riding naked in a luchador mask on the side of the highway.

We pedaled to the border, stamped out of Mexico, and rode the three miles farther uphill on empty stomachs to stamp into Guatemala. The date was April 3, 2017. After fifteen weeks in Mexico, we were crossing into Guatemala, where we expected to spend nine days traveling the 300 miles until reaching El Salvador. I sat outside the office with our bikes. Ville emerged from the immigration office with stamped passports, all smiles because the immigration officer had a wicked sense of humor. We always felt relief passing into countries painlessly, since it's common to be interrogated, frisked, full-cavity searched, or have one's things torn through. Outside in the typical chaos of border crossings filled with shops, restaurants, money exchanges, and peddlers, we found a working ATM and grabbed some breakfast. This sustenance was necessary because we had a massive climb ahead, 3,800 feet in fifty-four miles.

We stuffed our faces and saddled up. It was steep and intense but incredibly scenic and full of beautiful people. We passed through small villages where women sat weaving on looms in front of their homes. Scattered everywhere were various stages of coffee bean plants. We passed a group of women with babies tied in colorful blankets on their backs as they stood working in the fields. They smiled and waved as we passed.

The sun was fierce and unrelenting, but a light breeze swirled down the canyon. We stopped and watched a group of small children splash and play in a cistern of water. We all waved. While we climbed, trucks piled with giant white bags stacked and roped onto their beds high enough to defy the laws of physics passed us.

As we rounded a bend a small red pickup, piled high with white bags, had pulled onto the shoulder of the road. The driver was in the middle of the road, struggling to lift two of the bags off the pavement. They had toppled and split open when the haphazard rope job came undone. We pulled over, leaned our bikes against his pickup, dug out some plastic bags from inside the panniers, and walked to help the poor guy carry the bags back to his truck. I scooped up as many tiny, green beans as I could fit into the bags that were scattered on the pavement. Ville and the young driver hefted two bags out of the middle of the road and moved them next to the truck. One of the bags had a large tear in the side. Ville pulled out a pocketknife, punched small holes in the bag along the tear, and used wire to thread through the holes to close the tear. Then he and the driver lifted the bags back onto the heap and roped them down. He thanked us repeatedly, and as we climbed back onto our bikes he thrust two large bags of beans at us, insisting we take them. He said they were unroasted high-quality coffee beans on their way to Starbucks, and we were sure to find a roaster ninety-five miles ahead in Quetzaltenango. We accepted with hugs and pats on the back, and although we still had a very long way to climb, stuffed the bags into our panniers and continued. Upward and onward, albeit a lot more slowly under the weight of the beans.

My gears were in bad shape, clicking loudly like grinding metal, and not shifting correctly. Ville and I had pulled over onto the shoulder of the road to adjust the derailleur numerous times, but it didn't help. It started acting up the day before and gradually got worse. Thump, thump, thump, GRIND, thump, thump, GRIND. It was driving me absolutely crazy. I tried to ignore it until I needed to downshift, then more thump, thump, GRIND. URGH! It was during one such try at shifting when suddenly there was a loud SNAP. I looked down to see my chain snapped and dragging on the pavement. *That can't be good.*

We were only eight-ish miles outside Quetzaltenango, so close and yet too far to walk. Ville pulled out the chain breaker tool from our handy-dandy tool set. It might as well have been a surgical tool because never having used one before I hadn't the foggiest idea how it worked. After ten minutes of tinkering, Ville pulled out the pin and attempted to remove a link and reattach the chain. After multiple failed attempts on a battered and abused chain, guess I should have changed that a few thousand miles or so ago, we gave up and decided to thumb a ride to town.

The first pickup that flew past slammed on the brakes screeching to a halt, then threw it in reverse and came at us wildly, stopping just shy of my calf. We loaded the bikes into the back atop a bunch of smelly, black garbage bags, and slid onto the bench seat in the cab. I climbed in first, squishing next to the driver, a spicy, short Guatemalan named Celestino. He was on his way to Quetzaltenango and was more than happy to give us a ride.

The road was rough, littered with potholes, kamikaze traffic, and a massive winding descent. Celestino drove like a racecar driver, slamming the shifter into gears, banging into my legs, spinning the steering wheel wildly about, skidding close to the edge of the road, where a cliff loomed without guardrails, weaving between the craters in the road, and all the while glancing at us with a toothless grin and giggling like a schoolgirl. I had never seen anyone take corners in a car like Celestino. No one. I buried my face in Ville's shoulder.

We almost killed three dogs, two motorcyclists, and a couple of pedestrians, and had so many near head-on collisions with giant trucks and buses I lost count. Somewhere along the way, Celestino pulled over on the shoulder of the road and jumped out. Ville followed suit to see what was going on. Celestino proceeded to throw all his smelly garbage bags over the cliff down into the green forest below. Ville hesitantly picked up a bag. After packing every single piece of garbage with us until we found proper receptacles to throw them away, it was devastating for Ville to help this man chuck garbage into nature, but since he was giving us a ride, it would have been rude not to help him. Not every country has the luxury of scheduled garbage pickups, dumps, and incinerators like ours, so Ville just closed his eyes and chucked.

While reversing back out to the road, Celestino got one tire stuck in a giant hole and gunned the truck, RPMs squealing, until it caught traction and we went bouncing back onto the road. He slammed the gear box into drive, and we continued off toward town, my fingernails firmly planted into the dashboard and Ville's arm.

Celestino dropped us outside town, and we walked our bikes to a safe spot for me to sit with our panniers while Ville rode around to find a bike shop that carried our specialty-sized chain. Watching Ville as he rode away, I was reminded how lucky I was to have a partner who wanted me to rest while he went out on a wild goose chase in search of my chain. I felt the sting of tears in my eyes. In Finnish culture, it is very unusual to tell someone you love them, very rare for couples, and almost never happens between family members. Ville told me he loved me every day. He would tell me every time we said goodbye over the phone, every day when we left for work, and every night before bed. Even though most Finns were gun-shy about vocalizing their love, they did believe in showing it with actions. My Scandinavian Stallion showed his love for me constantly by making the meals, filtering the water, searching for hotels and safe places to camp, and going into the grocery store to do the shopping while I waited outside with the bikes and rested. When Ville returned with the chain, I told him again that I loved and appreciated him and everything he did for me, that every minute was precious, and that I was grateful to spend it with him. We hugged each other tightly, cried just a little, and rode a couple miles into town together to find our Warmshowers host and to roast six pounds of coffee beans.

"Friends, I think it is not possible with bikes," was the response from every person we asked for directions to Lake Atitlán. Using a map app on the cell phone recommended for cars, we assumed the naysayers didn't know what bad-ass cyclists we were and forged ahead. The map took us three miles down a steeply graded, winding dirt road. It was no cake walk, but it was passable.

"They must have meant this dirt road was impassable for bicycles, right, Ville?" I looked at him quizzically.

"I assume so," he responded, squinting at the screen of the phone, trying to keep us on the right route. "It hasn't been that bad . . ." He trailed off before we would be jinxed. We could do it; we had made it this far. After crossing the wash at the bottom of the hill, the road climbed steeply uphill with tight switchbacks that brought us standing out of our saddles and cranking on our lowest gears. The midday sun was brutal, and I was completely drenched in sweat and becoming increasingly depressed. I didn't want to say it out loud, but I hoped this was the unpassable part the people giving directions were referring to. I had a sinking feeling it was not.

Trees were sparse and we were open and exposed. We finally came upon breathtaking views miles up from Lake Atitlán, volcanoes with pointed cones and tiny Mayan villages scattered in the hills. It reminded me of Crater Lake in southern Oregon. Both were collapsed volcanoes with deep blue lakes nestled inside. The road ended at the overlook. Why were we up so high? It appeared as though the map app had led us to the top of the highest cliff for the view. We both looked down at the screen and couldn't believe our eyes. It directed us over the cliff and down what might have been a hiking trail but more resembled a crevasse. This passage would cover about a mile and a half to the next town.

"Shit!" we both breathed in unison.

"I am *not* going back all those miles," I said, my heart still beating wildly in my throat from the climb up, sweat burning into my eyes.

"Yeah, I'm not going back. Damn it! Well . . . what do we do, KG? I guess we just have to try it. What else can we do?" Ville said, deflated.

I wanted to scream or cry but none of that would have helped. So I trudged forward, gripping my brakes tightly, bracing for every bump, rut, rock, boulder, and bush in my way. For the first thirty yards you could call it a "mountain biking trail for advanced riders," but only a few minutes later it disintegrated into a boulder field. We dismounted, because it was impossible to ride our hundred-pound fully loaded touring bikes any farther. We tried to push the bikes over the boulders, all the while gripping the brakes to keep them from shooting down the hillside like a rocket, the sheer weight a massive struggle on my small body. The pain in my back was horrendous, but I couldn't quit. Not here. There was nowhere to go but down. *I hate this! Why? Why did I do this? Why am I here right now? Well, that isn't going to help anything. Suck it up, just keep going. You can do it, you can do it, you can do it, you can do it. Idiots put themselves in positions like this. I am a complete idiot.*

"Fuck this!" I yelled after I struck my shin on a sharp boulder and blood began gushing out of the cut. "I hate this!" I had never wanted to quit something so bad. But I was far too angry to quit. *Screw this mountain. The hell I am going to quit here.* I grabbed the handlebars, wrapped my battered hands around the brakes, and pushed on.

At best, I weighed 150 pounds, and with the bike's awkward mass on the steep hillside it took all my energy to keep the bike with me. And the "trail" was not wide enough for both me and the bike, so I had to scramble beside it through bushes. To make things worse, Ville and I were both wearing shorts.

We took turns, laying down our bike and helping the other one to lift the bike over boulders, step by slow agonizing step. A plant like a stinging nettle was everywhere, and my legs, hands, face, and everything that came in contact with it were on fire.

Farther down, the trail became so steep we debated getting our rope and lowering the bags and bikes separately down the mountain. Our emotions went in waves: frustration at the situation, denial that it couldn't possibly get any worse, sadness when it did, then depression that we were stuck. Our options were to go back up or keep going downhill, where it was worse. We rammed our pedals or sprockets into our shins so many times we lost count. I couldn't believe that we were in this mess because of a stupid app. I was too proud to admit that we were warned by the locals and didn't heed any of them. Then the zipper on my bra broke and my boobs were out there flapping in the breeze through my sweaty T-shirt.

Well, shit!

I was beyond caring. Both of us were maxed out, drenched in sweat, completely pissed off, and covered in bloody wounds. We pushed on. Step by step, the lake grew closer, and the steepness began to wane. Luckily, we had sustained no irreparable, bike-adventure ending damage, and thanks to our stubbornness we got off that hillside. It was our stubbornness that got us into that mess and back out of it.

Three and a half hours later, nearly in darkness, the trail brought us into a pungent garbage dump and, just beyond that, into the town of San Juan La Laguna. There we were kindly told by the local townsfolk we passed by, "not to go that way" while they pointed in the direction from which we had just come.

Uh, yeah, thanks. Noted.

It was nearly dark, but we were elated to finally be back on a paved road. We still had another mile climb up and over a giant hill into the town of San Pedro La Laguna. As we rolled into town, locals directed us up into the steep hills to where the more affordable hotels were. After we checked in, I took the absolute best shower of my life, watched the blood and pain run down the drain, and climbed completely exhausted into bed. I glanced at my watch. It said five minutes to eight. We both fell asleep the moment our heads hit the pillow.

Guatemala was spectacularly beautiful, but ass-kickingly hard. It had the steepest hill climbs we had yet encountered on this adventure, with death-defying descents, scalding sun, sopping humidity, washed-out roads that were potholed and crumbling when there was pavement, and pannier-high river crossings. But always we were met with the kindness of the Guatemalan people.

Just south of Villa Canalas, we were directed by a police officer to a "backroad," where we met with the hill climb of all hill climbs, simply trying to make our way back to the highway. The "backroad" started out steep, but then quickly became steeper even by Guatemalan standards. As we climbed, it became torturously, painfully, exhaustingly, and maddeningly steep.

I stared down at my speedometer, sweat pouring down my face. It had quit registering speed, we were moving so slowly. I stood out of the saddle, pushing all my weight into each pedal stroke, one after another after another. I had to put my foot down and rest, my heart throbbing in my throat, leaving a taste of iron in my mouth. I had never encountered an 18 percent grade before. It was as if the engineers had a limited budget for road building and yet needed to get a road from the bottom of the mountain to the top, so they just slapped the road straight up without one switchback. Every vehicle that passed had its RPMs pegged at full throttle and was squealing up the hill. This was not a pleasant experience with over a hundred pounds of rolling momentum trying to hurl us in the opposite direction down the mountain. I made it only twenty pedal strokes before having to break again. Eighteen. Nineteen. Twenty. Heart pounding, sweat pouring, standing there a sopping mess.

Three different Guatemalans seeing our suffering pulled over to ask if we wanted a ride. As tempting as it was, we graciously thanked them, declined, and stubbornly cranked onward and upward. It felt like cheating to get in the back of a pickup when the going got hard. We don't get to bypass the challenges in life, so it felt only right that we push through them on this journey. Besides, this was our adventure. We chose it, the good and the bad, the fun and the pain.

When the light filtered through the trees, teasing us that the top was near, I could hardly believe we had made it to the top without puking our guts out somewhere along the way. I counted 3.8 miles from the bottom of the hill to the top, which it had taken us well over two hours to climb. I was fairly certain I could have walked the hill faster. At the crest, we sat on the side of the road, bent over, panting, waiting for our heart rate to steady before climbing back in the saddles to continue down the other side.

The road fed into the CA1 Highway, where we coasted past the town of Cuilapa, passing a gas station/visitor's center with a sign out front with the silhouette of North and South America on it, a giant star right smack in the middle, and the words, El Punto Medio de las Americas (The halfway point of the Americas). I couldn't believe it. We had made it! We had ridden our bikes to the halfway point between Prudhoe Bay, Alaska, and Ushuaia, Argentina. We had accomplished something that had appeared to be an impossibility! It had taken 8,132 miles to get there, and over 289 days I had pedaled every one of them. Not a professional cyclist or someone fast or flawless but simply happy, wild, fearlessly free me. Me and Ville. Ville and I. We had done it. Together. The halfway point of the Americas made it clear how far we had come and where we were headed.

In the beginning of the ride on the Dalton Highway, a lifetime away, miles had dragged, time had stood still, each mile had felt like a hundred miles, and I feared hills because they were agonizingly brutal. Pain was the only constant. It had taken about a month, but somehow a mile had no longer mattered. I would acknowledge the hills, but they were no longer a means of torture, and pain was replaced by a Zen state of mind. My life had taken on a neat simplicity. We woke with the sun, ate, pooped, rode, rested when needed, stretched, pitched the tent when it was dark, and slept. Everything in between was an awareness of the beauty of life: observing people, places, nature, animals, plants, ecosystems, weather, and the passage of time. Riding for hours upon hours or mile after mile became as commonplace as breathing in and out, something the brain prompts the body to do without thought or action. At the end of each day, I would glance at my odometer, acknowledge the miles ridden as a personal accomplishment, and then zero the trip for the next day's ride. I quit dwelling on the past, quit focusing on the future, and only lived in the present moment. I truly felt alive!

17

Look a Gift Horse in the Mouth

We dropped down out of the mountains into a vibrant green valley, fields of row crops surrounded by towering palm trees with a view that went on for miles. Roadside vendors sold bananas and pineapples on tables or out of the beds of trucks. The sweet fragrance wafted in the air. After two days and sixty miles, we arrived at the El Salvador border and crossed over with relative ease, excited at the thought of starting another country, our fifth. It had taken five and a half months to travel 5,096 miles through the U.S. and Canada, over four months to go 2,770 miles to get through Mexico (although if the Mexican people had not been so hospitable it would have taken only three), and then only a week to travel 300 miles through Guatemala. Central American countries were much smaller than those we had already been through. We were excited to be getting some more countries under our belt. Plus, each border we crossed over brought a sense of accomplishment.

As we rode under the large blue and white banner that read: Bienvenidos a La Republica de El Salvador, a memory returned with vivid clarity. When I was a young child, I lived on the second story of a preschool and kindergarten my parents built and ran until I reached the age of twelve. There were five classrooms of children, teachers, and a cook on the main floor, who were there from six in the morning till about six in the evening, Monday through Friday. My parents hired Rosina, a woman from church, who came after school to help them clean and occasionally take care of us on the rare occasion my parents went out to eat without three kids in tow. Rosina was short, plump, and incredibly kind. She worked hard and never complained, and she always had a big smile on her face showing one front tooth rimmed with gold. She told us she was saving money to bring her son to the U.S. because she wanted to keep him away from gang violence in her country, El Salvador. When we crossed over the border into El Salvador, I thought of Rosina and wondered if her son had lived a life outside the gangs.

As a young child I had no clue where El Salvador was or that there were places in the world far less safe than my quiet, tiny mill and farm town. Now, twenty years later, I knew little more than I had as a child. The smallest and most densely populated of the seven Central American countries, El Salvador lacks access to the Caribbean coast. Extending along the northern border are ancient and eroded volcanic structures with average elevations over 5,000 feet. Of the 6.4 million Salvadorans, almost nine-tenths are mestizo (people of mixed indigenous and European ancestry).

In the late nineteenth century, coffee gave birth to the oligarchy Las catorce familias (the fourteen families), whose control of most of the land and wealth during the nineteenth and twentieth centuries ensured that economic growth revolved around them, as it continues to do today. Throughout the twentieth century, El Salvador endured chronic political and economic instability characterized by coups, revolts, and a succession of authoritarian rulers. During the 1970s, political repression, fraud, and human rights abuses eroded hope of democratic reforms and aided in the creation of guerilla groups opposed to the government. After a military coup in 1979, the country was plunged into the Salvadoran Civil War that lasted for twelve years. The Chapultepec Peace Accords were signed in 1992, officially ending the civil war after the economy was in shambles, damage to the infrastructure was evident, and 75,000 people had lost their lives. Postwar, El Salvador was hit with a severe hurricane, a series of deadly earthquakes, and presidents mired in corruption and scandals. Moreover, failure of land reform and pervasive poverty contributed to continued crime and violence in the country. In 2017, El Salvador had the highest murder rate in the world, when over 4,000 people were murdered due in large part to gangs, organized crime, and the drug trade. Two of the most notorious gangs in the world, Mara Salvatrucha (MS-13) and the 18th Street Gang (Mara 18), originated in El Salvador in the 1970s before spreading throughout the U.S., Mexico, Central America, and Canada. I did not realize El Salvador had such a violent past until after we rode through it.

My thin wool shirt was littered with holes scattered like buckshot across my back from the months of blazing sun. The rivers of sweat had been cascading down from under my bicycle helmet for hours since we left the border and began climbing into the sunbaked hills, soaking my shirt and shorts. I grabbed for the hydration tube that carried three liters of water from a bladder zipped into my frame bag to just over my handlebars and within easy reach of my mouth, forcing more water down. My lips were dry, my mouth parched. I had sucked down over a liter an hour and still I watched the water hit my pores and evaporate, leaving salty streaks on my skin, and I had still not peed. Not in hours. Actually, now that I thought of it, I had not peed all day.

I guzzled a bunch more water trying to compensate, filling my belly until it bulged. Sometime within the next half an hour of riding, I finally felt the urge to pee. I left Ville to hold my bike on the shoulder of the road and skittered into the bushes in an overgrown vacant lot and squatted to pee. Only the tiniest amount came out, followed by a burning fire. In my young life I suffered through a handful of bladder infections, so painful it had always ended in emergency room visits followed by the maximum amount of antibiotics allowable. I knew this fire was a bladder infection. We were in the middle of nowhere in the mountains between the border and a village called Chancuva with no clue where to find a doctor. This brought instant anxiety and tears to my eyes. I pulled up my pants, waddled back to Ville, and told him the grim news. He suggested we ride until we found somewhere to pull over and get cold water and electrolytes. With my burning fire, I climbed back in the saddle and kept pedaling south until we came to a roadside tienda and makeshift restaurant, specializing in bagged chips and soda.

Ville told the sweet, smiling lady behind the counter that we needed water and electrolytes. I went to find her toilet, basically a hole in the ground with a ratty half-used toilet paper roll next to it. And still the fire. The tears burned my eyes. I couldn't hold them back. As I walked back out to Ville, I was in so much pain I could not hide my tears. The woman looked really concerned. Ville explained my predicament and she immediately took charge of the situation. She doused paper towels in cold water and made me sit down in a chair and put them on my stomach. She ordered Ville to get onto the back of a motorbike with her portly, prepubescent son, who looked barely old enough to walk, let alone drive a motorbike. Ville kissed me, climbed aboard, and they zoomed off in a black plume of smoke.

Unable to talk over the deafening roar of the strained motorbike engine, Ville said he clung to the back of the bike as it bumped off the pavement onto a dirt road, bounced and weaved around potholes for another mile before they turned into a dead-end street. The son drove the motorbike right onto the front porch of a block-building without a door surrounded by a mishmash of wood and concrete houses and buildings. Inside, a bookshelf against the back wall was littered with pill bottles and labeled medical boxes. A young man popped out from behind a curtain and stood inquisitively behind the counter as Ville and the son attempted to explain the situation and my symptoms. A young wife then appeared from the back of the shack, which Ville noticed was possibly their house, with a young baby on her hip and toddler in tow. Through broken Spanish and sign language, the young man gave them a package of pills for pain and another package for infection. Ville profusely thanked the young couple and turned to go.

"Wait, wait, Gringo. Can I ask, what are you doing here?" the young man said in Spanish, implying both El Salvador and the middle of nowhere.

"My wife and I are traveling by bicycle from Alaska to Argentina. About ten months and 12,000 kilometers so far to get here." Having given the same response so many times, Ville had perfected his responses to any question about our ride.

"Do you like El Salvador?" the husband asked, a common question for us.

"Oh yes! We love El Salvador. People are very friendly," Ville said.

"What do you think of the food here?" the husband asked, the second-most-common question we were asked.

"The food is very tasty. I really like the pupusas," Ville added.

The young man pauses, looking inquisitively at Ville. "How old are you?"

"Thirty-six."

"Where are your kids?" the young man asked, genuinely confused. This was quite a common question since we crossed the Mexican border. In Latin American culture, family is important, and children are the lifeblood of the family. By the time a Latina is in her twenties, it is very common to have at least one child.

"We don't have any kids," Ville responded with an awkward smile.

The young man looked shocked. Then his face softened. He glanced over at his wife, the look of pity swept across their faces. The young man bent down, pulled out a small box from below the plywood counter, placed it on the countertop, and slid it towards Ville.

"Es un regalo," he said. Ville looked down at the gift and the bright red name across the package: VIAGRA.

For all the negative things about climbing, pain, suffering, and exhaustion, the one glorious positive was elevation gain, because that effort, especially in Central America, where the land mass was narrow and relatively flat, meant lower temperatures. That was why we chose to take the route, CA-8 Highway, that crossed into El Salvador through the mountains and not the CA-2 Highway along the coast. It would take us five days and 233 miles to travel through El Salvador, winding through mountains before we would drop to Highway 2 along the coast to avoid the capital, San Salvador. After La Libertad, we would zigzag northeast through humid jungle, passing through Zacatecoluca, San Miguel, Santa Rosa de Lima, and El Amatillo at the border of Honduras.

After a long-labored climb into the mountains from the border of El Salvador, we found ourselves riding through the beautiful Ruta de las Flores for thirty-eight miles. We stopped at tiny villages along the way eating mangoes and coconuts and licking the stickiness from our fingers after we rode away. But the celebrations ended as quickly as they began when the road dropped steeply from high in the mountains down to the coast, the heat and humidity swallowing us. My mood descended with our elevation, and I became seriously depressed.

And then my antibiotics quit working.

I had squatted to pee behind a bush on the roadside and the same burning fire returned with a vengeance. I felt completely hopeless. *What was I to do now? AGAIN, in the middle of nowhere!* My bladder was on fire and sitting on a bicycle seat was the last thing I wanted to be doing, but we were again a few miles away from a town. It was well over a hundred degrees, humid enough to cut with a knife. I buried my face in my hands and let the tears come. I had had enough. Biking all day in the heat was one thing, my least favorite thing, but I just couldn't bike in this much pain! I wanted to feel better. I needed to feel better!

Ville wrapped me up in a loving hug, wiped away my tears, and promised everything was going to be okay. He stuck out his thumb and flagged down a passing pickup. The cab was full of people, while others stood holding onto a metal rack in the back. They pulled over without hesitation, helped load our bikes in the back, which left almost no room for us. Not one person complained; they only smiled. They were on their way to the only pharmacy in the next town—"No hospital," they informed us—and were happy to take us with them.

Even though this type of kindness had happened so many times throughout Latin America, I was still stunned every time it came our way. They didn't receive anything from us; they refused money and were not after accolades or pats on the back; they put up no walls around themselves and were genuinely kind to us. It was impossible not to smile, even through my pain, so I hung tightly onto the rack sandwiched between Ville and our bikes and smiled.

After waiting my turn at the pharmacy, which looked more like a convenience store than a medical facility, I walked up to the counter to tell the pharmacist about my symptoms. She put three giant, white pills on the counter, explaining that they were the strongest antibiotics they had. I needed to take them for three days. Ville bought nine pills (in case I needed more later in the ride), and the pharmacist gave him a disdainful, are-you-trying-to-kill-her? look over the top of her glasses. I wanted to tell her there were so many other ways he was trying to kill me, antibiotics were the least of it. She recommended I stay out of the sun while taking them, as if that were even an option on a bike adventure. Ha! Good one.

Over the next few days of riding in the heat, even while wearing long sleeves, my sunscreen sweated off and I turned beet red. The physical exertion was hard, but adding heat, humidity, sleep deprivation, bad roads, a tight budget, and health problems tested my will to keep going. We took reprieve from the midday heat in American fast-food chains because they were the only places with air conditioning and consistent Wi-Fi. My refusal to ever enter a fast-food joint back home went straight out the window. The heat made me crazy and desperate. I became giddy when I saw them and practically skipped inside the door, basking in the coolness and stuffing my face with fries and burgers. Sometimes, I would order a milkshake for dessert.

We typically rode for days without taking showers, my least favorite thing about the adventure. I longed for a shower every night I had to pull my salty, smelly shirt over my head and put on a slightly cleaner shirt to sleep in. My scalp itched from the sweat, and I craved even a cold, bucket shower to rinse off. Ville and I were regularly accompanied by a ripe cloud of stink. Our clothes were so grimy and sweaty they could stand up on their own. We looked homeless. We were broke, lived on bicycles, slept each night in a tent, and our possessions consisted of only what could be carried in four small bags. We had very little, which also meant we had little to lose. We were unencumbered and free.

This freedom empowered us to keep going, to keep riding around the next bend in the road, to climb over the next mountain pass, to the next village, to the next country. We felt unstoppable. If there was a fear of failure, I don't recall thinking about it. Each moment was a success. We were alive, breathing, healthy, and experiencing the world together. Even though we were exhausted and filthy with more hills to climb, we were truly happy.

Ville and I rode into La Libertad only to discover it was Easter and the coastal town was packed with Salvadorans, so we rode all over town before begrudgingly paying double for a dumpy motel near the highway. Had we known Easter was a time for family beach vacations with unrelenting partying, we would have opted to camp instead of paying for a hotel. We found out the hard way after a few families rented the adjoining motel room and partied until five in the morning. Sleep deprived, we got up, packed, and left to begin riding while it was still dark outside.

In the cool of the morning, the miles we rode were easy and pleasant, and the people we passed along the road were incredibly friendly. While Americans lived in their cars and roads were for driving, many Mexicans and Central Americans lived on the roads; walking, biking, riding in horse-drawn carts, waiting for buses, sitting on porches, lying in hammocks, pushing carts, pedaling rickshaws, riding motorcycle taxis, sitting in snack stands, selling fruit, soda, water, gas, you name it. Our days were filled with people, smiling, waving, and saying, "Buenos dias." There was the occasional person who looked past me or through me, but almost everyone smiled. They would say, "Buenos dias" or "Buenos tardes," sometimes "Buen viaje" and I even received a few "I love you's." And in the moment, when our eyes met and we smiled, I hoped it made that moment or their day and their week a bit better. It made all the difficulties and challenges melt away and the whole adventure worth it.

After five days and 233 miles in El Salvador, we crossed the border into Honduras and onto some of the most horrendous, patchworked, bumpy, shoulderless, trafficked roadways packed with the speediest, most aggressive drivers we had yet encountered. The potholes in the highway had been filled with asphalt mixed in wheelbarrows. Without a shoulder or room to move over, truckers ran us off the road into the dirt embankment a few times. Luckily, we escaped physical harm, but it was terrifying and left us dreading the road. In the thirty feet of thick brush between the edge of the road and the fields were corrugated metal shacks and people selling fruits and vegetables. Many of those shacks were homes to entire families.

Historically, Honduras has also seen its share of political and economic instability. After its independence in 1838, power yo-yoed between liberal and conservative factions throughout the nineteenth century. In the twentieth century, most of Honduras's elected presidents were embroiled in corruption, scandals, conflicts, and coups. From 1963 to 1979 the military was in power. Then, in 1979, El Salvador and Nicaragua's revolutions brought on a cycle of violence. Throughout the eighties, the U.S. sanctioned border areas for attacks against Nicaragua's Sandanista government, ran camps for training Salvadorans in counterinsurgency to combat El Salvador's Civil War, and gave substantial economic aid. The U.S. presence supported the further militarization of Honduras and brought about dissention and protests within the country. In 1998, Hurricane Mitch, washed away crops, roads, and population centers, killing several thousand Hondurans and displacing over a million. It ruined the country's economy and infrastructure and caused widespread misery and unemployment.

In 2009, during a coup d'état, leadership of Honduras was taken from President Zalaya by the military and National Congress, and Roberto Micheletti was elected president. The international community, including the UN and the Organization of American States (OAS), condemned the ouster. In response, Honduras withdrew from the OAS. Lacking leadership, the country's infrastructure deteriorated. People appeared to be fending for themselves and barely surviving. One would expect, especially if you followed the news about Honduras, that it was seriously dangerous. With the second-highest murder rate of any country in the world (second to El Salvador), many travelers rushed through it or skipped it altogether. But we found the same kindness from Hondurans as we did everywhere else.

After just two days and eighty-seven miles in Honduras, we crossed into Nicaragua, where the temps dropped from over one hundred degrees to somewhere in the nineties. The beautiful road stretched out in front of us, freshly paved with a spacious shoulder. I was so happy that I wanted to lie down on the pavement and kiss it. We pedaled on and passed mile after stinky mile of sugar cane fields, where semitrucks with giant knobby tractor tires pulled five container cars loaded full of sugar cane along the roadside on special tracks made for them. The cane was so pungent I felt it linger in the back of my throat. From the border, we traveled 210 miles southeast, passing through Chinandega, Leon, and into the capitol, Managua. We passed bony white and brown cattle being herded by young guys on horseback down the middle of the highway. The landscape was so flat I could see for miles ahead, the blue sky so large I felt too small to matter.

We made our way into Managua, where every single hotel was out of our budget. We were left contemplating just how far out of town in the dark we would have to ride to find something affordable. Just before throwing in the towel, we happened upon a fancy hostel, run by a German man, Jonas, who took pity on us and gave us two nights lodging for far less than the advertised price after we asked, looking frantic and exhausted, where we might find affordable accommodation. We thanked him profusely in disbelief of our dumb luck. Managua was a crowded, sprawling, concrete city, where we watched a basketball game played by people in wheelchairs in the park, hiked up to the top of a hill overlooking the ocean, walked along the Malecon along Lago Xolotlan, and relaxed on clean sheets with showered bodies. It was glorious.

Jonas insisted we visit Laguna de Apoyo, a lake in the crater of a volcano thirty miles southeast of the city. We made a slight detour from our route to Granada to climb up and into the crater only to discover it was a tourist trap full of unaffordable hotels. Disappointed and deflated, we rode from place to place, forced to settle on a hostel with a room large enough only to cram our bikes in next to a modest mattress for a whopping ten dollars a night. I know ten dollars sounds like a deal, but considering what we had been paying, it was highway robbery. Just as we finished cramming our bikes and gear like Tetris blocks into the room, the woman at the desk came to our room to inform us that she had meant the room cost ten dollars for each person per night. As we began wrestling our bikes back out of the room to leave, the woman felt sorry for us and insisted the ten dollars was adequate payment.

This little side trip was a terrible idea. Wanting to salvage something positive from the experience, we planned to take a dip in the lake and refresh ourselves and wash away the frustration and resentment. We made our way down to the water's edge, where we noticed that all the fancy hotels had roped off their private beaches for vacationing gringos. We walked farther to the public beach and swam with the locals, the only two gringos. We bobbed in the lukewarm water while chatting with the locals happy to be enjoying the volcano surrounding us.

Each morning, we rose at the ungodly hour of five to beat the heat, although the temperature never dropped below a sweltering 85 degrees. At around eleven, we were forced into fast-food establishments because the pavement became so hot you could fry anything on it. While we fixed a flat tire outside a Burger King we met a young, kind Mexican American family whom we chatted with. Dressed in collared shirt and slacks, the man introduced himself before introducing us to his wife, who stood next to him in a beautiful white dress with a toddler resting on her hip. A child of about six held his father's hand and fixed us with his large brown eyes. Originally from Mexico, the man told us they now lived in Arizona. We told him we loved Mexico and that we had received nothing but kindness while traveling through the country.

After fixing the tire, we walked inside the air-conditioned restaurant and surveyed the menu. The family came to sit with us and set down burgers for us for lunch. The man told us what we were doing was inspiring and that if we had had such generosity while traveling through his home country he wanted to keep the kindness alive. This was proof that kindness was contagious.

We returned to our bikes in the sweltering heat and rode along the Carretera Panamericana, which was scorched pavement surrounded by fields of white dry grasses and gnarled trees. The sun baked our skin, the sky opened wide above us, and the road stretched out before us. The miles ticked by rather lazily.

Discovering a Warmshowers host who had a hostel in El Gigante on the Pacific coast, we decided it would be fun to take a detour to the beach, so we turned west on a side road twenty miles over baked hills. Fifteen miles south of El Gigante was the fishing village of San Juan del Sur, which we visited while on a backpacking trip in 2009. We expected the same white sand beach and cool, refreshing waters to be a reprieve after four days in the Nicaraguan sun. It was euphoric to stand in the ocean letting the sweat and exhaustion float away. After a long soak, we were welcomed into a restaurant by the owner to take some much-needed showers. We pitched our tent under a tree on the sandy beach and fell asleep to the sound of the crashing waves.

"KG! Wake up! Something is at our tent!" Ville shook me awake.

Groggy, I rolled over, rubbed my eyes, trying to adjust to the darkness, and sat up. There, in the glow of the moonlight, was a large, snorting pig, rooting with its snout right next to Ville's side of the tent. Having spent my teen years on a farm, it was not my first time seeing a pig, and I was annoyed to be awakened in the middle of my slumber for a dumb pig.

I sighed. "Ville, it's just a pig," I mumbled before grabbing the sleeping quilt, throwing it back over myself, and falling back to sleep. Ville, on the other hand, had grown up in the city and had only ever seen a pig in the movies, movies of dead bodies that were fed to pigs to eliminate evidence of murder. He nervously lay awake for a long while, sure the pig was going to eat our panniers, all our food, and possibly even the bikes. Eventually, the pig got bored and moseyed off down the beach in search of murdered bodies to eat or, more likely, food. Only then did Ville fall back to sleep.

Ville and I found that crossing borders early in the morning was our best chance at dodging all the chaos: money changers, hawkers, lines, and people directing you where to go or providing the "correct" forms in exchange for money. After 270 miles and seven days in Nicaragua, it was at first light we found ourselves biking the last five miles or so to the border of Costa Rica. The sun was not yet peeking over the barren hills to the east.

About three miles before the border, a hideously long line of semitrucks had stopped, awaiting entry into Costa Rica. Auto traffic and, in this case, semitrucks importing cargo, were required to fill out paperwork and sit through inspections before they could cross over borders. Foot traffic with nothing to declare, which is what we were considered, were able to enter the customs office directly. So it was with great joy that we passed the line of semis. At that early hour, there was no oncoming traffic. As we passed by each truck, I started waving, calling out, "¡Buenos dias!" and smiling at every driver, unusually perky at such an early hour. While sitting in their rigs, standing outside them, sitting in chairs, and even lying in hammocks, the drivers waved, smiled, and yelled, "¡Buenos dias!" and "¡Buen viaje!" And the happier they got, the happier I became. What an amazing start to the morning.

The border crossing was a breeze, and we didn't get charged entry, for once. As we climbed into the humid, tropical jungles of Costa Rica, the semitruck drivers began to trickle over the border one by one. They gave us plenty of room, honked, waved, and yelled things like, "¡Buen viaje, amigos!" as they passed by. Because we had made the impersonal personal by smiling and saying "Buenos Dias," we now felt like friends. It felt amazing! Kindness had inspired more kindness. World Peace, such a hippie-dippy unachievable notion, could actually work. For the rest of that day and for many days after, we were treated warmly by truck drivers, and it made our world peaceful.

The vegetation in Costa Rica was vibrant green, the climate far more humid than in Nicaragua. Birds and parrots squawked around us. Sweat poured out of every pore, cascading down my face, dripping over the front of my panniers. The antibiotics I had to take were still messing with my internal thermometer, so when the temperature was hot, I was boiling. We camped that night in the yard of a Red Cross, the staff allowing us to use the bathrooms to shower, our tent pitched in weeds surrounded by battered Red Cross trucks and vans. We spent another night on a football field, jolted awake by a flock of squawking macaws overhead only to discover a horse grazing next to the tent when we climbed out.

After 125 miles and seven days, we arrived in Punta Arenas, where we were welcomed onto the porch of a Warmshowers host's modest home in a run-down part of town. After relieving ourselves of panniers, we followed him out to the beach to watch him surf just before nightfall. While chatting with him on his porch later, I was eaten alive by swarms of mosquitoes. We were forced into our tent early because it had a net that protected us from the vicious blood suckers. We had a fitful sleep because this area of town was more active at night than during the day. It then made sense to me why there were safety bars around every porch. Much like a jail cell, our tent was behind bars on the porch locking out the active night crawlers on the street.

Early the next morning, we found the bus station in town, where we booked tickets to the capital, San Jose. We planned to catch a flight in a few days' time to head home to Bend. As an immigrant, Ville held a green card, and the rule was he could not be out of the U.S. longer than a year without the government potentially revoking his card and resident status. Because the trip to Argentina would exceed the timeline, we found the cheapest flights back to U.S., hoping that two weeks there would be long enough to keep his card valid and us on our adventure.

The bus terminal was chaos, as bus terminals usually are, a great reminder why we were happy to be on bicycles and our own schedule. After a lot of begging and bribing, we got our bicycles and panniers secured under the big bus and loaded up for the two-hour bus ride to San Jose. We planned to stay a couple nights near the airport at the home of Edu, our friend and San Cristobal de las Casas Warmshowers host, and his family. We also planned to leave our bikes with them for the two weeks we would be in the U.S.

As the bus sped wildly along the windy highway up into the mountains on its way to the city, I couldn't help but think of how far we had come since Bend and how the airplane could transport us there in just hours. It seemed insane that my legs had pedaled me all the way to Costa Rica. I was excited to see my family and friends and thrilled for a break from my bicycle seat and the constant sweating.

We had been on the road for almost a year, traveled 8,900 miles through eight countries, and we were about to be teleported back to Oregon in May, trading summer for spring and transforming from touring cyclists to couch potatoes. I missed my family, but I was happy to be on my bike, happy to be on our adventure. I was actually a bit unsure how I would feel. *What if I didn't want to fly back to Costa Rica and keep biking south? Could this happiness and love for the ride disappear in just two weeks?* I was about to find out.

PART III

Panama, Colombia, Ecuador, Peru, Bolivia

18

A Mosquito Almost Ends It All

We had been in Bend for five weeks because I had become horribly sick, the sickest I had ever been, sick enough to nearly end the ride. We delayed our flights hoping we would continue if and when I recovered. I was unable to climb the stairs to bed, hardly ate or drank. By the second week I was sitting up, weak and frail, and by the third week I was upright and walking, a far cry from exercising, let alone riding a loaded bike all day. Ville was worried I might not pull through. This was the only time during our trip, despite the bike accidents, toothaches, and other illnesses we weathered, that I was afraid the whole thing was over. Although my tests had come back negative for both the Zika and West Nile viruses, my doctor was confident I had picked up a virus, likely passed to me by a teeny-tiny mosquito, smaller than my fingernail somewhere in Central America. Against her orders we returned to our bikes and our Adventure in San Jose, Costa Rica.

We landed and bussed to our friend's house and even had time to squeeze in a stop at a bike shop to get a tune-up and have the new bottom brackets we brought back with us installed. Because the bus terminal was in the center of downtown San Jose, we had a death-defying and hair-raising ride there. The bus that took us back to the coast, back to the exact spot we had left off five weeks earlier. However, we were no longer the same people. Everything felt foreign: the landscape, the people, the bikes. Onward we pedaled.

I glanced down at my odometer. I had ridden only three miles since I last checked. The cars that passed me felt deafeningly loud. *Had they always been this loud? Had I forgotten how loud they were? Why did my legs feel like lead?* It took so much energy to push the pedal down to get a full rotation. *Had it really been this hard before?* It was the first time in five weeks that I had sat in the saddle on Blue Bullet, broken a sweat for any reason other than a fever, or done any real exertion other than climbing up the stairs to go to bed at my parents' house. Geez, I felt like a complete and utter beginner back on the Dalton Highway. The only reminder of time in this saddle was the amount of dirt caked into the butt crack of the sumo-wrestler squeaky toy on the left handlebar, and the rubber of my brake lever, worn paper-thin beneath my hand. My back ached, my hands hurt, and I was sweating profusely again. I glanced down, only .8 mile had passed. *Damn. This was going to be a really, long day.*

July was the rainy season in Costa Rica, dreary and gray. An accurate representation of our moods while we adjusted to being back on this bicycle journey. I was not well. The virus was still inside me; I could feel it in my aching joints. Plus, I felt a pinching pain in my spine every time I rolled over a bump. And I was tired. I became exhausted and worn out much faster than normal, but at least I was upright and alive. It could have been worse. It can always be worse. And like hell was I going to let a virus take me out of this adventure. As miserable as I felt, I was not lying on a couch wasting my life away. We were back seeing the world! *You can do this.* The power of words, telling yourself you are strong, that you can do anything, and that you will. *You can do this. Just keep pedaling.* So far, so good.

We had agreed to stick to a lower fifty-miles-per-day average until I felt stronger and, luckily for me, Ville suggested we call it a day a little earlier than normal that first day. He asked if we could camp in the yard of a restaurant where we had stopped to eat dinner. As we unrolled our mattresses to set up camp around the back, an older woman scurried up and unlocked a door to a small, dark room with a small bed inside, ushered us inside, and insisted we stay there instead of in our tent. She refused payment and hurried off to make us some tea. I undressed and climbed my aching body into the shower, pulling the plastic shower curtain closed behind me, startling the largest, hairiest, ugliest spider I had ever seen. It streaked from near my feet at the bottom of the curtain, to the shower head in a fraction of a second. I froze.

"Ville!" I yelled. "Ville!!" I yelled louder. I huddled in the corner, only an arm's length from the gigantic arachnid. *Oh geez, I really hope this thing can't jump.*

I had grown up with spiders. I had spent my teenage years on a farm, our hundred-year-old farmhouse was crawling with them. I had learned to live with them. I was not scared of any of them, even though two species we found quite regularly were the deadliest spiders in the world. But none of those spiders were even the size of this spider's head.

"What?! What happened?" he yanked open the door and ripped back the curtain.

I stood frozen. "Look at the size of that spider," I whispered, as if it would hear me and lunge. I pointed at it hiding at the base of the shower head. "Please, kill it," I begged, my arms folded over my chest.

"Holy shit! Look at the size of that thing!" Ville stepped backward, with a grimace on his face. "I don't need a shoe . . . I need a gun!" He laughed, then disappeared and came back quickly with a shoe. He took numerous swings at it, but it was fast and moved like a ninja. It appeared to be able to jump. I desperately wanted to crawl out of the shower, but I was trapped between the beast and the wild man swinging a shoe. Ville seemed nervous, which only made me panic more.

"Dang, this guy is fast!" Ville said, recoiling, steadying himself for the next onslaught of whacks with the shoe. Finally, he made contact with the spider, pinning it against the shower wall. When he picked up the shoe, there was a massive, sticky, yellow, gooey mess, with pieces of legs left, dripping down the wall. It made me shudder.

"Yuck!" we chimed in unison.

"Did you see how big that thing was?" I asked anxiously, wide-eyed and shivering. "It came out of nowhere."

"I'm just glad you didn't ask me to carry it outside and let it go," Ville said with a dead-pan stare. He was right, of course. I always tried to save every living thing, carrying worms from a rainy sidewalk back to the grass or shooing beetles off a trail so they wouldn't be stepped on. But this had been different. I was naked, exposed, trapped in a shower the size of a coffin with an unidentified spider the size of my hand. This was war. We shook the shower curtain vigorously in case any spider friends were hiding and checked every corner of the room before going to bed. Fortunately, we had no other spider encounters that night. Nor did we have any more through the rest of Central America. Mild, pleasant days, interrupted only by rain showers constantly rolling through, defined our ride through Costa Rica, although, stifling heat and humidity were constant companions at lower elevations.

We were disappointed to discover we had to pay sixteen dollars to exit Costa Rica, and then felt devastated once we discovered Panama was a letdown to bike through. Although the road widened, as did the shoulder, we saw fewer motorbikes, noticed less foot traffic and a notable increase in the number of cars. The traffic moved faster, the cars were larger, and the drivers more aggressive. Less foot traffic on the road meant fewer opportunities to interact with people and more with road-raged drivers. It reminded me of biking through the U.S.

Compared to Costa Rica, the highway in Panama was relatively flat, and the landscape was severely deforested to make way for ranching. We were nearly killed by careless drivers unconcerned with speed, making right turns directly in front of us and running us off the road. It was complete hell. My blood was boiling, my stress level was through the roof, and I imagined taking a baseball bat to the back of every car.

We found a relatively inexpensive motel to stay in for Ville's birthday. When I gave him the choice of doing absolutely anything he wanted for his special day, do you know what he wanted to do more than anything else in the world? Bike all day. Yeah, I know. I couldn't believe it either. We had plans to see our friend Devin, who had been working in Panama for an NGO, in a few days' time, and he was kind enough to connect us with a few different Peace Corps volunteers to stay with along the way. The kindness of friends was the highlight of Panama.

We spent our four-year wedding anniversary in our tent in a fire station completely drenched. We were sandwiched between a fire engine and an office full of loud, crude-talking firemen, punctuating each sentence with raucous laughter. We wrung out our clothes, climbed inside the tent, lay down on our air mattresses, and reflected on what a wild ride the last four years of marriage had been over the loud roar of rain pelting the roof. *Well, at least Ville knew how to keep things interesting*, I thought, laughing. I suggested that maybe for our next wedding anniversary he could take me somewhere nice, maybe even spring for a hotel room, somewhere we might celebrate our anniversary without an audience.

We crossed the infamous Bridge of the Americas over the Panama Canal and cheered the whole way over, illegally taking up one entire car lane to keep the traffic from running us off the bridge. We biked into Panama City and stayed in a hotel that just might have been a brothel, sandwiched between giant skyscrapers, banks, and malls. The next day, we packed our bicycles into boxes after realizing we were too broke to sail over the Darian Gap to Cartagena, Colombia. The only "safe" alternative to sailing was to fly. Otherwise, we would have to machete our way through one hundred miles of treacherous jungle.

19

Energy Juice

"Perdón, señor," Ville said, walking up to a pudgy man dressed head to toe in official black airport-security garb. "¿Podemos reparar las bicicletas aqui?" He asked politely, pointing to the open area between the baggage claim belt and a wall of windows in the Cartagena Airport where we might assemble our bikes.

It was July 17, 2017, and we had arrived late that afternoon on a flight from Panama City. We would ride just under a thousand miles south in Colombia, climb into the Andes Mountains and pass through Sincelejo, Medellín, Popayán, and Pasto. This route was not planned beforehand. I had never been to South America, and I was excited to experience it.

"¡Si, si, claro!" The mustached man nodded his head excitedly and pointed toward the corner at the far end of the belt, where there was no one left waiting to pick up their luggage. "En la esquina."

"¡Muchas gracias, amigo!" Ville replied, smiling, shaking the man's outstretched hand and returning a giant, matching smile. The man patted Ville on the back with his other hand.

"No problema. ¡Bienvenidos a Colombia, amigos!" he exclaimed.

If this were any other international airport in the world, they would never have let us assemble our bicycles right there next to the baggage claim belt inside the cool, air-conditioned building, but this was Colombia. They were happy to let us do it.

The boxes looked banged up, and we had to patch my bike tire twice, but the strangest mystery of all was how Ville's brake lever had been completely sheared off on the top, a feat accomplished, seemingly, with the assistance of a grinder. There was no plausible reason for it. You had to grip or compress the brake lever to access the metal that was ground off. Yet somehow the box was completely intact. Colombia.

When we emerged from the airport the heat swallowed us again. Our shirts stuck to our sweaty skin even at dusk. Frantic to get to our apartment rental before dark, we circled streets, asking for directions, only to be repeatedly told that biking in this area after dark was extremely dangerous. Always great to hear when you're lost and have no other choice. We finally found our place, carried all our bags up multiple flights of stairs, and enjoyed a cold shower.

The next morning, we opted for a 5 a.m. start to beat the heat, but my rear tire had another flat to change, and then another, a mere mile down the road. Dammit! Flats sucked, but multiple flats in a hot busy city made us really cranky, enough to push us over the edge. I *hate* heat. Burning sweat poured into my eyes while I crouched over Ville, both of us trying to change the tire on the shoulder of the road, when some street kid appeared to try his hand at rifling through Ville's frame bag.

"Come on, fuera chico! Fuera!" I yelled after him, standing up and making a move toward him. He looked mangy and sad. His face was dirty, and he had a broken shoe. I tried to harness my teacher's patience despite the sweat and frustration of my flat tire. I scrounged for a few pesos out of my handlebar bag, held my hand out, dropped them in the kid's dirty palm, and watched him run away. I turned back to Ville and continued working on the tire. I had never wanted to climb so badly, to climb into cooler temperatures and away from the humidity. After pulling out more than eight metal shards from my rear tire with the needle-nose pliers, it held enough air to ride on until we got out of town and found a bike shop where we could stock up on more tubes. Ville also bought a new chain.

As we left the coast through the center of the country we rode through mangrove swamps and passed a small, dead alligator on the shoulder of the road. "Don't worry, Ville, it's just sleeping," I said, a joke we used to ease sadness over the deaths of so many creatures we passed along the roads, meaningless deaths caused by the human need for speedy transport. Earlier, seeing tiny hummingbirds, butter-flies, hawks, owls, rabbits, deer, and even a young mountain goat lit-tered along the roadside, I wouldn't talk for hours, fuming, asking why we need to drive fast vehicles—for what purpose? We miss all the beauty in the world. It took me to some dark places. Too much time on a bike will do that sometimes. We watch the world running by in hyper speed, like a cyclone that passes by, leaving destruction in its wake. We humans don't know what we have until it's gone. So, instead of dwelling on it, we lightened the mood. The joke was less hilarious, however, when we passed an enormous, dead python stretched out in the middle of the road. I would rather have seen it living.

We passed herds of water buffalo, flank-high, munching on greenery in the marshes, zipping armadillos skittering in front of us, squawking macaws flying overhead. We saw many kinds of spiders on their sticky, outstretched webs, so many vibrantly colored birds it would make a birder swoon, a handful of sloth signs (although we didn't get to see any), and even a couple of iridescent, giant, blue butterflies that stopped us in our tracks. We left the coast at Cart-agena, opting for a hillier scenic route for the next 400 miles. Al-though it was still sweltering, it was better than the bustling, coastal route. We patched seven flat tires and chalked it up as a new record.

Questioning whether the airline had also bent my rear wheel, I put on my new Schwalbe tire that I had been carrying since Costa Rica. It seemed to do the trick.

Twenty miles before Sincelejo, I was pedaling along in my meditative reverie, the brush and tall trees thick along the highway, the heat rising off the pavement making me sleepy, when there was a crashing sound of breaking branches and what sounded like an elephant charging from the brush to my right. Instead, a wild pig came squealing out from the brush, nearly startling me off my bike, as I swerved and narrowly missed hitting its flank.

"What the hell was that?" I yelled.

"What the . . . ?" Ville swerved, too, just missing hitting the wild beast as the dusty-brown pig continued its charge. We stopped to watch the snorting, flailing pig swerve to the right, then the left, ears flapping as its little feet went clop, clop, clop along the pavement before diving back into the brush from where it had, only moments before, sprung.

We folded over with laughter, hardly believing we were nearly involved in a head-on-head collision with a pig. If that was how I left this earth, I wanted it etched on my gravestone.

Ville and I rode right through Sincelejo, a large, sprawling, concrete city known for bullfighting and music, about one hundred miles south of Cartagena. We stopped briefly for breakfast at a café for cyclists adjacent to a spectacularly designed bike path on the way into the city, after passing heaps of jersey-clad cyclists out for their weekend bike ride. We could hardly believe it. We ate our breakfast surrounded by cyclists watching the Tour de France on a small flat-screen TV on the wall and felt like we belonged. We reminisced about how long it had been since we had seen cyclists enjoying riding for the sheer joy of it and agreed that it was in Ixtlán del Río, Mexico. That was six months and about 6,000 miles ago.

Another giant perk we discovered in Colombia was good food with portions fit for a touring cyclist. Along the roadside, we enjoyed an assortment of restaurants, open-air cafés, food stalls that typically served a giant vegetable soup followed by a heaping main dish of seasoned white rice, black beans, eggs, fried plantains, and a slab of beef, occasionally complemented with a pile of fries. I imagine being a vegetarian or vegan here would be difficult.

The roads in Colombia were a mixed bag; we saw everything from narrow roads without bike lanes to giant bike paths that wound through towns. But the cyclists, motorbikes, cars, box trucks, and semitrucks all seemed to share the road cohesively. No one seemed to be in much of a hurry. On numerous occasions, a curious motorcyclist pulled up alongside us as we cycled for a chat about where we were heading. Even a few police officers checked in on us to make sure we were alright. Luckily, the Colombian people were out-of-this-world friendly and the scenery was beautiful and bio-diverse, leaving us to gawk at giant Colombian mahogany and oak trees, savannas full of swamp grasses and sedges, rolling hills of vivid greenery, desert scrub brush, and dwarf palms.

Five days and 320 miles after riding out of Cartagena—as the Tour de France raged on in Europe with Colombia's Rigoberto Uran winning stage 9, Chambery, after a fierce battle over three hellish climbs—we climbed up and out of the heat; 7,723 feet in one, grueling, forty-five-mile day, and realized why Colombian bicyclists were so damn good in the hills. The Andes Mountains were in their backyard. I had not realized we would be climbing in the Andes Mountain Chain until we were in them. And that first day in the Andes was only the beginning.

I never learned about the Andes Mountains in school, not even where they are located in relation to the U.S., because it had seemed more important to teach me about the Civil War, the capitals of all fifty states, multiplication tables, and Psalty the Singing Songbook. (I went to Catholic School.) It came as quite a surprise to me to learn that they spanned from Colombia to the end of Argentina, roughly

5,500 miles, and are the longest continental mountain range in the world. Who knew?

We had started that first climb after arriving at the Sauce River, following its bank uphill while passing brightly colored concrete and wooden houses. Towering above us, the houses and buildings were built into the thick vegetation along the banks. We passed a number of waterfalls, one after another, cooling the air with their mist. We passed large PVC pipes that gathered water from high above us and sprayed it onto the should of the road for passing trucks to pull underneath and get a good wash. We found ourselves standing up, out of our seats, during long, steep stretches, the occasional truck driver giving us a thumbs-up or cheering us on as we climbed. We would smile, wave back, and dig deeper, inspired to keep pushing, climbing upward into the clouds. The climb was long, grueling, and steep, and soon we were sweaty enough to pull over and stick our heads under the cold, refreshing spray and get a wash as well.

Hours later, we pulled over for a rest on the side of the road and watched a large, wooden boat full of people cross the river to the far bank. As we watched about thirty of them disembark, load into trucks, and disappear up the forested hillside, we were informed by a local man that they were workers heading up the hill to the coca farms. I imagined we were in the right country if we wanted to score some kilos of pure, uncut cocaine. It would even make us bike faster. However, we had no interest in becoming drug mules, so we carried on.

In a downpour of icy-cold rain after a grueling twelve-hour climb late that evening, we finally summited in the village of Yarumal. We were nearly halfway through the country. We had been ill prepared for the day's climb, miscalculating how many snacks we would need. We had relied on chocolate bars until they began melting in Central America and we switched to roadside food stalls, which had worked out fairly well until this day. After checking into a modest motel room tucked back behind a restaurant, we inhaled our dinner, then climbed, shivering, under a pile of wool blankets. The temperature dropped to 40 degrees in the elevation. We were asleep before our heads hit the pillow.

The following morning, we climbed on our bikes into the mountain air, the sun peeking out between low clouds, the winding two-lane road quiet. We passed farms with black and white–speckled dairy cows; the fragrance of meadows and wildflowers trailed us as we passed. The hills proved challenging on sore legs, leaving us spent when we finally arrived at our Warmshowers host's house after forty-six miles. Dr. Lenin's home sat nestled on a hillside, an array of farm animals roaming the gardens and every delicate, colorful flower you could imagine hanging from baskets or flowing from pots surrounding the farmhouse. I wished we could stay longer to relax and soak it in, as our host insisted we do, but we had already promised to meet another host in Medellín the following day—the downside of planning ahead.

After a short climb, we came to a large grassy overlook and pulled over to enjoy the view. We lay our bikes down on the grass, walked out, and stood at the precipice of a giant cliff. The wind tangled my hair and flapped my clothes about. I looked far down into the valley of the canyon and could not see the bottom. I closed my eyes and took a deep breath, pulling in as much air as I could and holding it until my lungs burned, then blew it out into the wind. I opened my eyes as a pair of giant birds circled the updrafts directly in front of me. I felt bigger than I had ever felt, bigger than the canyon, larger than life. I looked over at Ville, also standing at the edge of the cliff watching the birds, and felt a deep happiness beginning in the pit of my stomach and expanding to fill me.

I was grateful to be there and for health, wealth, determination, perseverance, luck, and the kindness of others. It was everything that had brought us to so many beautiful places. As beautiful as the one in front of my eyes. Although there were many trials and tribulations, Ville and I were getting to experience it all together. After all, what is a life without the memories created in it? How fortunate was I to create these memories with Ville? And I knew, without having to say it out loud, that Ville felt the same. But I said it anyway.

"Ville, I am grateful for you. Thank you for being here with me," I said, trying to choke back a tear and the emotions that came forth with it. "I want you to know, I really love you."

He looked over at me, "Wow, KG. . . . I love you, too. Thank you for saying that," he said, his voice breaking with emotion, his eyes filling with tears. We embraced in a big hug, not caring if anyone saw us.

Either of us could die at any moment, and I did not want to regret the words that I never said.

Life is too short to care.

On the steep descent, we came upon a slow-moving semitruck. The tight, hairpin turns slowed the driver down to first gear. He was trying to avoid picking up speed, careening off the edge, and plummeting to the thick forest. The strain of the RPMs, pegged at their max, was deafening. I couldn't see around it because it took up the entire lane and we were approaching a blind turn. But even so, I gauged that I had enough room to squeeze past it, passing on the left, even if a car were coming uphill in the oncoming lane.

So, I went for it.

As I gained speed, moving to the left of the truck into the oncoming lane, another semitruck appeared in the oncoming lane. I had enough room to squeeze between them. Not a lot, but enough. Enough to catch my breath, feel the pounding of my heart in my chest. Just enough to feel alive. As I moved back into the right lane after passing the truck, Ville pulled up alongside me, having squeezed between the trucks right behind me. We were then flying at breakneck speed down the hill. I glanced over at him, and he looked at me—we both had giant grins.

We passed about fifteen more trucks like that. The remainder of the descent lasted for over an hour, longer than a roller-coaster ride and a hell of a lot more fun!

The road fed into a busy highway at the bottom of the canyon, passed through the town of Bello, and opened into Medellín, a giant metropolis cradled in giant mountains. As we entered the city, the shoulder disappeared, and the chaotic traffic zoomed inches from us at excessive speeds. I could no longer hear myself think. I wanted off this busy highway. Now.

We passed a young guy in a wheelchair on the busiest section of highway, saying hello as we passed. When we stopped at the next intersection, he pushed himself up behind us and asked us for a ride. He grabbed onto the back of Ville's rack and let himself be pulled along waving his free hand wildly in an attempt to direct traffic around us. After spending about a half an hour, he yelled out his thanks on a descent and let go before disappearing up a side road. We continued into the city.

Only the facades of houses we saw were painted, leaving bright-orange brick and mortar exposed. It gave the appearance of everything being left unfinished, yet it was hip and cool. We drank beer at a microbrewery, visited the Fernando Botero Museum (Medellín-born figurative artist and sculptor who depicts figures in a large, exaggerated style), walked around looking at Pablo Escobar murals (it seemed he was revered as a saint in his hometown), shared food with our host family, and enjoyed seeing the sights for a few days.

We left the city on a Sunday and found the highway closed to all auto traffic, the lanes filled instead with cyclists, walkers, skaters, rollerbladers, and the like. It was incredible. As I was riding along, enjoying a stretch of road without cars, I saw something out of the corner of my eye. At the last second, whatever it was flew straight at me and into my mouth. It landed on my tongue. Frantically, I grabbed at it, realizing whatever it was had hooks on its legs and was stuck to my tongue! By the time I was able to get it out of my mouth, I discovered the hitchhiker was a large, shiny blue beetle, the size of a quarter. My tongue was left coated in sticky, foul-tasting gunk. I spat it out, rinsed my mouth with water, but by then my tongue had gone numb. Seriously? What are the odds? Was it aiming for my mouth? More importantly, do I really ride with my mouth open that wide all the time?

I rinsed my mouth out again and kept riding. After a few hours, the feeling in my tongue came back, and Ville and I had a good laugh about it. We had a long, slow, easy climb away from the city, summiting after only 3,810 feet (an easy climb by Colombian standards). We pulled into the parking lot of a restaurant for lunch, where we were stunned by cheers and a standing ovation from a large group of cyclists. They pulled us inside to sit with them. They threw large plates of food down in front of us and wanted to hear all about our ride. We took pictures with their bike group before they waved and left us to head back toward the city, and it was only upon our own departure that we discovered that they had paid for our meals before they left. We couldn't believe it. How kind the Colombians had been. We climbed back onto our own bikes and headed south.

Over the next week, we climbed, descended, and climbed some more, over 570 miles from Medellín to Ipiales. We weathered downpours, mud that ran in rivers, and miles and miles of road construction with some very friendly construction workers. We saw air plants that covered sagging powerlines in cloudy mists and sugar cane fields in the heat of the valleys. We were bought a meal by a restaurant owner in the town of Chinchina, an area rich with coffee plantations, and stayed in trucker motels and sex motels by night. We were warned by the locals of "dangerous areas" ahead, referring to Black neighborhoods. We received the same kindness and smiles from these communities as all the others we passed through. I realized racism had no borders.

I was cranky, sweaty, and fatigued. Cycling in Colombia was exhausting, but the upside was spectacular scenery with little traffic and hardly any tourists. But we had to work for it. Five miles of low-geared ascents, followed by a white-knuckled descent. Repeat. My legs felt like lead, and my muscles burned with lactic acid buildup. The hills were getting me into cycling shape after the five weeks I spent sick in Bend.

We loved meeting people along our journey, those in the "in-between" areas rarely seen by tourists. While cycling through one such village, we passed a group of six, young, well-dressed boys walking along the road on their way to school. We yelled greetings to them, and they giggled, cheered, waved, and began running alongside us. We slowed our pace as they jogged alongside us, telling us their names, asking ours and a million other questions. They wanted to know about our bikes, where we were from, why were we there, why we were riding, and was I a girl? We asked about their lives, homes, and school. We teased them, and they laughed along. They asked where we were biking and were surprised by our answer. After we left them a mile later, waving, and calling out their names, I felt happy and fulfilled. The laughter of children has the power to lift anyone's spirits.

Hours later, we drank "Energy Juice," a concoction of fresh-squeezed orange juice, quail eggs, and mystery fuel, blended on the side of the road by two ladies. The vibrant color patterns on their dresses were a sharp contrast to the darkness of their skin, wrinkled and leathered from years spent working in fields, their bright white smiles infectious. We chatted about the area and their livelihoods selling juice to passersby. The lightness in their stories and jokes left me believing they were truly happy.

Passing through small villages and tiny towns, the produce came from the yards surrounding the restaurants. The gastronomy of the area revolved around chickens, soup with necks, feet, liver, and heart followed by a plate of rice and the remainder of what was left of the chicken. Sometimes vegetables floated in the soups, but chicken was king.

Days later, we descended. Down, down, down we went until we found ourselves in a wide-open, arid desert I called Death Valley. Ville had multiple flat tires during our descent, forcing us to pull over at a small roadside tire shop, in the middle of nowhere, out in the baking sun. We worked on one tire for a couple hours, finally digging out a small metal shard left behind by an exploded semitruck tire and now lodged deep into the tire, one of the many we had dug out along the way. That day, the mechanic's seven-year-old son came out to help, which made the time pass more pleasantly.

We climbed to Pasto past the town of Chachagui, where giant homes had swimming pools inside gated communities. In the pouring rain, we arrived at an altogether different climate and altitude, where we checked into a hotel, met a young bike-touring couple from France, Léo and Virginie. It was rare to meet other cyclists, so it was a treat to talk to someone longer than five minutes. Before leaving Pasto, fifty miles north of the Ecuadoran border, we replaced our bike chains and cassettes, having put over 5,000 miles on them, and enjoyed calorie loading.

20

2 Fast 2 Furious

Having stayed at Ipiales in southwestern Colombia, yet another dumpy border town offering nothing but a place to sleep, we arrived at Ecuador's immigration office, which was full of people even at 6:30 in the morning. Of course, the computers were down. Two days before our arrival, Colombia granted temporary transit visas to Venezuelans, who were desperate to flee the conflict and chaos going on within their country. Venezuela had been in a downward spiral for years, with growing political discontent, further fueled by sky-rocketing hyperinflation, power outages, and shortages of food and medicine. Thousands died and millions fled the country. Over the five hours it took to get stamped out of Colombia, hundreds of people gathered in lines that turned into hordes and then into disorganized chaos as everyone impatiently awaited their turn.

Immigration officials locked gates to keep agitated people outside the building, while one lone agent worked ever so slowly (seven different booths sat empty, inefficiency at its finest). While we waited in line, we talked with those around us. I felt saddened by their stories.

Venezuelans were leaving behind everything they owned, taking only what they could carry in a trash bag, desperate to find work and a better life anywhere else. I couldn't imagine being in their shoes. To leave everything you have worked so hard for because your currency had so devalued it became a struggle to afford food. My heart ached for them.

After finally getting through the line, stamping out of Columbia, riding about a hundred yards, and stamping into Ecuador, we found a roadside food stall. The roads in Ecuador appeared to have recently been paved. There was a bike lane, and the grades were bicycle friendly. It was a great start. We peddled rolling hills of green checkerboard pastures littered with black and white cows. It was beautiful and reminiscent of the landscape in France, according to our new friends, Léo and Virginie, who had joined us.

With the elevation around 9,000 feet, we were biking in pants, layered clothing, and rain jackets. We bought warmer down jackets before leaving Bend and were happy we did. The temperatures dipped severely at night. The hills were the perfect foreground for the glacial-capped mountains. It was stunning. We pulled over constantly to take pictures or video.

The plan was to take a little R&R once we reached Quito, the capital of Ecuador, 150 miles from the border and perched high in the foothills of the Andes. It was also home to our friend Freddy, who lived in a spacious, boutique hotel, where he ran a trekking service, having guided multi-day expeditions all over the world for several years. Freddy was middle-aged, about my height, built like an ox, well dressed, a polyglot, and a cosmopolitan Incan. Built from the ruins of an ancient Incan city, Quito was a blend of European, Moorish, and Incan architecture. We met Freddy in Myanmar a few years before on a backpacking trip through Southeast Asia and stayed in touch, planning to visit him on our ride to Argentina.

All that stood between us and Quito, Freddy and R&R, was 3,000 feet of climbing up sixty-seven miles of mountain road. After a long descent into Ibarra, we arrived at a hotel. From the front gate, it looked quite fancy; stone walls, a gated parking area, a front desk, and hotel rooms accessed from inside the building. A true hotel. A teenage boy worked the front desk, which wasn't abnormal in Latin America. We checked into our room, lugged all the bags and bikes inside, then Ville jumped in the shower, and I walked out into the lobby to call my parents.

I sat down on a velvety couch, made myself comfortable, and began catching my parents up on the latest news. As I sat there, I heard moaning, soft at first until it began to escalate with the sounds of slapping. I looked around and realized that a few of the hotel room windows opened into the lobby where I was sitting. I would have given anything to move, to take my call outside, or in the privacy of my own room; however, the Wi-Fi would not work in our room or anywhere outside the lobby. I strained to hear my parents over the volume of the love making coming from the occupants with the open window. I spoke louder, trying to drown out the noise that seemed to get louder and more grotesque. I hoped my parents couldn't hear them on the other end of the line.

After an hour of torture, the noises finally came to an end (pun intended), and although impressed by their stamina, I was ecstatic for some peace and quiet to finish my phone call. When the couple exited the room, I was surprised by who I saw. The man was the age of my grandpa, portly and well-dressed. He looked like an introverted accountant. And the shy, middle-aged woman on his arm could easily have passed as the town librarian.

Never judge a hotel by its entrance, I guess.

We started climbing before dawn. We climbed and climbed for sixty-seven miles. As we rounded switchback after switchback, we slowly ascended high over a river running through the canyon floor. As the temperatures rose, we began passing houses with patches of shade from the trees in the yards. We passed banana trees, the sweet fruits hanging in bunches, beckoning to be eaten. We followed streams that trickled along the roadside, watering plants and livestock along the way. Locals waved from their yards and doorways as we passed.

"¡Buenos dias!" We yelled.

"¡Buen vieje, amigos!" They yelled back.

Freddy met us on the outskirts of town after our seven hours of climbing and took us to dinner before heading back to his house. After we settled in, he informed us he had agreed to a side gig; he was to drive five hours east into the Amazon rain forest, pick up a couple students, and drive them back to Quito for their flights home. He asked us if we wanted to ride along and, of course, we agreed. We left the next morning.

It was a wild five-hour drive; we climbed up and over a 12,000-foot pass, through cloud forests where rain had washed away large sections of road and debris had scattered over the rest. The automobile moved significantly faster than our bicycles. I was scared shitless. Freddy, presumably, was also a racecar driver, so we managed to make it alive to Puerto Misahualli.

Heat and humidity swallowed us whole when we stepped out of the car. Within minutes, my shirt was stuck to my sweaty skin. I felt gross. We wandered around the center of town, passed by an open-air restaurant, and decided to eat lunch before picking up the students. We noticed a woman laying small, white, wiggling things on a barbecue grill next to us.

"¿Perdón señora, que son estos?" Ville leaned closer to the woman, pointing at the white things.

"Chontacuro," she said, smiling.

"Oh! Those are larvae," chimed in Freddy. "You can eat them. They are great protein."

The woman wiped her hands on a towel, picked up the bucket, and let us look inside. Floating in water were fat white larvae with black heads and tiny pinchers. They looked less than appetizing. I shook my head.

"You can eat them alive," Freddy said. We both looked at him incredulously.

"No, I'm serious," he said smiling. "People eat them alive. They cook them for tourists." Freddy asked the woman if we could try one alive.

"Si," she nodded. "Bite the head off first, because of the pinchers." She pointed down in the bucket at the squirming larvae. "You can eat one if you want." She held the bucket out.

"Okay, I'll try one," Ville said, reaching into the bucket and pulling out a pulsing blob. I shuddered.

At a nearby table sat a group of teenage girls who had taken notice that Ville was about to chow down on this bundle of protein. Suddenly, they surrounded our table, cell phones out, videos rolling.

Ville took a deep breath, stuck the larva in his mouth, bit down on the head, tossed the head on the table in front of himself, and chewed quickly, trying to kill the beast before swallowing it.

The girls erupted in squeals, groans, cheers, and retching noises. I shook my head again.

Freddy laughed. "It's full of protein . . . it's full of protein," he kept repeating.

"Loco," the woman said, referring to Ville. I couldn't agree with her more.

R&R with Freddy lasted three days before we started hiking. We hiked in El Boliche National Park, Pasochoa Mountain at 13,780 feet, and Ruminahui Mountain at 15,488 feet. Freddy was the Godfather of Ecuador. He knew everyone, and they knew him. Because of his connections, we were able to hike through private lands to easily get to the trailhead up Pasochoa Mountain. At the mouth of the crater, the clouds parted long enough for us to see into its throat while a pair of Andean condors circled. Condors are the largest flying, as well as one of the longest living, birds in the world, with a wingspan of almost eleven feet and lifespans up to seventy years.

Later, from our tent, we watched the glaciers on Mount Cotopaxi turn bright pink before fading to black. Unfortunately for us, Mount Cotopaxi, Ecuador's highest peak at 19,347 feet, had begun to stir and emit toxic gases, leaving us unable to climb it during our stay. Instead, we summited Ruminahui the following day, our legs leaden. On a bicycle we sat upright using leg muscles to propel us forward and we never set foot on the ground other than to stop. The bottoms of our feet were like those of newborn babies. Hiking with backpacks, we hunched over under the weight and our poor newborn baby feet hurt like hell.

I was pleasantly surprised that we didn't get sick from hiking in high elevation. I had half expected to be vomiting halfway up. It must have been all the mountain passes we climbed that had helped us climatize. When we had climbed 14,500-foot Mount Whitney while hiking the Pacific Crest Trail I became so dizzy on the way up I needed to take multiple breaks to rest and suck wind, bent over with my hands on my thighs. At the top, I had a headache that eased only as we made our way back down to camp. I had nervously expected the same.

After a week of hiking, it was time to get our butts back in the saddles. We thanked Freddy for his kindness and continued. It was a rude awakening to be riding again, but the scenery became more and more breathtaking as we headed south on the Carretera Panamericana, and we soon forgot about our aching legs. On our route toward Cuenca we passed through the towns of Ambato, Cajabamba, and Chunchi, where we were again the only gringos, drawing lots of curious gawkers and mouth gapers. The climbs we encountered were obscene, anywhere from five to twenty miles as we battled intensely cold headwinds in mist and rain. In the small town of Chunchi, we sat on a picnic bench eating our dinner of spaghetti from our pot and watched the sun slowly set behind the most gigantic, green mountains I had ever seen, while casting bold pink, purple, and orange colors through the sky and clouds far below. It was spectacular. It is hard sometimes to believe such beauty is possible.

Once we left Quito we were viciously attacked by dogs multiple times a day.

We began carrying rocks and sticks to fend for our lives. It was always surprising when a dog charged full speed at us, fangs exposed, snarling and snapping at our exposed legs. It was hell. In the developed world, I liked dogs, I used to have a husky named Timber. In Ecuador, I hated them. Had nightmares about them. Wished they were all locked behind fences. The mangy, homeless ones seemed too busy scrounging for food to attack us. It was the dogs protecting a house that were the real danger. Ecuadorians did not intend to create vicious attack animals. In the rural areas, they lacked police protection, so the dogs protected and served.

Yelling didn't help. Stopping the bike and trying to rationalize with them did nothing. They barked and lunged, alerting their friends to the buffet they were about to make out of us. Throwing rocks and swinging sticks was what the locals did, and it seemed to be our only defense against them. So that is what we did. At least five times a day. It was my least favorite part of being in Ecuador.

We rode into the colonial town of Cuenca, another "eternal spring city" located in the highlands of Ecuador in the southern third of the country. It was a touring cyclist's dream. The city was large enough to find novelties like Indian food, pizza, and gelato, and small enough to be without big-city chaos. We rested for a day, parked our butts on benches in the Parque Calderon, and ate gelato in liter bowls watching the townspeople. Between the two of us, we shamelessly ate a whole gallon. It was gluttonous and wonderful. We continued south to Loja, climbing arid mountains of muted browns and yellows, manzanita and scrub brush growing along the roadside.

That night, we stealth camped up a side trail that split off from the main road, under a giant, fragrant eucalyptus tree a short distance from the road, and watched the sun set and the shadows creep up the sides of the mountains as light left the sky. The following morning, we ate breakfast at a food cart inside a gas station and stopped just before dark near the town of La Chorera. We had to make a big decision: take the inland route of the Ecuadorian and Peruvian Andes or the faster, flatter coastal route through Peru. Ultimately, we chose the inland route through the Andes because we were sure to be stuck in stifling heat along the coast. Plus, we were on this adventure for the views, which were guaranteed in the mountains. Even if the inland route would add an additional month of riding, it seemed worth it. For better or for worse, we headed south out of Loja on the E682, which, according to the map, ran 120 miles to the border of Peru.

How bad could it be?

The highway turned into more of a "country road," and the mountains grew substantially larger as we made our way south. We struggled to find flat spots to pitch our tent because the hillsides were so steep. Our struggles only worsened on the E682 road. In this elevation, the air temperature plummeted once the sun disappeared. It was the rainy season. The cold wind howled up the canyon.

On the first day, as the sun set behind the mountainous walls, we began to search for a level spot for our tent, becoming ever more desperate as we climbed. We passed by a family waving from their yard, Ville rode over to introduce himself and asked if they minded if we camped in their yard. The grandparents, who owned the land, welcomed us immediately and told us to pitch our tent on their porch under the roof of their single-roomed stuccoed house in case it rained. Their nephew and his wife chatted with us while we played with their two young kids in front of the house. A priest arrived, and we were invited to join the family at evening Mass at the church down the hill. We sat with about fifteen of the townsfolk in a packed little church.

Three young boys in the pew in front of us turned and stared wide-eyed at us. I asked their names, and they dove behind their mothers' skirts, peeking out shyly with big brown eyes. I doubted they saw many visitors attend Mass.

Outside, after the Mass, we were handed steaming, hot tamales and coffee, and watched a small firework show in celebration of Virgen del Cisne. Being treated as friends by such kind and generous people was touching. Even though, by the developed world's standards, the people we met in the developing world were poor, the feelings of community, love, and acceptance of each other were palpable. The importance of family and community appeared to be of utmost importance. The children were happy and kind to each other. The parents gave them the space to play without helicoptering over their every move. The older children looked after the younger ones. They embodied the saying "It takes a village." Children seemed to be loved and embraced by the entire town.

What made these families so different from mine or other American families? Less office work for one. More human connection. Their priorities were not efficiency here. They also lived with far less. Less stuff meant less money needed to pay for stuff and more time for human connection. What had efficiency bought the developed world? More time. More time for what? More time spent at work, away from family, away from spouses, creating more efficiency. It seemed completely mad. Was it possible to opt out? They sure had in southern Ecuador.

Globalization hadn't ruined those villages in the Eucudorian Andes. It was like riding through a portal to a time when connections were with people in town and possibly in the neighboring one, but that was all. News traveled by word of mouth instead of the 24-hour news cycle. Climate change was felt on their skin, felt with the changing of the seasons because they had less distractions to keep them in denial of it.

They were more like us, and we were more like them.

We had lived in a tent, four bags, a bicycle, and $800 a month. We were the epitome of inefficiency at home and yet efficient here in the developing world. That was why the response we received about our adventure varied greatly from people in the U.S. who couldn't understand how or why someone would choose to do what we were doing to people south of the Mexican border who told us how fortunate we were to experience so much beauty on such a journey.

Ville and I lived in a world focused on human connection. We received news by word of mouth, we were emersed in nature, and we enjoyed having less stuff. Was I happy? I had never been happier in my life.

We passed a road sign that read Road Construction Update but was faded and appeared to be long forgotten. Just beyond the sign, we climbed into the National Park Yacuri, full of birds, waterfalls, butterflies, and expansive views. After the summit, we dropped steeply down a canyon searching for flat spots to pitch our tent. In the fading day's light, and just shy of the Peruvian Border, we pulled over at a little pink church. It was the only building we'd seen for the last few miles. In the yard, a man, two young girls, and a little boy bent over spreading coffee beans onto a large mat to dry. We asked the man, Stalin was his name, if we could camp nearby, and he unlocked the church doors for us and told us we could sleep inside. I brought out packages of cookies and gave them to the kids. They were extremely shy, hiding behind each other, but after some coaxing, they accepted and ran off giggling. I watched them play tag in the forested hillside.

I am at a party, not quite sure where, but the room is packed with people, voices in conversation all around me. I discover a glass Pyrex pan full of a piping hot risotto of some kind. I hunch over the pan, pick up a spoon, and start shoveling it into my mouth. It is creamy and delicious. Before I know it, I look down and have eaten over two-thirds of the pan. Shit! Now I am trying to hide the fact that I ate so much, anxiety creeping that someone watched me or knows that I totally pigged out.

And then I woke up.

I was in a tiny church in a three-house, one-church town called Canadá, thirty-eight miles north of the Peruvian border, lying next to Ville on our air mattresses. My tummy was growling, and I was disappointed the risotto was only a dream.

Outside, a hard rain on the roof sounded like white noise on an old TV set. Pictures of the Stations of the Cross hung on the walls. I was reminded of Catholic School, when I had to attend Mass every Friday with my class and every Sunday with my family. As a child, I hated it. What child wants to sit for hours listening to adults monologue about nothing they can understand? None I know. No wonder I didn't enjoy school and would rather play sports. It made sense that I was now getting my education in the real world instead of a classroom. Guess I hadn't changed that much since I was a kid. I still had my sense of wonder.

Early the next morning, we rode away from the church and waved goodbye to Stalin and the kids. Only twenty-two miles to the border of Peru. I was excited and ready to enter a new country. A mile later, the pavement disappeared. Then, the gravel road beneath our tires became so steep that I had to take breaks every switchback to shake and knead the cramping from my hands after braking so hard. The road turned into a boulder field and then to thick, slick mud. My excitement drained as we descended, and I realized the jagged scar on the mountain across the canyon was the road we had to climb back up. It was exposed to the boiling midday sun. I hated the boiling sun.

We crossed the creek at the bottom of the mountain and began climbing that jagged scar. The scrub trees were not enough to block the sun's intensity. Sweat poured into my eyes. I sucked water from my drinking tube, only to watch the sweat run down my arms. The climb took an hour. After twenty-two miles we reached the town of

Zumba. I had a splitting migraine, and there was no border crossing in sight. We checked into a motel to take a cold shower and rehydrate. My head was in a vice, and I felt nauseated from the pain. Lying in the darkness was all I could manage.

I woke in the morning to the sound of wind blowing the rain against the glass of the motel window, my migraine no better than the night before. The catch-22 was that I felt nauseated from the pain and couldn't fathom food but needed to eat to continue or take medication for the pain. I couldn't imagine riding my bike, but I couldn't imagine staying in that room another day either. I forced down some greasy food with a handful of pills, and we saddled up and headed out in the pouring rain.

We spent two more days climbing and descending in the rain, having to dismount and push our bikes up or slide down muddy roads littered with boulders until we finally came to the Peruvian Border. We stamped out of Ecuador and crossed over a bridge above a river to Peruvian immigration. We sat in the grass, waiting for the immigration officer to return from his lunch break. Two European couples in four-wheel drive rigs had been waiting there for two hours. They were pacing, arms flailing as they wailed about their predicament to anyone who would listen, which no one was. I assumed they hadn't spent much time in Latin America yet. They would learn it in time, as we had.

I remembered crossing through Mexico when I was still on American time, impatiently expecting things to operate on my schedule. We waited through federales checkpoints, for food to be made, for people to arrive, for things to be fixed, for permission to camp, and for immigration officers to get to us. Each time I became less on U.S. time and more on Mexican time. As we continued south, we more comfortably operated on Latin American time. Everything moved at a much slower pace. No one was in a rush. I became less impatient. After all, I had the time to wait.

We sat by the river watching the water flow, grateful to have a break from the hard bicycle seats, and listened to the Europeans bitch. Once the immigration officer arrived, we stamped into Peru and checked into a six-dollar hotel room, four miles from the border in Nambale, to clean off the mud and refill our bellies. I pulled on clean underwear, shorts, and a T-shirt that smelled like the bar of soap I'd used to clean them with in the motel sink in Cuenca. It was euphoric to be clean and out of my cycling clothing for an evening, even though I had to hand-wash my clothes and hang them around the room before lying on the bed and putting my feet up. I had ditched cycling shorts with a padded crotch once my nether regions became used to the seat. I now wore fitted shorts under baggier shorts to help with friction. At the time, I was wearing a red wool T-shirt, having thrown away a pink shirt a month ago because it was full of holes and smelled like a dead horse. In Cuenca, I had found a black permanent marker, and colored in the words "2 FAST 2 FURIOUS" across the chest of my red shirt, just for fun.

One could call me a minimalist because, other than my rain gear and sleeping gear, that was all I wore. It seemed impossible to survive on so few clothes, but I had. I'd survived over a year, almost fifteen months to be exact. I imagined telling the former Kristen, the one who hadn't yet cycled from Alaska to Peru, that she would live on so little for so long. She wouldn't have believed it. But the more I thought about it, yes, of course she would believe it. She had to. It was the only way to begin an adventure like this—to believe anything and everything is possible.

21

Joy Ride

After three days spinning our tires in mud, it felt thrilling to be on firm pavement again. The grade was also manageable without us sucking wind. We made it thirty-five miles from the Peruvian border to the town of San Ignacio with relative ease, got money out of an ATM, and continued. We passed through fields of flooded rice patties with giant mountains far in the distance. Then we were back climbing a steep canyon because everything had become steep canyons. Since the canyons had steep walls, we had to be more creative looking for a flat spot to camp. We passed a hand-painted sign Llantera (Tire Shop) and a small wooden lean-to set back from the road with a big empty lot in front. In the yard was a wrinkled man tinkering with something.

"¡Buenos tardes, señor!" Ville called out, as he rode through the lot and stopped directly in front of the man. "Perdon, is there a safe place we can camp nearby?"

"You can camp here," the man replied with a big smile, while setting his tools on the ground. He had big ears and a big nose, skin the color of coffee, and his clothes were covered in oil and stains. He whistled through his missing teeth when he spoke.

"Do you mind if we camp in that lean-to in case it rains?" Ville pointed toward the shed on the other side of the empty lot.

"Of course! Of course!" he replied excitedly and stood up. We walked our bikes to the shed, making small talk along the way. The shed was just over head high, with three walls, open in the front, a dirt floor, and a tin roof. It was constructed with a mishmash of left-over wood, no shingles. It would be something to store a lawnmower or garbage bins back home. Inside had a couple of posters of naked ladies tacked up on the wall, from the eighties and early nineties, judging by the teased hair styles and amount of pubic hair. The place was perfect.

"¡Muchas gracias, amigo!" We thanked him profusely before he made his way back across the lot.

We set up the tent inside the shed while a handful of turkeys, ducks, and chickens clucked, squawked, and skittered around us. These were Peruvian breeds; they didn't look like the turkeys or ducks from home.

We had pulled our food bags and cookstove from our panniers when the man reappeared and asked if we would like to join his family for dinner. We gladly accepted and grabbed both our food bags to contribute. We walked inside the single room house made of salvaged materials and a tarp and sat down at a small wooden table next to the man and his adult son. His wife set down two large plates in front of Ville and me: on each, a large, heaping pile of steamed rice next to a small, bony fried fish. The eyeballs were still on the fish, unblinking. I thanked her profusely. In front of her son and husband she set down plates of steaming white rice, no fish, then returned with a final plate of rice for herself and sat down, with a large smile on her face. It was obvious that she intended to feed us the fish that had been caught earlier that day and have her family eat only rice.

"No, no! Please. We aren't very hungry. Look," I pleaded, pulling out food from my food bag and spreading it out on the table. "We brought our own food. We want to share it with you." I pushed the oranges, nuts, and cookies toward them. "We are just fine with some rice. We have food."

They refused, repeatedly, telling us that they had already eaten. That they were full. I knew they were lying, I felt awful.

"Please, let us at least share the fish," I begged, although I could tell it was already falling on deaf ears. We had planned to cook a pasta dish for that night, and it would have been awkward to retrieve it along with our pot and cookstove to make our dinner in their home. I didn't know what to do. I wished we had more food with us to share, although I knew they wouldn't have taken it.

The following morning was the same. We were served duck eggs and leftover rice. They told us how grateful they were to have us there, how they rarely had guests, and how it was such an honor for them. The feelings were reciprocal. I reached into my pocket, pulled out two necklaces, each featuring a copper tag with WE LOST THE MAP hand-stamped on it by one of my closest friends from back home, and handed them to the couple. When they looked them over in the palms of their hands, held them up, and tied them around their necks, I noticed tears in the woman's eyes.

They told us they were going to church that morning. They were sharply dressed; clean, ironed white shirts, he in slacks and she in a skirt. When we waved goodbye and went to pack up our belongings, the couple walked out to the road together and thumbed a ride. I felt honored. I was struck by how giving and selfless they were. I had a long way to go before I would ever be that generous, although I vowed to strive for it.

Just before we were ready to leave, my stomach tightened, and I urgently needed to poop. Ville handed me the roll of toilet paper from one of his bags, smiled, and said, "Enjoy the view."

"Thanks," I said, and walked over to the edge of the cliff, where sat a three-walled, hole-in-the-ground toilet, and dropped my pants.

A raging river of gurgling snowmelt churned in the ravine far below where I squatted, and as I scanned upward I saw the sun was cutting a shaft of light over the monstrous Andes mountains.

What a breathtaking place to take a shit.

A few days after sleeping in the lean-to, we took a side trip up an unmarked gravel road detouring off the 5N road to a village called Cocachimba. There, we hiked up to see one of the world's largest two-tiered waterfalls, Gocta Falls. The height of the falls is around 2,530 feet, although the locals claim it to be larger. Whatever the accurate height of the falls, it was spectacular. Standing next to the large pool at its base was like being in a shower, the mist swirling around the cavern where ferns and moss grew on rocks. We watched a village soccer game that evening played with questionable Andean rules, the occasional child or stray dog becoming part of the game.

The next day, while riding along in my mindless reverie, Ville announced suddenly from behind me, "KG, we are running out of cash."

I pulled over to the shoulder and stopped.

"We need to find an ATM. And I need to check the map because I think we cannot make it to the next town without getting money somewhere." He said, pulling the phone out from his front handlebar bag and zooming in to the app with the map. "It looks like about eight miles ahead there is a Y in the road and then a town called Chachapoyas," he said, with a deep sigh. "Damn, the town is like . . . um . . . ten miles from the road. And a really steep climb."

"Why don't we get to the Y and make a decision," I suggested. He agreed and we rode on.

When we arrived at the Y in the road, we looked up at the road that switch backed up the side of a mountain toward Chachapoyas, and I decided I would rather run out of money than climb it. Ville suggested I sit with the bikes and gear, and he would hitchhike up to the town to get money. I felt like a jerk, but I just didn't have the strength to go twenty extra miles climbing mountains in the wrong direction. I agreed.

After five minutes of standing out at the Y in the road with his thumb out, a giant dump truck pulled over, and Ville climbed up and inside the cab, waving goodbye before closing the passenger door.

I was sitting in a patch of grass alongside the empty road, our bikes stacked against a street sign, eating an apple, appreciating sitting instead of pedaling. It started sprinkling, but within a couple minutes it was pouring.

About twenty feet up the road was a tiny yellow building, fully enclosed with windows with the word *policia* scrawled on the wall. I made a run for it, planning to stand under the awning for shelter. I noticed two young police officers sitting inside at a small desk. I smiled and waved at them, and they waved back. After five minutes of standing there, one of them came out to invite me to sit inside. I got nervous, not because they were threatening or made me uncomfortable, but because my Spanish wasn't very good. I could understand a lot by that point but froze when I had to speak, jumbling my words, and usually mixing Finnish in by mistake. But I didn't want to refuse and seem rude. So, I agreed, thanked them, and sat down on a wooden chair inside the office.

The chair felt harder than my bicycle seat. A mess of papers piled on the desk sat between us and a couple of pictures of a drooling baby and a toddler. If I had to guess, I would have guessed both police officers were older than me, but I knew they likely weren't. The guy to my left was younger, fitter, and had a name tag that said Castillo. The other was shorter, ate well, and was fidgeting with a ball point pen. When was the last time they had a foreigner pop into their office, I wondered, guessing it didn't happen often. To my dismay, they were obviously bored and full of questions.

We exchanged hellos and the usual banalities about where I was from and what my husband and I were doing there in Peru. After moving beyond the surprise, then denial, about how far we had come by bicycle, Castillo asked the standard, "Do you have children?"

"No," I said, smiling. "No niños."

They looked sideways at each other, then back at me.

"¿Porque?" Castillo asked, surprised.

"Because we are biking from Alaska to Argentina instead of having kids," I said in butchered Spanish. Ugh, I really wished I hadn't agreed to sit in the office. I glanced out at the rain on the window. I debated walking back out and waiting in the rain for Ville to return, but there was no way to do that now without making it awkward. Damn.

"Is something wrong with your husband?" Castillo asked, dead serious. "You know . . . can't make kids." This would be a question my sister might ask me, with liquid courage, after I confided in her we had been trying to have a child for years. But in Latin America it was the most normal question to ask a complete stranger.

"Well . . ." Castillo said, pausing and glancing over at the other cop before continuing, "there is a bar in a town up the road. They have beer. I can take you there and give you help to make a baby if you want."

Neither of them laughed.

I wanted to laugh out loud, as if someone just delivered the punchline to a hilarious joke, while simultaneously crawl into a hole. If I hadn't spent months in Latin America, I would have been offended and stormed out, but I knew he thought he was helping me. As if offering to help me patch a tire or rescue my cat out of tree. Just all in a day's work for a Peruvian police officer.

After composing myself, I looked at him with a wry smile and said, "No gracias."

"You sure?"

"I am very sure. Estoy muy seguro."

"What state are you from?" He continued, unfazed. Ecstatic that the subject had changed, we chatted about where I was from. Where they were from. How many children they had. Castillo had one child and the other cop had four. They wanted to know what I thought about the president of the United States, if I had ever been to Hollywood, and what I thought of Peruvian food.

Finally, after what felt like days but was only a couple of hours, Ville stepped out of a car. I jumped up from the hard chair, opened the door into the rain, turned, and thanked the cops for letting me sit inside.

"KG!" Ville exclaimed, walking toward me with a giant smile on his face, his handlebar bag strap slung over his shoulder.

"God, am I happy to see you!" I said, hugging him tightly.

"Wow! Guess I should leave you alone more often," he joked, hugging me back tightly.

"Funny," I responded. "Boy, do I have a story to tell you later."

"Oh yeah?"

"Yeah. Hey," I said suddenly, pulling away from our embrace. "How was your trip? Did everything go okay?"

"Well, I chewed coca for the first time."

"Oh yeah?"

"Yeah, I was getting sick from the altitude, climbing up that hill so fast, and the driver offered it to me, saying it would help."

"Did it help?" I asked, as we walked back to our bikes.

"I think so. I don't know. I didn't throw up, so I guess it helped." And then, suddenly: "I got attacked by a dog."

"What?! Really?! Are you okay?" I asked, as I climbed back on Blue Bullet and he climbed onto Rufio.

"Yeah, some guy picked up a rock and threw it at it, and the dog ran away. But it was charging right at me!"

"Geez," I said as I pulled back out onto the road, Ville falling in behind me. I waved at the cops sitting at their desk as we passed by the office and they waved back.

"I had to walk all the way through town to the main road to hitch a ride back," he said, riding alongside me so I could hear him.

"Sorry, babe."

"That's okay. It wasn't too bad," he replied. "Hey, were you able to get out of the rain?"

"Oh, yeah. Sure did," I said, and proceeded to recount my two-hour conversation with the police officers, ending with the generous offer to impregnate me.

"Oh, wow!" Ville said, laughing. "Did you take them up on the offer?" He joked.

"You know it. I mean . . you were gone for like . . . two hours. What did you expect me to do?"

"That's my girl."

Riding bikes from Alaska to Peru was the hardest thing I had ever done, and the route through the Peruvian Andes was the most difficult part of the ride, far more difficult than I could have imagined. It made the ten days we had spent biking on the Dalton Highway seem like a joyride. It wasn't the grades of the roads we traveled on that were the killer—they were actually quite pleasant. At least the Peruvian road engineers realized there were a lot more things traveling on them other than automobiles, so pedaling in our lowest gears was mostly doable. The difficulties came from the sheer distances we rode to climb up and over each mountain pass, along with the rapid altitude changes, and extreme temperature fluctuations. They would prove to be extremely difficult and dangerous.

At elevations above 5,000 feet one should acclimatize slowly as they climb, but at elevations over 15,000 feet it is imperative to do so or one risks irreversible brain or lung damage. When Ville and I hiked the Annapurna Mountains in Nepal, a ten-day trek that crossed over Thorung La Pass at 17,769 feet, we climbed a maximum of 2,000 feet a day; then on the ascent above 10,000 feet hiked a maximum of 1,500 feet before stopping to set up camp, going on 500 more feet and then returning to camp. The reason for the slow ascent was to avoid problems such as acute mountain sickness (AMS), a condition where blood vessels leak fluid into surrounding tissue, causing the brain to swell and press against the wall of the skull; high-altitude cerebral edema (HACE), late or end stage AMS; or high-altitude pulmonary edema (HAPE), in which vessels in the lungs constrict, causing fluid to leak into the lung tissue and eventually into the air sacs. Late stages and sometimes early stages of AMS will result in permanent damage to the frontal cortex that can leave people with an impaired ability to plan, focus, and make complex decisions. When we were within a day's hike of Thorung La Pass, we watched as another hiker experienced a headache that suddenly turned to blindness in one eye because the optic nerve in his eye had detached due to his too rapid ascent. He was rushed down the mountain on the back of a motorbike, hoping the damage would reverse itself. It had been a wake-up call to us that AMS was no laughing matter and needed to be taken very seriously.

When hiking the Annapurna Circuit, we had the time for a slow acclimation, where walking up to 2,000 feet and back down 500 feet was attainable in one day. On bicycles in the Peruvian Andes, we would climb through 2,000 feet of elevation gain in an hour or two. We did not have the time for slow acclimation.

Ville and I rode out of the town of Leimebamba and climbed twenty-five miles over the Calla Calla pass at 12,000 feet in a single day. I felt dizzy, delirious, and breathless as we neared the summit, but found my bearings on the rapid 38-mile descent. The single lane road was unguarded, winding, and full of switchbacks that dropped us through arid desert and scrub brush with the occasional chicken, piglet, or cow sauntering out of our way as we zoomed past. With the aim to camp somewhere before the heat at the bottom of the canyon, we stopped at a village mid-descent and asked if we might camp in a schoolyard. There, we made some friends.

A young man named Emilio showed us to a small building that had been used as a locker room, where we set up our tent inside.

Adjacent to the locker room was a fenced concrete soccer field. After disappearing for a moment, Emilio returned with a throng of kids and a soccer ball. We played together for an hour, laughing and trash-talking, the same as Ville and I had done since we were kids. Ville took a break from football to set up our cookstove and cook our dinner next to the field, attracting quite a crowd. A few indigenous Incan women, who spoke only Quechua (13 percent of Peruvians speak it as their mother tongue), gathered around Ville and stood giggling and whispering to each other while he cooked. When Ville asked Emilio, the only other Spanish speaker, why the women were laughing, he responded: "They have never seen a man cook before."

Early the next morning, in the middle of the Andean Mountains in northern Peru, we descended into a deep gorge and crossed a bridge that spanned the Maranon River at 1,000 feet, then began our ascent of another road that climbed 11,000 feet in twenty-eight miles. I sweated profusely. Drip. Drip. Drip. Almost at the summit, my head pounding from dehydration in high-altitude sun, UV rays growing stronger the higher we climbed, I threw in the towel and asked Ville if we could camp. He found a flat spot with unobstructed views of the Andes in a cow pasture above the road and hidden from sight. We carried our bags and bikes through an opening in a fence, pitched our tent atop a layer of hay, then watched the sun set. It was extraordinarily beautiful.

When I awoke the next morning I sat up in our tent and watched the sun cast rays of light that peeked and danced through the clouds far down into the valleys and canyons below. On the same hillside in the distance, we watched a farmer make his way slowly toward us with a small herd of black and white–speckled cows, singing and whistling as he went. We packed up and made our way back down to the road, completing the climb over the summit as the road narrowed and the shoulder dropped away, the winds gaining strength as the vegetation fell away in the high altitude. On the other side of the pass, we dropped into the small town of Celedín, ninety miles from Leimebamba, where we checked into a hotel and splurged for once on having our clothes washed in a machine by a woman in town, instead of hand-washing them in the sink as we had become accustomed to doing. We had another glorious sixty-five-mile descent before another full day of climbing to Huamachuco, 490 miles south of the border. Ten miles of potholed, patchy pavement south of there, we were forced to take a graveled and sandy unpaved road to stay in the mountains as opposed to dropping to the coast, but our 1.5-inch tires were unequipped for it. Wider than the standard Tour de France cycling tire but not as wide or knobby as a mountain bike tire, they are ideal for riding on pavement, not loose dirt, which is where we found ourselves.

We spent two days and sixty-five miles on loose dirt roads, pushing, pulling, grinding, and swearing up and over passes. Occasionally, we experienced gravel and even boulder fields, which would have been fun on mountain bike tires and shocks, but our bikes didn't have shocks. Without shocks, the gravel and boulders chattered our teeth and rattled our eyes crossed. We took lots of breaks to keep our sanity, what was left of it, in check.

We stopped at a bar to eat lunch and then pushed on toward the town of Angasmarca after the waitress told us it was a short, easy climb. Not quite. It took us three more hours to climb over the pass and drop into Angasmarca, long after the sun had set and the moon was on the rise. Calculating distance became irrelevant on the route through the Peruvian Andes; it no longer mattered to us or the Peruvians we met. Distances were told to us in driving hours, which did not convert to cycling time.

We paid ten dollars for a basic room in a hospedaje, and I was thrilled to discover the shower had hot water. My fingers were frozen from the descent in the dark, and my body sore from the road chatter. I turned the temperature up as hot as possible and stood under the shower head until my skin turned bright red. We had thirty-eight miles to the next town, Pallasca, and after a hot shower and a night in a soft bed I was ready for it.

I woke in a damp cavernous room. As my eyes adjusted to the darkness, I tried to recall where we were, much like a habitual drinker will after a hard night on the bottle. The pieces clicked together. We had found this hospedaje in the central square, agreed on a very basic room with two child-sized beds across the room from each other because we were too exhausted to continue hunting for something better in the dark. I glanced over at Ville, still asleep in the bed across the room from me. I rolled onto my back, pulling the blankets closer to my chin, the fragrance of livestock hitting my nostrils. The ceiling had to be about twenty feet high, the tile floors made it so much colder in the room. I had drunk so much water the previous night, trying to stay hydrated from the strenuous climb, that my bladder was screaming at me. I sat up, found my flip-flops, slipped them on over my socks, and walked down the hall to a communal bathroom. When I returned, Ville was awake and changing into his riding clothes. He kissed me and gave me a quick squeeze before making his way down the hall to the toilet. Getting dressed was one of my least favorite parts of the day. At least I knew what I was wearing.

It had taken us thirteen days, 326 miles to get this far. Since crossing into Peru, we took only a half a day off our bicycles. I was completely worn out.

We found a small food cart in the central square, where we bought eight egg-and-avocado sandwiches; *hockey pucks* was the name we had given to these Peruvian breakfast sandwiches. Today was a downhill day. We were always pumped when it was a downhill day because we got to enjoy the fruits of our labors. We had a few muddy rivers to cross at the beginning of switchbacks, mud that sucked our tires and took all our focus to get through. We were on a single-lane road that hugged the cliffs, no guardrail, and we could see far down below us the river that cut through the steep canyon. The sun was shining, although it was cold, cold enough to wear my long sleeves under my jacket. There wasn't a soul around. It was us and the mountains, as barren as if we were on Mars. I was happy and smiling. My cheeks began to ache I was smiling big. I was lost in a happy trance as we flew past blind corner after blind corner.

I noticed an abandoned shack as I flew past, then I heard dogs. A pack of four sprung off the porch and started charging me. I screamed as loud as I could, "Dogs!"

But it was too late.

They just missed me as I flew past, but as Ville rounded the corner they lunged at him. He said he didn't see them coming.

He slammed into one of the dogs with his front tire. It yelped. He lost control of his bike and went down hard. I screamed.

"Get off him!!! Get out of here!" I had turned into a wild girl. I was off my bike, running toward Ville, the other dogs were on top of him, snarling, barking. I picked up rocks, threw them, one after another after another. Missing, hitting, missing, missing, hitting. Ville was blinking, coming to. Trying to sit up. There was blood. Lots of blood dripping off his arms, his legs. The dogs retreated toward the shack, but they kept barking and snarling. The front door flung open. A young girl stepped onto the porch, a look of complete shock on her face.

"I am going to kill your dogs!" I yelled. She shut the door. The dogs ran away. I am not proud of what I said to her, but I wasn't thinking. And more than likely, they were not her dogs, only strays.

After chasing the dogs away, I turned and ran to Ville, helping him to stand up.

"Oh, no! Ville, I am so sorry, are you okay?!" I looked over his wounds. He looked dazed.

"I'm okay, I'm okay, KG," he said, trying to calm me down, rotating his elbow so he could scan the damage. "Fucking dogs!" he yelled. Blood was dripping down his arms and legs, bloodying his green shorts and wool socks. The front of his shorts had been shredded in the fall. His long-sleeve shirt was ripped in three places.

"I don't know if I'm hurt . . ." he muttered. He moved his limbs checking for breaks as the blood continued to drip. His left knee began to swell.

"I don't think anything is broken," he said finally. There was a lot of blood and road rash with deep cuts but nothing to stop our adventure.

I picked up his bike and moved it next to a giant creosote bush on the side of the road in case a car came around the corner. Then I realized I had thrown my own bike down in the middle of the road and moved it to the side as well.

A woman from up the hill asked if she could help us. She had a white buttoned shirt and a multicolored skirt worn by many of the indigenous Peruvian women, her dark hair pinned in a neat bun on top of her head. She asked us if we could walk up to her house so she could help us. We thanked her but knew there was nothing more we could do than wash the wounds and apply antiseptic. Next to the road was an above-ground well covered with a piece of wood. We asked the woman if she thought it was okay to use it. She said, "Si! Si!" So, we pulled water up in the bucket and began pouring water on Ville's wounds, trying to wash the blood off.

The problem is, water on an open wound, especially road rash, feels like burning fire. Pouring water over the wounds magnified Ville's pain. But it had to be done.

"Ugh! God that hurts! Geez!" he gritted his teeth. I had to rub my hands over his skin to rinse off the blood and clean out the gravel. The water ran pink in the grass. I looked closer at his arms. There were so many tiny pieces of gravel in there, there was no way to pull it all out. I inspected his side and rinsed that, too. It looked like someone had taken a cheese grater to his body.

"Ville, I'm so sorry!" I just kept repeating, as I washed his open wounds. The woman sat and watched us, clicking her tongue and turning her head from side to side as if to say, "What an awful thing that has happened."

"Ville, I really think you need to let me put antiseptic on those. All I have is hand sanitizer. It's going to hurt like hell. I am sorry in advance," I said, running back down the hill to my bike and digging out the medical kit. After packing and repacking so many times, I knew exactly where everything was. Could find it blindfolded. I ran back with the kit, pulled hand sanitizer and antiseptic ointment out of the bag, and started to apply it in globs to bloodied and grated skin.

"KG!! That burns like hell!" He groaned, turning away and closing his eyes, teeth clenched.

"I know! I know! I'm sorry! But there is so much gravel in there, I really think you need this on there," I argued with him. "I said I'm sorry. I warned you."

We must have looked like quite the spectacle. I wondered what the poor woman was thinking, we were speaking in English, and I doubted she understood us.

"KG . . ." Ville tried to raise his left hand over his head, "Damn. I broke a couple of ribs."

"Really?!" I stared at him in dismay.

"Yeah, really."

"How do you know?"

"I've broken ribs before . . . damn . . . yep . . . shit . . . it hurts like hell," he said, as he slowly bent over, stood up, ran his hands over his ribs, and then tried to raise his arm over his head again. "Well . . . that sucks."

"Yeah, it sucks. Are you going to be okay?"

"Oh, yeah."

"Can you keep riding?"

"Girl, please," he joked. At least he still had his sense of humor. "Of course, I can still bike."

"Good, then get the hell back on your bike and quit your bitch-ing," I responded, cracking a smile for the first time since the fall.

After an hour of cleaning wounds, we packed up and inspected his bike. The left handlebar was bent, but after some finagling we were able to bend it back. The front rotor was bent, hit by his side pannier in the fall. He loosened the brake, moving the pad far from the rotor so it would not catch every rotation. We repeatedly thanked the neighbor woman for coming to help. She said if we needed any-thing else we were more than welcome to come to her house or stay with her. We thanked her again, climbed on Blue Bullet and Rufio and decided to keep on keepin' on.

We had over a fifty-mile descent along a canyon that day.

Ville drew lots of attention. Multiple Peruvians asked if he was okay or if we needed help. He thanked them, said no, he was fine, and we continued. Blood continued to drip down his legs, arms, and side until it turned goopy, then hard.

Five hours later and eighty-five miles from Pallasca, we reached the bottom of the canyon, where a river joined an even larger one that flowed to the sea, at which point we turned upriver and began to climb a new canyon road. We had reached our limit and decided to call it a day as soon as we could find a good place to camp. The canyon did not allow for flat camping options, so when we rode past a small young girl in front of a stuccoed hut surrounded by mango trees I suggested to Ville we ask if we might camp in her yard. Ville rode back to the small girl, who listened and ran inside to ask her parents. A moment later she reappeared with three more kids in tow and said we could camp in their yard. As we followed her through the yard, she introduced herself as Ana, Sammy was her little sister, and the other two boys were neighbors, Paul and Maricielo.

These kids were so excited to see us. Their smiles and excitement were contagious; bouncing up and down, speaking rapidly to us, and insisting on holding our hands as we followed them into the orchard, a canopy of mango trees above us. We picked a spot a short distance from the house, for privacy, although the kids didn't seem too concerned about privacy.

"Oh, no!" Sammy wailed, when she noticed the dried blood on Ville's arms and legs. "Oh, no! Oh, no!" The rest of the kids came closer, inspecting his wounds.

We leaned our bikes against a mango tree, and I brought out the medical kit, planning to do a more thorough job of wrapping the wounds for Ville to sleep, mainly to protect the wounds from bacteria, but also so he didn't bloody all our bedding. There was no way to wash it. The kids begged to help. I gave them the ointments and bandages and watched as they wrapped everything up tightly. It was adorable.

Ville pulled the tent from his back rack and unrolled it. The kids insisted on helping us set it up. We talked them through step by step, and they took turns blowing up our mattresses and then tucked them inside the tent. They zipped together our sleeping quilt and begged to sleep with us. We had a two-person tent, and there was no way to fit four kids. Begrudgingly, they went inside as the sun set. We climbed into our tent and fell asleep. Without the fear of rain, we left off the rain fly.

We had a fitful night of sleep; at four in the morning, roosters began crowing, and shortly after that I opened my eyes to see four grinning faces looking at us through the netting. It was the only time in my life I could recall laughing so hard that early in the morning. We cooked and ate oatmeal together. I pulled out my toiletry bag and began brushing my teeth, at which point Sammy pulled out my nail clippers and my brush and asked for a detailed explanation of what they were. For each child, I carefully clipped fingernails, combed hair, and rubbed on peppermint oil, that I carried to help my migraines. I shared cookies and stickers, things carried to give to children as we passed by.

They cradled the stickers in their palms so delicately, as if I had given them the biggest treasures.

I pulled out four red-tailed hawk feathers from a stack of feathers I had been collecting since Alaska. When I told them, they couldn't believe it. It might as well have been feathers from the Moon. I wondered if they knew where Alaska was.

They were so happy they hugged me.

Then they scurried around the yard, collecting poopy duck and chicken feathers, which they gifted me, and I excitedly taped them to my seat post, fine additions to my collection.

Ana ran into her home and emerged with a little journal and asked me to write English words down for her to practice, which I promptly did, adding the Spanish translations for her. When it was time to leave, Ana ran inside and emerged with her parents, mom carrying a drooly baby. Ville and I walked to the road and waved goodbye as we continued up the canyon, the kids chasing us for as long as they could run before getting tired.

My heart swelled with gratitude for having met them. Those poopy feathers, my mementoes of Ana, Sammy, Paul, and Maricielo.

22

Filet of Guinea Pig

The next terrible fall was my own.

We had ridden 110 miles from Ana's yard to the town of Huarez, climbing over 10,000 feet through Canon Del Pato, a road that passed through thirty-five tunnels cut into the Cordillera Negra Mountain Range, where it meets the Cordillera Blanca Mountain Range. The Rio Santa flowed between the ranges. Waterfalls cascaded from above and flowed over the road before joining the Rio Santa on its way to the Pacific Ocean. Temperatures reached over one-hundred degrees and dropped as we climbed.

Huaraz is a jump-off point for trekkers looking to hike in the adjacent Huascaran National Park. When we reached it, we took three days off to recuperate. We needed it after Ville's fall, the heat, and the climbing. We showered, made love, ate, and slept.

It was a sunny cold day when we rode out of Huaraz. We turned east onto an unmarked dirt road that zigzagged into the Parque Nacional Huascaran, promising spectacular scenery, and planned to arrive in the village of Huallanca fifty miles later. As we climbed, it began to rain. It wasn't long before we were soaked and shivering.

We passed fields with grass-roofed rock huts and sheep inside rock fences. There were no trees in the high-altitude plains. Sheep herders waved, wearing little more than thick wool jackets, pants stuffed into leather boots, and colorful knit hats.

After the rain stopped, we camped in a beautiful spot next to a creek in a meadow with views of peaks cloaked in puffy clouds. At 14,000 feet, the cold seeped into our bones, so we stripped out of our wet clothes and put on all our wool layers to warm up. After some struggles with our gasoline stove because of the altitude, we feasted on spaghetti, which helped warm us. In the morning, after a giant breakfast of bacon, eggs, French toast, hot coffee and . . . Ha! Man, just daydreaming a little there. I meant, after our breakfast of oatmeal and mashed bananas, we packed up and continued the slow climb on the gravel road that wound through the mountains.

It began to rain, and we became soaked through again, but we climbed higher. Then it began snowing. I lost feeling in my fingers. We passed petroglyphs tucked under a rock cornice. We continued to climb through whirling snow, as if we were riding through a snow globe.

The snow turned into a hailstorm, disorienting us. We had no choice but to continue. Still we climbed. I couldn't feel my gloved hands and my cheeks hurt. As we reached a sign that stood at the peak we began to descend. Without shocks, my bike chattered, the elevation made me feel lightheaded and drunk.

Suddenly, my feet slid off the slippery pedals. The metal struts had been worn down after riding thousands of miles. I came down hard on my tailbone on the tip of my bike seat, and a sharp pain shot up my spine. My feet hit the gravel, and the speed of the bike launched me into a front roll. I landed flat on my back, heavy Blue Bullet coming down on top of me and bouncing off.

I lay there. The snow landed on my face. I was paralyzed. In shock.

Suddenly, I was crying, gasping for air. Far away, I could hear Ville yelling. In slow motion. Blurry. Then he was leaning over me.

"KG! . . . KG! . . . Are you okay?" It was like he was under water. *Why couldn't I hear him? Was I dead? If I wasn't dead, I should be.*

"Please. Please, Ville, don't touch me. Don't move me," I whispered, the words sounding as if someone else had spoken them.

I needed to make sure I wasn't broken before he tried to move me. Training as a lifeguard had taught me that. I gasped for air. I took a deep breath. Then another. I was in pain, but I hoped I could move without anything being broken. I started moving my arms. They worked. Snowflakes continued to fall on my face. I moved my legs. They worked. My tailbone throbbed like someone had hit it with a baseball bat. Well, that wasn't good. Not the first time I had broken that, either. What the hell was wrong with my husband and me? Were we gluttons for pain, punishment, and injury or what? I had broken my tailbone years prior, in my early twenties, when I had sat down while trying to land a jump in the snowboard park at Mount Bachelor. It had burned like hell, and I couldn't sit without serious pain for a month. It was definitely broken again. Shit! Now how the hell am I supposed to sit on a bike seat?

I turned my head from side to side, then sat up with Ville's help. Tears ran down my cheeks. I was damaged but not broken. My back was seriously bruised, my tailbone throbbed, I ached all over as the swelling began, but I was okay. Whatever okay meant.

I stood up.

"Oh, God, KG. I thought you were dead," Ville said quietly and moved in to hug me softly.

"I'm okay . . . I think. Geez, I really hurt, though." I wiped away tears and melted snow from my face. "We need to keep going. I can feel the swelling. I just want to get to town and get off the bike," I said, slowly walking back to Blue Bullet, lying there on its side, panniers flapping.

"KG, are you sure? I mean . . . I . . . think we can try and find a ride . . ." he trailed off because he knew as well as I did that that was not an option. Only two minibuses passed us the entire day. There was no one coming along.

I had no choice but to keep going.

No choice but to climb back on the hard leather saddle of Blue Bullet with a throbbing tailbone. I tried not to think about it. I still couldn't feel my fingers. Dammit, I wanted off this mountain!

"I'm sure," I said adamantly. "Let's go."

I climbed onto the seat and started down the mountain. Ville apprehensively followed behind me. Somewhere along the way down, the gravel turned to pavement. Switchbacks unfolded for miles upon miles in front of us. The snow turned to rain that eventually stopped and the sun came out.

I still couldn't feel my fingers. They had gotten too cold. I was worried I wouldn't be able to compress the brake levers to slow myself down the mountainside, but I didn't say it out loud. *Just keep going, just keep going, just keep going,* I repeated in my head, trying to drown out any other thoughts. My tailbone throbbed. I ignored it. I pulled over to shake my hands trying to get the blood circulating in them. From behind, Ville called out for me to look at him, and when I did I saw that he was taking a video of me. I straddled Blue Bullet and tried to smile and wave at the camera. In this video, I can be seen waving with a weary smile on my face, the clouds moving swiftly over the mountain and switchbacks of roads in front of us. It looked spectacular! Only I knew that the smile masked how miserable I felt and the serious pain I was in.

Hiding pain and pushing forward.

We must have been followed by an army of guardian angels working overtime to keep these two circus freaks safe, because it was a miracle that neither one of us had died by then. Thanks, guardian angels, you all deserve medals. And maybe a raise.

Thirty miles after my fall, we found ourselves on the main drag in the small town of Huallanca. I couldn't believe I had made it. My legs shook, and I thought I might collapse if I got off my bike. I was so drained I let Ville make all the decisions: pick the hotel, do all the talking and negotiating. He paid for a hotel room with the promise that there was hot water for a shower. I couldn't wait for a hot shower, needed a hot shower to ease my throbbing back and warm my freezing body. I was shivering before I had even undressed. I pulled off my clothes, stepped into the shower, and the water was ice cold.

I cried.

I let the tears run down the drain with the ice water scrubbing my body as quickly as possible. I would need to get in bed under the wool blankets to get warm. I tried to tell myself there were far worse things in life: hunger, famine, human trafficking, and genocide. I was devastated and in pain, so it was hard to listen to myself.

I toweled off, pulled on my wool sleeping clothes—pants, a long-sleeve shirt, and socks—and crawled under the covers while Ville left to shower. At least I was alive. If I had broken my back, Ville would have had to leave me alone up there in the freezing snowstorm to go search for help, which was over thirty miles away. Things could have been so much worse. I shivered at the thought of it. I had to push these thoughts out of my mind, focus on the present.

Ville returned and climbed under the covers with me, snuggled up in the big spoon position, and stroked my hair. I rubbed his arm feeling his scabbing skin. We were both very grateful to be alive.

"I can't take any more of these shitty, gravel, potholed, washboard roads," I said. Ville and I were riding out of Huallanca. My tailbone still throbbed. We agreed to take the less direct route on the 3N Highway to avoid another gravel road. My tailbone ached so bad I couldn't imagine bouncing on a gravel road. We descended into a narrow canyon along a river and became enveloped by canyon walls. The scenery was spectacular.

And then it began to rain.

The rain was unrelenting enough that by afternoon, when we passed through the town of La Union fifteen miles later, we were covered in mud. The dirt road that zigzagged through town had become a tire-sucking mud that splattered onto us as trucks, cars, and buses rolled past.

We climbed up and out of a gorge as the rain continued to pour, the mud covering the bikes, panniers, and our legs. Ville's brake pad began to squeal, so we stopped to rinse it with drinking water, only to discover that it had disintegrated. Because the bicycle shop in Orange County had put the wrong rotors on, the spare brake pads we had no longer fit, so it took an hour using our Leatherman to fix the problem, all the while being splattered with more mud by passing cars. Darkness fell before we could reach the town of Chavinillo, so we camped early on the side of the road in some bushes.

As we climbed the six miles into town we passed a young boy in a white and blue school uniform walking along the road to school.

"Would you like a ride?" I called out as I slowed next to him. He nodded. I pointed at the rack on the back of my bike and told him to climb on.

He did and slid an arm around my waist to right himself. I steadied myself and started pedaling. It took a moment to get accustomed to the added weight.

His name was Eduard. He was nine years old, shy, and weighed the same as a large sack of potatoes. My legs began to burn. Up the road, we passed an indigenous Peruvian woman dressed in a white shirt, colorful skirt, and a hat, with a multicolored blanket wrapped around her back. Eduard said, "Es mi madre."

"¿Esa es tu madre?" I asked in surprise.

"Si," he nodded.

I slowed and asked if he wanted me to stop. When I did, he slid off and began walking with her. I smiled and waved, and we continued, unable to carry his mother on the back of either bike.

Eduard came running after us, "¡Espera!"

We stopped, and he asked us if we wanted some picante de cuy (guinea pig in spicy sauce) with white rice.

I looked back at Ville, "Why not, right?"

"Si, gracias," I said. His mother caught up to us. She smiled, untied the pink blanket from her back, and laid it on the ground. Inside were multiple metal containers that held food. She opened a container and held out what looked like white rice covered in sauce and half of a small greasy animal body with a clawed arm sticking out. It would be a stretch to say it looked delicious, even for a starving cyclist, but we were grateful. It was food. We were not picky eaters, and we were, after all, hungry. We both smiled and accepted the containers of food.

"Muchas gracias, señora," we chimed.

"¿Te?" his mother asked, stooping to pull out a large thermos and holding it toward us.

"Si, gracias," we both said, nodding and rooting inside our back panniers for our titanium cups.

She poured us each a steaming cup of tea and fastened her blanket with one fell swoop back onto her back, smiling broadly at us both.

Ville reached into his wallet and handed her a handful of peso bills, worth about two dollars. She shook her hand no and gestured that it was a gift, at which point Ville insisted, and she took it, folding the money into her shirt. We ate the greasy little pigs, agreeing that they tasted like pig, fed the bones to a couple stray dogs, slurped down the tea, and realized Eduard was waiting to take the containers back to his mother, who had continued up the road. He told us she walked every day to his school, where she sold the meals she had cooked. Eduard climbed back on the back of my bike, and we continued up the road to his school.

I had not realized when I had offered him the ride that his school was over two miles up the road. This meant he walked over two miles each way. I thought of all the car rides, carpools, and buses I had taken to school, but not once had I ever walked.

I pulled a small package of cookies out of my frame bag and handed them to Eduard. He thanked me graciously, smiled broadly, and ran toward the front door of his school, as kids giggled and teased him about the ride he had taken to school with two gringos.

The remaining climb to the village of Corona del Inca, sixty miles from Huallanca, wasn't too bad, but the thirty-five-mile descent on the backside, quite literally and figuratively, went downhill. First, the pavement disappeared, then dogs began attacking us as we passed, then the gravel got deeper, followed by washboard on the road that chattered our teeth, all while Peruvian drivers flew unnervingly close to us in little Hondas and Toyota station wagons, as if training for the next Fast & Furious film. The buffs we pulled over our mouths saved us from about seven pounds of dirt in the lungs, and our sunglasses had to be constantly wiped of dust, making it nearly impossible to see. On the decent, we passed an exorbitant number of crosses and memorial sites: pictures, sodas, candles, and memorabilia, that are left along the roadside to honor those who have perished there. I wondered why nothing changed and they continued driving like Vin Diesel on unguarded gravel road in the mountains.

By sundown, we neared the bottom of the canyon that opened into a large valley and the sprawling city of Huánuco. We found a decent hotel room with a little Peruvian Twist and checked in for a night. Ville had coined the term Peruvian Twist for the unexpected little nuggets of fun we found in motels: a toilet that floods, a sink that doesn't work, a shower that produces only a trickle of water, or, my personal favorite, a zap of electricity while in the shower from the electric water heater wired incorrectly. Water and electricity do not mix. We were lucky we didn't die. Although, that would be one spectacular way to go. How did she die? Oh, she was electrocuted in a Peruvian shower while on her way by bicycle from Alaska to Argentina. Such a shame, such a shame.

In Huánuco the hotel's Peruvian Twist was a flooding toilet. Ville went to tell the woman who ran the place. Instead of fixing it, or calling someone to fix it, she simply handed Ville a mop.

The following day, we climbed fifty-five slow uphill miles, passing villages, communities, and the occasional lone house. Most of the houses we passed in the Peruvian Andes were made of mud, with tin, grass, or clay roofs, and most lacked windows and sometimes doors. Toilets were often a wooden or tin shed that surrounded a hole dug into the ground far from the house. Water often came from wells or was hauled by bucket from the nearest water source, and laundry was washed in buckets, rivers, or a sink outside the home. Peruvians grew and raised what they needed for survival: pigs, chickens, sheep, burrows, turkeys, grains, corn, herbs, veggies, and guinea pigs. It was a simple life that relied on manual labor for survival.

Often, we would pass women dressed as Eduard's mother had been, walking along the roadside with herds of animals, taking them from field to field for grazing, from home to town to sell, and often with young children in tow. It exhausted me even to think of living in their shoes. What would my life have been like if I had been born in a Peruvian village? Would I have been able to go to school? Would I have been allowed to play soccer? Would I be upset that my brother was out playing while I washed clothes? Would I have married young? Would I have had children and, if so, how many? Would I feel that I lacked opportunities, or would I not know those opportunities existed? Would I be happy? I wondered what the women thought of me when they saw me pass by on a bicycle. I had not seen any women on bicycles in Peru.

That evening, Ville and I reached a tiny village nestled into a gorge just as the sun was disappearing behind the mountains. We spotted a building with an illuminated Hotel sign out front, and I held our bikes as Ville knocked on the door. The woman who answered said, "No, we don't have any rooms. This is not a hotel," at which point Ville asked her about the sign. She said, "It's an old sign" and shut the door.

This inaccuracy of things is quite common in Peru; never assume that a hotel sign or restaurant menu means a room or the food listed is available. Waiters often told us they didn't have what we wanted to order, or even our second choice. We'd then tell them to bring whatever they did have, which was usually chicken parts soup—necks, hearts, livers, feet, and mystery parts—followed by the rest of the bird with white rice. I was very grateful to have food, but I was very tired of eating chicken.

We had also discovered that many Peruvians explained distance in the time it might take to drive instead of in kilometers, making it a challenge to convert the time it would take on a bicycle. Even when the distance was given in kilometers, it was often grossly inaccurate. Much later, it dawned on me that the majority of Peruvians did not own or drive cars, therefore they rarely knew distance other than in ride time. What they lacked in the knowledge of distance, they made up in kindness; they always wanted to help us or supply an answer, even if it was the wrong one.

We pulled over in front of the next "Hotel" sign, and while I watched the bikes, Ville again went to the door to inquire about a room. As I sat there astride the bike, my heart rate slowly returning to normal, I took in our surroundings. There were a few houses and closed shops along the road ahead, but no other hotel signs. The road continued to climb out of sight. It looked like we were already at the edge of town.

I was imagining myself in a hot shower and about to get off my bike when Ville suddenly marched toward me.

"Yeah, we are not staying here," he said in a huff, clipping his handlebar bag back onto his handlebar.

"Why not?" I asked, deflated. So much for my hot shower.

"They want way too much money. Let's go. We will find something else," he said, climbing onto the seat and pedaling back onto the road.

"But, Ville . . . I'm pretty sure we are almost through town."

"There have to be more places. Let's just look up the road a little farther."

"Fine," I muttered with a huge sigh, climbed aboard Blue Bullet, and followed him to the road. I passed him and moved into my place out front.

We rounded the bend, more houses and empty buildings, rounded another, more of the same.

"Ville, I don't think there are any more hotels. Maybe we need to go back. How much was it?" I ask, turning back so I can hear him.

"Nine dollars," he says, as if I should be as flabbergasted as he is at the ludicrous price.

"Nine dollars? Are you kidding?"

"KG, we have not had to pay more than six dollars," he explains.

"Yeah, I get that, but I am so spent. I really don't think there are any more hotels, babe. Look, we are already at the end of town," I said, sighing deeply. "I can't keep going. Can we please go back to that place?" I plead.

"Well, not really. I think the woman got a little upset with me . . ." he trailed off, embarrassed. "I don't think we can go back there."

"You're kidding." I stopped the bike and looked at him with a well-you-better-march-right-back-in-there-and-apologize-mister look. "What happened?"

"Well, I kind of tried to negotiate the price down and she was one of those, nose in the air types, KG, and I mean, look around, look at this town," he said. I was *not* amused. He continued, "I can tell you're not very interested in seeing things from my point of view." He tried to make me laugh: "I can see that you don't have a very open mind right now, but maybe we can talk about this later."

"What happened?" I look directly at him, fighting back a smile.

"She asked me to leave," he said bluntly. "We can't go back"

I sighed deeply, rolled my eyes, and climbed back on the bike to keep riding and find somewhere to camp. Which is quite hard to do when you are above 12,000 feet and there are no trees, shrubs, or anything but wide open high plains.

"Don't worry, KG, we will find something," he tried to sound positive.

I just really want off this hard saddle. My tailbone throbbed, and my butt was killing me.

After about ten more minutes of climbing and passing only a few buildings, we saw an old couple walking toward us on the side of the road, heading in the opposite direction.

Ville pulled over next to the couple as we passed and said, "Disculpe" (excuse me). They stopped. He asked them if there was a hotel or somewhere safe we could camp nearby. The man paused, thinking.

"Ah!" he exclaimed. "I have an idea!" He told Ville he owned a small apartment building in town. It wasn't much, but we could have a room for the night if we would follow them back down the hill. Ville accepted graciously, and we both thanked him repeatedly. Back in town, in front of a large blue building, he showed us to a room that was more like a broom closet. No bathroom or kitchen, it was big enough to fit only our bikes and our tent, which we had to set up because of the number of spiders crawling everywhere. As we walked across the rotting and broken floorboards, I glanced up at the ceiling where the paint was peeling and hanging, which also looked as if it may cave in at any moment. The room was so pungent with mold and gasoline that it was a bit hard to breathe. I was not quite sure how we would make it through the night.

As soon as we erected our tent, I stared hard at Ville over the top of it with smiling eyes, "Nine dollars, huh?"

"Well, I love you," he said, which is his response he often uses when he is in hot water with me and would like me to forgive him.

He walked over creaking floorboards around the tent and pulled me in for a big hug.

"You're lucky you're good looking, pal," I joked. "I guess I'll forgive you. But only this time."

He leaned down and kissed me.

"I love you, too."

There was a knock at the door.

We opened it and saw a sweet, middle-aged lady standing there with coffee and sandwiches. We accepted them, thanking her warmly. The woman's name was Rosalita, and she lived in the building with her sister. We walked out into the dirt patch in front of the building, sat with Rosalita and her sister, and ate our sandwiches while we talked. We learned both women were seamstresses who made blankets, potholders, and scarves to sell while their husbands both worked at an American-owned mine up the road.

A chicken that had been circling us squawked and jumped into Ville's lap, pecking at his sandwich.

Everyone laughed, and the women's five-year-old daughter came running over to shoo the chicken away. We told them of our dislike for chicken and, in particular, crowing roosters. They told us they had just eaten their rooster a few days prior. We talked until dark and then went back to our palace to sleep.

As annoyed as I had been about missing out on my hot shower and a bed free of mildew and spiders, I wouldn't have traded the evening spent with those sweet ladies to get it. Those were the moments we had cherished along our journey and, usually, they happened when least expected. Plus, it was a memory shared with Ville that I would be able to chide him about whenever he gave me a hard time. Nine dollars.

"I don't know why my head hurts," I said as I steered my bike as close to the edge of the cracked pavement as I could, allowing cars plenty of room to go around Ville and me. There wasn't a designated bicycle lane, only a faint, yellow-dotted line in the center of the road. Ville checked for cars, then moved up alongside me so he could hear over the howling winds blowing over the plains. Out in a field was a pack of white alpacas grazing with towering, glacial-wrapped mountains behind them. One lifted its head to watch us as we passed by, then resumed munching, undeterred.

"Sorry?" he yelled, straining to be heard over the wind.

"I said, I really don't know why my head is still hurting!" I yelled.

"Still?"

"Yeah, I don't get it. It's not like I'm dehydrated. It's freezing up here. I'm barely sweating." I wore my rain jacket to use as a windbreaker from the cold winds.

"Maybe it's the altitude?"

"It could be. But it's so weird. We were up at 16,000 feet last week and I felt a little drunk, but not this bad. My head is killing me!" I yelled, while leaning backward and trying to stretch out my spine. My vision began to blur. "I hope it goes away once we start going down."

We had been riding high in the altiplano, at over 14,000 feet, for two days, and my head throbbed the entire time. When we arrived at the intersection that might take us to the town of Cerro de Pasco, the world's highest city with over 50,000 inhabitants, we decided to skip the side trip because we had heard it was a dump due to rampant mining. It was an extra four miles out of our way, and my head was pounding. All I could focus on was getting down to lower elevations, hoping my head would improve.

That night we stayed in a hospedaje, and the owner let us lock our bicycles in his cellar against a couple stacks of pungent alpaca hides. We were disappointed to discover the shower did not work. This was becoming a pattern.

When Ville and I got married, he told me he was going to take me to beautiful places all over the world. What he neglected to tell me was that I was going to have to ride a bike to them, that I would be sleeping in sex motels or on an air mattress, that I would be washing my clothes in sinks, that I would need to get used to smelling like alpaca hides or a long-distance trucker who rarely bathed, and that I would likely lose all feeling from the waist down. He would say it was the language barrier. I would say he knew I would hate it but that I would also love it more than anything else. I just hoped the feeling in my crotch would come back someday.

We passed through the small town of Junin and started on the hundred-mile descent to the city of Huancayo. We stopped on a bridge in the city of La Oroya, the fifth-most-polluted city in the world and watched the river run black beneath us. Smokestacks spewed thick, black smoke choking out the blue sky. I thought of the fish, birds, plants, and animals that had died because of that plant and it made me angry. Then I thought of the workers, about their families, children, and surrounding community and it made me really sad.

We pedaled on.

Twenty miles later, Ville paid five dollars for a room above a restaurant and again the shower did not work. I wet a towel in the bathroom sink, undressed, and washed myself the best I could with cold water. I looked into the mirror and didn't recognize the woman looking back. Her skin was so dark, cheeks and nose a rosy red, hair highlighted honey brown from the sun. I pressed the cold towel to my temple, my headache having disappeared only moments before we arrived when we had finally reached lower elevations. I was grateful not to be in pain anymore.

By nightfall the following day, we reached the city of Huancayo, 1,170 miles south of the Peruvian border, halfway through the country, and were thoroughly disappointed. We had high hopes for amenities, such as restaurants and hotels, but the city lacked it all. Most of the streets were dirt, brick, and concrete buildings scattered haphazardly about, as if layout of the city was an afterthought, or not even a thought. We took a rest day in town because we needed one but were happy to continue.

Over the next two days, as we climbed, the roadside crosses and shrines were a constant reminder of danger. Occasionally, we would pass a cluster of crosses where either a bus or minivan had plummeted over the edge and down to the river hundreds of feet below. Sometimes, there were stuffed animals and toys left near crosses. The sadness I felt from seeing those was hard to shake and would sit with me for hours. And sometimes, pieces of the wreckage were still present, twisted, mangled, and left behind in the thick vegetation, so recent that the crosses and shrines had not yet been set.

In the next village, we scored a seven-dollar room with a working hot shower and a TV. After Ville showered, washed, and hung his clothes, I climbed in the shower, and he ventured out to look for food. He found a food cart nearby and after ordering lomo saltado—stir-fried beef with onions, tomatoes, and French fries—a crowd gathered around him. When they discovered he spoke Spanish, he was bombarded with questions from the curious locals who had watched us ride into town. He was a celebrity. By the time he made it back to the hotel with our dinners, the food was cold. I didn't mind—food was food—and Ville was jazzed to have connected with people.

Early the next morning, we rode out in drizzling rain after a breakfast of caldo de gallina—boiled rooster soup. It tasted like eating the rubber sole of a shoe. I rounded a tight curve where a creek poured over the road and moss grew. My balding tires slipped right out from under me, and I went down hard, straight onto my knees. The jarring pain shot up my legs and into my back. I lay tangled in my bike, stunned, the water pouring over my legs.

A small Peruvian man, who had been working on a road crew, tried to help me up. Ville arrived, and they both lifted me from the pavement. It was all I could do to keep the tears inside. I was in serious pain, but I didn't want the Peruvian man to see me cry. I swallowed tears and slowly climbed back on my saddle, thanking him for helping me, and pedaled on. Ville followed. The pain turned to anger.

I wanted to scream. I wanted off this shitty road! The only way to get off was to keep going. I let tears fall as I pedaled. My knees began to swell, and I ached deep inside.

By nightfall, we made it to a quaint town full of drunken people celebrating the anniversary of the town's founding. Even old ladies were weaving joyously all over the main street with beer bottles in hand.

Ville stopped next to a man sitting on a curb surrounded by a bunch of empty beer bottles and asked him where we might find an inexpensive hotel. He slurred so much we couldn't understand a thing he said. He pointed at a yellow house up the street. Ville went inside to inquire about a room. He came back in a huff because the woman wanted twelve dollars for the night. I hit Ville with one of those deadpan, disdainful, you're-not-going-to-do-this-to-me-again-are-you? looks, which he ignored. I followed him down the road out of town. When we came to a police station, adjacent to a large, dirt soccer field, Ville struck up a conversation with an officer standing outside and asked about camping in the field. I looked over at the field and watched a couple stray dogs and pigs nosing at the dirt.

"Of course you can camp there, friends!" The officer replied with a toothy grin.

"¡Perfecto! ¡Muchas gracias, amigo," Ville said excitedly and looked at me.

I think you can guess the look I gave him.

That night it poured so hard that our battered rain cover hardly kept any of the rain out. The wind howled down the canyon, blowing our tent sideways. It felt as if we were in a washing machine. When we awoke, most of our clothes and sleeping quilt were soaked. We packed them up, planning to air them when the rain let up. The rain turned the soccer field into a mud pit, making it difficult to disassemble the tent, pack up, and walk our bikes back to the road.

"Damn," Ville muttered. "My tire is flat."

"Twelve dollars, huh?" I looked hard at Ville. Mud covered our legs and panniers, and caked our tires, including his flat one.

It was still drizzling.

We walked the bikes back to the Main Street, found a small restaurant with a wooden table out front under an awning, sat down, and ordered some breakfast while Ville patched his tube. Inside we met a middle-aged, well-dressed couple from Lima. They joined us at our table, insisted on buying us more breakfast. We thoroughly enjoyed their company. Peru takes but it also gives. By the time we said our goodbyes the rain had let up.

23

Altitude Sickness

Without the rain, we had a fairly pleasant ride to Ayacucho, a city with thirty-three churches (one for each year Jesus was alive) and a violent past that includes the Battle of Ayacucho—an important battle in Peru's War of Independence—and the site of terrorism by the revolutionary organization Shining Path. We took a few days off because we had traveled 1,340 miles in Peru. Our next big push was to Cusco. The route had ten massive passes to climb, and the summits varied between 10,000 and 13,000 feet. Altitude sickness was a real threat, and climate would range from a humid jungle to snow-capped peaks. My parents planned to meet us in Cusco, and together we would visit Machu Picchu, the ruins of an Incan Empire.

On the way to Cusco, 380 miles, we pedaled Blue Bullet and Rufio up 61,600 feet of elevation gain and 60,000 feet of descent.

That was almost exactly sea level to the top of Mount Everest and back down. Twice.

We covered 230 miles in six days, climbing seven passes in a complete blur. My thoughts passed slowly, as if oozing through my brain in a thick liquid. I began to breathe more easily when we reached lower elevations.

Near Chincheros, I sprung a fever. It was all I could do to make it to a hotel and crawl into a bed. I was relieved to get out of the heat. I hadn't been sick since Mexico, so I'd had a good long run, but my luck had finally run out. I hated lying still, especially when I was sick.

We made it to Uripa after I recovered and had five more passes varying between 7,000 and 13,000 feet. I had never yo-yoed through such elevation and felt dizzy and delirious with every pass. Anything over 10,000 feet left me struggling to breathe, to pedal, to think, to talk, to sleep, and to push forward. The snow-capped mountains surrounded and towered above us. I felt small and insignificant and yet larger than life.

We descended into Abancay, located in a scalding hot, desert valley. We had no intention of staying. We ate our lunch of lomo saltado and continued twelve miles up and out of the heat. In a weak effort to climatize, we hoped to camp halfway to the summit. Anything over 8,000 feet should be gained by a thousand feet per day. A 13,000-foot pass should be summitted in six days or more. We summitted in a day. And besides, we still had a few hours before the sun would set around six o'clock. As the light faded from the sky, we had descended to an elevation of about 8,000 feet. It was time to camp.

As we neared the 13,000-foot summit, climbing the last 7,000 feet in twenty-five miles, we were rewarded with sweeping views of countless snowy mountains as far as my eye could see. The Andes were infinite. Even at 13,000 feet I could see nothing beyond them. I struggled to breathe, as if someone were sitting on my chest. On every inhale and exhale, I could hear my lungs wheezing. It was time to get down.

Do you know what it feels like to descend 7,000 feet in thirty-six miles?

Like a bird in flight.

You are weightless. Your mind is empty. You do nothing but take in the scenery and remember to brake when necessary. You feel free.

Nearing Cusco we noticed more wealth and western-influences. Instead of seeing homes of mud with corrugated metal roofs, we saw brick homes with tiled roofs, windows, and doors. Farms were larger and fenced. This was more like the world we had grown up in, but now it felt foreign. I didn't want our simple life to change. In the Peruvian Andes there were no cell phones, televisions, computers, billboards, fast-food chains, or lattes. We weren't over-stimulated with the clutter from our previous life. Life was simpler, and we found beauty in that simplicity. We spent quality time with some of the people we met, and when we parted ways we knew we would never see each again, but the brief connections were so significant that it made it acceptable.

Cusco was a stark contrast. Single-lane roads widened to multiple lanes choked with traffic and congestion. We saw buildings instead of mountains. In place of pigs, cows, sheep, turkeys, and guinea pigs were herds of westerners, aimlessly waddling with maps and cameras.

We looked forward to the arrival of my parents. At the airport on the outskirts of town, we watched their plane land outside the small terminal. My heart raced. When my mom and dad stepped through the security gate, tears flowed, and hugs were shared. My parents had only been to resorts in Mexico and a five-week vacation through central Europe, so this was a new traveling experience for them. They were like curious puppies. Although their luggage was delayed, my mom carried a duffle bag of much-needed-and-anticipated bicycle parts, knowing we would be screwed without them. She would think to do something like that.

We spent two weeks together, visiting Machu Picchu, the Urubamba River Valley to see ruins in Ollantaytambo, a salt mine called Salinas de Maras, Moray, and Chinchero. We ate at indoor markets, tasting the animal legs, beaks, and brains on display. The look on my mom's face reminded me that this display was once foreign to me, too, before I became a traveler. Ville and I reveled in being off our bicycles, sleeping in, walking, drinking lattes, staying up late, and waking up in the same place two days in a row. We all thoroughly enjoyed spending time together. What's special about reuniting with family is that they deeply know us. We can laugh at inside jokes.

It felt wonderful to be with family we knew so well.

It felt like being home.

24

Caravan of Misfits

After my parents left, I felt a deep sorrow in my heart, and with every beat I could feel it spreading into my chest until it was a tight knot. I stared out the window of the tourist bus at a flock of bright, pink flamingos wading in a shallow riverbed that ran along the road that stretched from Cusco back to Juliaca. One of the birds lifted its head out of the water, holding a wiggling fish in its beak, and swallowed it whole. At least I'm not that fish, I thought.

Ville and I stayed another night in the hotel before catching a tourist bus back to Juliaca. In stark contrast to the local bus we had taken to Cusco, there were no preachers, lottery tickets, or elixirs being sold.

I missed my parents already. Our adventurous lifestyle was a sacrifice that required extended time away from family and friends. Why did a broken heart feel like your heart was actually broken? Mine was broken. I knew they would be there when we reached the end of the world and made our way back to Oregon.

We roughly calculated that the remainder of our adventure would take four months, considering we needed to arrive in Ushuaia in mid-summer. Snow and freezing winter temps would still be possible in Tierra del Fuego then, but they were guaranteed if we arrived late, so it was critical that we arrive on time.

Ville and I made a new friend back at Casa de Ciclista, PacMan. He was a wiry, spastic guy in his early forties from Buenos Aires who was on a bike tour to wherever the wind blew him or with whomever he happened to meet along the way. Today it happened to be us.

We spent two days in Juliaca replacing bike parts with the help of PacMan, who assured us he knew what he was doing, although we weren't sure. What did it matter if parts fell off along the way? We would just put them back on again.

After much deliberation, Ville and I decided to head northeast of Lake Titicaca toward the Bolivian border, having been told there was far less traffic than on the southern highway route. No one knew if the immigration office was open, but we decided to risk it. If it were closed, we would have to backtrack to Juliaca and take the trafficked route. PacMan decided to follow along.

The altiplano was a series of intermontane basins lying 12,000 feet above sea level, beginning northwest of Lake Titicaca in southern Peru and extending about 600 miles southeast to the southwest corner of Bolivia. The altiplano was flat and treeless with violent winds that hit us from all directions. But, save for the winds, the route from Juliaca to Puerto Acosta, Bolivia, was fairly mellow compared to the highway between Cusco and Lake Titicaca.

My Spanish was decent by now, not perfect, but I could understand quite a lot. However, I couldn't understand a damn thing PacMan said. Because there was less traffic, he insisted on riding next to me and talking at me. He spoke in rapid fire, pronouncing the Spanish "ll" in the Argentinian fashion as a *sh* instead of as a *y* like I was used to. Did he care that I couldn't understand anything? Not one bit. I would nod as if I understood and interject a "Si, si" or "Claro," meaning "what you just said is clear and understood by me." I think he talked to keep himself warm. Every now and then, he would add a loud, honking laugh. It was nauseating after riding in silence, but I knew he meant well, so I forgave him.

He offered to ask a farmer if we could camp in his field while we waited at the road. He returned hysterical after being bitten by the farmer's dog. Flailing arms, gesturing toward the farm, then back at his arm. I quickly pulled out my medical kit to help. Upon further inspection, the dog bite had been a small nip, leaving a flesh wound the size of a nickel that hardly broke the skin. There wasn't even blood. My baby nephew had sustained worse. To appease PacMan, I cleaned the wound with antiseptic and covered it with a bandage. We then found a room in a hospedaje for the night.

Arriving at a small village, Tilali, we stamped out of Peru and continued ten miles to Puerto Acosta, where a single-roomed concrete building was Bolivia's immigration office. The village looked like a ruin, and there was not a person in sight. We leaned our bicycles against the wall and walked through the open door. Behind a desk sat an immigration officer who looked about thirteen years old. Next to him sat a plump officer in a military jacket with missing teeth, who asked for our passports. He sat back in his chair while the Man-child inspected each of them.

The young officer asked for our vaccine cards.

"Ville," I whispered quietly, so neither man could hear me, "I don't have my vaccine card with me. Who the hell asks for a vaccine card? In Bolivia?"

Ville flashed a look that said "Damn it, KG" straight at me, before turning back to the officer and sliding his own yellowed vaccine card to him.

Ville launched into a long-winded explanation about how my vaccine card had been stolen recently while we were traveling in Peru. The officer raised Ville's card in the air, inspecting it from all angles as if it were his first time inspecting such a card, then slid it back to

Ville. I wondered if he could read it. Ville didn't skip a beat, charging on about football teams, the weather, how excited we were to try Bolivian food, yada, yada, yada, and before we knew it, the officer stamped Ville's passport and said, "That will be $160 for the visa for the American."

"Wait, what?!" I almost threw up.

"Si, $160 por American tourist visa," he repeated, looking at me calmly. "Good for ten years." It would take us two weeks tops to ride through Bolivia. I was fuming, but there wasn't a damn thing I could do about it. Did I want to enter and ride through Bolivia or not?

Ville pulled out his wallet, unrolled a wad of U.S. twenty-dollar bills, counted them out, and laid them on the desk, where the officer counted them in front of us. I tried not to think about how much food that would have bought us.

I was the only one who had to pay for my entry. Why? Reciprocity. Bolivians paid the same amount for a tourist visa to enter the U.S. Couldn't blame Bolivia, but it still stung.

The Republic of Bolivia is landlocked by Brazil on the north and east, Paraguay and Argentina on the south, and Chile and Peru on the west. Only one-third of the country is in the Andean Mountains that divide into two ranges, Eastern and Western Cordilleras. There is a high plateau in the center that is cold, barren, and virtually treeless. One reason Spain built its empire here was to extract silver using enslaved Indians to work the mines. The Spanish racial and social apartheid continues today.

The paved two-lane northern route above Lake Titicaca, the highest navigable lake in the world, was beautiful. Occasionally, we had views of the lake as we passed through small villages, where Bolivians waved and moseyed about their day. Through all 645 miles of Bolivia, we would be riding on the altiplano, which hovered around 13,500 feet. We skipped the capital city of La Paz, taking a long dirt-road detour instead. As PacMan jabbered next to me, I stared at a glacial-covered mountain range reminiscent of the Grand Tetons in Wyoming. From camp we watched a lightning storm swirl over the rocky peaks.

When we reached pavement again, Ville's back tire wobbled and Handyman PacMan sprang to our rescue, pulling out tools that looked heavy-duty enough to fix a locomotive. The guy carried everything; it was mind-blowing. Need a chain saw? He had one. Car jack? Check. Crane? Didn't ask, but I am sure if I had asked he would have pulled one out.

We camped in an open field and watched as another touring cyclist approached wearing a florescent orange jacket. His name was Camilo. He was a government engineer from Bogota. We invited him to join us and got to know him while making dinner on cookstoves— ours a miniature stove the size of a matchbox attached to a gas can the size of a water bottle while PacMan and Camilo each had giant car-camping-stoves and kitchen-sized frying pans piled high with French fries and steaks.

Camilo, a twenty-four-year-old single guy who owned his house, part of which he rented to pay for travel, had taken leave to ride South America. He had dark skin, disheveled black hair, patches of facial hair, and was about the same height as Ville but with a slightly larger build. He was mellow and witty. He punctuated everything from talking about good food to good-looking women with his fingers together in front of his mouth, saying, "Ooooh, ooooh, ooooh." He had pedaled along the coast from Colombia through Peru and planned to ride through northern Argentina before heading east toward Rio de Janeiro. There, he planned to party with beautiful Brazilian women. Ooooh, ooooh, ooooh.

While we ate and listened to Camillo speak Spanish at a decipherable speed, the winds suddenly picked up. West of us loomed an ominous sky. There wasn't time to run or hide.

"Oh, no . . ." I said, feeling a sense of foreboding.

Suddenly, sand pelted our faces, legs, and hands.

"¡Perkele! God damnit!" Ville yelled over the howling wind. "A sandstorm!"

I set the pot of food in the sand and covered it with my body, burying my face in the hood of my jacket and pulling my hands and legs in like a turtle. I hadn't been in a sandstorm before and, unfortunately for us, this would not be the last.

How long could they last? I wondered. I tried not to inhale sand or think how claustrophobic I felt.

I remembered watching my dad sandblast a wooden sign in his shop as a child. At high velocity, the sand ate away the wood within seconds. My legs felt like that wood. It was painful and disorienting.

When the wind subsided, we shook sand out of everything, our food, hair, tent, and teeth. The monstrous black cloud was now in the east, gobbling up everything in its path.

We slept slightly on edge, hoping there wouldn't be another sandstorm during the night. Luckily, there wasn't.

The next morning, we woke, made breakfast, pooped, and packed up, while PacMan talked at us. Now we were a real-life, traveling circus, a party of four. Sometimes PacMan talked at me, sometimes at Ville, and sometimes at Camilo, but always at one of us. Camilo carried nearly double what we did, and PacMan carried slightly more than that. At least PacMan's wheels seemed built to take the weight; Camilo's were not. Almost daily he broke a spoke. With a shared wheel-size, Ville felt bad and gave him some spares. Then, more of Camilo's spokes broke. He told us he refused to buy any more because he was saving for beer. *Ah, to be young again.*

The weather was cooler in high altitude, so we wore rain jackets most days to protect us from the wind and sand. We struggled to find food and water. Bolivians lived on far less than the Peruvians in the Andean villages. Save for the few cities, we had to stop at numerous roadside food carts, stalls, and tiendas to gather all the ingredients to make spaghetti and oatmeal. We bought fruits and vegetables spread out on blankets. Restaurants served chicken and rice. We bought bottled water because there weren't many springs, rivers, or lakes. None we cared to drink out of anyway.

Most Bolivians lived on the altiplano, where they herded sheep, llamas, goats, and pigs. We spent our days waving as we passed them by. They were incredibly kind, allowing us to camp in their fields, but quite shy, too, leaving us alone. Towns were filled with disintegrating sand-block buildings, caved-in roofs, garbage blowing down streets with minimal vegetation. I felt like I was in the film *Mad Max*.

In a village outside a brick plant, we asked a man standing behind a low brick wall in his backyard if we might camp somewhere nearby. He pointed up the hill at a small church with only the frame and metal roof completed. We talked with the kind man awhile before retreating up the hill to the church. While we slept on the dirt floor the man and his family slept in a car parked in their backyard, the roof of their home having been blown off and now covered with a tarp. We gave the kids stickers, but wished it was a house.

In the city of Oruro, 255 miles south of the Bolivian border, the four of us shared a hotel room. We enjoyed a hot shower after a week without one, re-supplied our food stores, failed to find Wi-Fi, and moved on. For four days we pedaled through open spaces, watched afternoon thunderstorms and rain showers roll through, followed by pink and orange sunsets. We played games, shared stories, and laughed until our sides hurt. Often at the silly antics of PacMan.

If we told a story, PacMan had a better one in which he was the hero who jumped higher, ran faster, finished quicker, and did it better. He claimed to be a black belt in karate, although I hadn't seen ninja kicks quite like his. He loved to do them. All the time. Making lunch, he jumped up and did ninja kicks; telling a story, he would interject with ninja kicks; playing a game of throw-the-rock-and-see-who-can-knock-a-can-off-a-post, he pulled out his good ol' handy-dandy ninja kicks. It was quite entertaining.

When we retreated to our tents PacMan often talked at us until we zipped the tent closed. Unfortunately for Camilo, a native Spanish speaker, he got the brunt of it. One night, Camilo climbed into his tent, turned on music on a travel speaker, and zipped his tent closed while PacMan squatted outside talking for half an hour before it got so dark he had to retreat to his tent. An incredibly kind and generous character, PacMan gave Ville clothes to replace torn and damaged ones, offered us his two backpacking chairs at almost every camp, always shared his food, and was the first to help when bicycles needed repair. But he was a character.

It felt good to have friends again.

We rode 390 miles to the border of Argentina. We pedaled for three days by small lakes of white salt scattered along the horizon. On the last evening we camped in a wooden lookout tower on the side of the highway with views of the Salar de Uyuni, the largest salt flat in the world. It is what remains of a prehistoric lake that went dry, leaving nearly 4,500 square miles of white salt rock formations and cacti-studded islands. Still in sleepwear, we awoke to a bus full of tourists below and sent PacMan down. He ran them off with his camera and ninja kicks. We rode an entire day on the Salar de Uyuni and ended up with sunburns. Twenty miles from the border of Argentina, Ville discovered his sleeping pad was missing and spent a day hitching rides from a drunk, cocaine-sniffing dump-truck driver and a Dakar Rally driver to retrieve it.

It was an eventful ride through Bolivia.

PacMan and Camilo had left us to go their own ways and it was just me and Ville again.

PART IV

Argentina, Chile

25

Desert Blues

Vegetables, bananas, and watermelons laid out on blankets, giant tour buses, sacks of rice stacked high, bags of chips, cases filled with liters of soda, smiling brown faces, and rolls of peso bills waiting to be exchanged, greeted Ville and me as we rode up to the immigration office of Bolivia to stamp out and then onto the Argentinian office to stamp in. We had finally made it!

Argentina.

We walked up to the kiosk and waited in line. We breezed right through. Ville and I had waited for this moment for an eternity and now it was finally here. The border of Argentina, the final frontier, the country where we planned to finish this wild and crazy bike adventure. However, all I could see in all directions was more desert.

It was not only anticlimactic, but it was depressing.

Worse still, we had over 3,480 miles to Ushuaia, according to our phone app. Coast to coast, the continental U.S. could be ridden in 2,340 miles. This was the equivalent of riding from San Diego to Jacksonville *and* halfway back again.

Damn.

Argentina was huge! Who knew? I sure didn't until I looked at the map on our phone. Bolivia was dwarfed by Argentina. I looked up to see the desert stretched out in front of us and felt utterly depressed. I loathed deserts, which was bizarre because I was born and raised in a high desert. I've called the desert my home, felt happy there. But a long-distance bike ride through a desert was different. The land was flat and stretched out far too long. I liked the distances in the mountains, where the terrain was uneven, rapidly changing, and unpredictable.

We received our entrance stamps and pushed on into the wide-open desert. As usual, the only plan was to ride south. We would decide the route along the way.

We rode for twenty days and 987 miles in the north Argentinean desert, yo-yoing between complete misery and a grudging acceptance, until we reached the city of Mendoza. The headwinds were fierce and unrelenting, and there was hardly a tree, building, or Burger King for reprieve. The four-foot-wide shoulder we had in Bolivia, disappeared. The distances between towns were seventy to eighty-five-miles, which was too far to push each day, day after day. But we didn't have a choice. We had to reach towns to replenish our water. By day the sun boiled our skin, and by night the wind blew away our tent. Sex motels would have been a welcome respite. The cost of hostels and hotels was far out of our budget, so we made do with twelve-dollar campgrounds. To stay under budget, we stealth camped in scrub brush without showers and bathed in gas station sinks. We hoped roads would improve—possibly there would even be a shoulder or a bike lane to ride in—but it never happened.

Each morning, we rose at first light, pooped in a hole out in the open, struggled to keep the stove lit long enough to cook oatmeal in the high winds, then climbed back out on the two-lane road. When we tired of being pelted in the face with sand and wind, or when our shoulders were seized up and in need of a shake out, we would break for lunch, sit in the sand, eat our bread, salami, and cheese. With trepidation and dread we would climb back on our bikes and continue south until the sun was setting and it was time to scout for a camp spot. We struggled to find a sheltered spot. Sometimes it was a dry wash, a large scrub brush, or the road embankment; we couldn't be picky. For dinner we often ate veggie pasta because meat spoiled in the heat, but now we dreamed of PacMan and Camilo's steaks and French fries. In this manner we passed through late November and the first half of December.

After riding with PacMan for two weeks, listening to his incessant, "Well, in Argentina, they do *this* better and *that* better," we thought that simply crossing into Argentina we would enter a heavenly oasis so out of this world that we might never wish to leave it. What we found instead was more of what we found in the rest of the developed world: fancier cars that drove at excessive speeds and failed to move over, and an unfriendly, unwelcoming barrage of "can't camp here, this is private property" and "try down the road, I am sure there is a campground somewhere." Gee whiz, thanks for nothing.

We were so disappointed in Argentina, that we became angry when we were denied permission to camp in yards, on farms, or behind police stations. Angry when a grocery store opened hours late. Angry that they ate meat as if animals were dispensable. Angry that everything we needed was closed during siesta hours.

Luckily, it had nice people, too.

Two hundred miles shy of Mendoza, after two and a half weeks in the Argentinan desert under the blazing sun, an oasis of trees appeared in the distance. As we neared, we realized they lined the highway, like a welcoming party on the way to the town of San Jose de Jachal. We passed buildings along the highway, then houses, then a YPF gas station with an Auto Club of Argentina. We pulled over to ask about camping and noticed an abandoned fenced campground directly behind the gas station.

"¡Si, si!" The gas attendant nodded excitedly and disappeared inside to get keys. We followed him to a big gate, which he swung open for us to walk through.

"¡Muchas gracias, amigo!" We thanked him, and Ville shook his hand. We leaned the bikes against the fence and walked around the campground, scoping out a place to pitch our tent. The ground was hard clay with large, scraggly oaks growing randomly. Crumbling brick tables with dusty sinks and outlets stood next to a few of the tent spots; however, none of them had water or electricity. No matter, we were excited to have a place to camp. We agreed on a spot under a large oak tree, hidden from the road, and pitched our tent.

"Hey, KG, want to watch one of the movies I downloaded on my cell phone before bed?" Ville asked, giddy.

"Sure!" I replied. "What do you have?"

After eating dinner and brushing our teeth, we climbed into our tent, where we agreed on a comedic film, *This Is Spinal Tap*, a mocumentary about an eighties metal band. Ville set the phone on his mattress, and we lay on our bellies as the movie started. A thunderstorm cracked in the distance.

Boom! Lightning struck close by, and the skies opened, pouring heavy rain.

"Ville, should we check on the tent?" I asked nervously.

"No, we should be fine," he replied, not taking his eyes off the cell phone screen.

An hour into the film, the phone fell over. Ville righted it. It fell over again, and again he righted it.

Near the end of the film, I asked Ville to pause the film so I could take a pee break. It was pitch black outside. As I zipped the door open and reached for my shoes, which I always put in the vestibule directly outside the door, there was only one shoe there and it was floating in a sea of water.

"Ohhhh, noooo!" I said, stunned. "Ville! My shoe is floating!"

"What?" Ville asked, leaning over and looking out the door. I reached for my headlamp, clicked it on to see dark brown, murky water that was only half an inch from the bottom of the tent door. Were it to rise, we would be floating in it.

"Oh, shit."

I started laughing. Then Ville was laughing. We couldn't stop. We were so screwed but couldn't stop laughing! We laughed until our sides hurt and we struggled to catch our breath. How didn't we notice the water submerging our tent? The phone had buoyed up and down while we watched the movie because our air mattresses had become floating devices. And still, we had not noticed.

Rookies.

We picked up our tent, everything still inside, and carried it above the water, setting it down on higher ground. We climbed back inside, got comfy, and resumed the movie.

26

Outcrazy the Crazies

Apart from a red rock canyon and a lush tropical forest, northern Argentina was a thousand miles of desert. We passed through the little towns of Cafayate and Chilecito, each an oasis littered with vineyards, cafés, restaurants, and overpriced hotels that catered to wealthier travelers but nothing for us poor touring cyclists. We muscled onward without so much as a glance at what we couldn't have. By the time we hobbled into Mendoza we were ready for time off.

Ville and I had spent only one day off our beloved bicycles since our departure from the less-than-glamorous Juliaca, Peru. We had covered 1,740 miles in that time, passed through two borders, made and lost two traveling buddies, got sunburned, peeled, browned our skin again, and shocked some tourists. I was thirty-seven years old but felt like I was eighty. I was no longer writing my doctor, asking about various ailments I picked up along the way because I knew she would either suggest that I rest (not possible) or quit riding (not an option), and so I did my best to ignore the pain, lathered myself in butt cream, and hoped my body parts didn't fall off.

The sprawling, beautiful, hip city of Mendoza, located 230 miles east of Santiago, Chile, was a much-needed reprieve, with its leafy streets lined with Art Deco buildings and a plaza around every corner. The city was alive with music, dance, and cheap, tasty malbecs. We had emailed Warmshowers hosts and brothers Mauro and Nico a week prior to our arrival, and they had agreed to house us in a studio space in a garage made of concrete and cinderblock for four glorious days and nights. When I wasn't slamming out continuing education courses online for my real estate license, in case I needed a job when the tour came to its end, Ville and I walked the streets, listened to concerts in the park, and watched tango. The thought of being a real estate agent again felt awful. I wasn't sure if I *could* go back to that life.

Back on Ruta 40, heading south from Mendoza, the washboarded gravel road zigzagged through more desert. We rode through the sprawling city of Malargüe in the foothills of the Andes surrounded by nature reserves and a ski resort, although we stopped for only lunch and ice cream before continuing.

In the tiny village of Buta Ranquil we were given permission to camp in the parking lot of a police station. In the morning, I went inside to use the bathroom and walked past the morning briefing, where ten officers sat listening intently to their captain give orders and thought how absurd my life had become. I was sleeping in the parking lot of a police station in Argentina and listening to their morning brief through paper-thin walls while pooping. *If I thought this was completely nuts, what did the cops think?* Even though they encountered colorful individuals in their line of work, I doubted many were dirty, sweaty, bike-touring American women who camped in their parking lot and used their bathroom. By the looks they gave me, I was almost certainly the first.

As we continued south, the scenery improved. In Chos Malal we found a campground nestled next to the Neuquen River. The next morning, we took pictures at a sign along the highway that read "Argentina Neuquen, Ruta 40, KM 2623, Chos Malal" next to a large, concrete monument in the shape of a wave. The towering monument marked the halfway point down the length of Argentina. Another half to go.

With hundreds of miles of desert and strong sidewinds, minutes stretched into hours, and hours into days. My mind wandered, but the constant howling wind in my ears brought me back. I was sure I'd go crazy if I had to listen to it any longer, though I knew I would have to. All I could see was more desert. After a few days of teetering on the brink of madness, we reached our breaking point and decided to go to Chile.

But we would have to climb over the Andes again to get there.

We headed west, leaving Ruta 40 onto Highway 242 toward Temuco, midway down Chile, and began climbing over the Andes, where we encountered stronger and more hellish headwinds blowing east off the mountains. At least the sun was shining. We passed a small grove of monkey puzzle trees and stopped to gawk at them. Native to Patagonia, the prehistoric-looking, evergreen trees were tall and scraggly with razor-sharp needles and looked about as friendly as cactus. Halfway up the pass, we stamped out of Argentina, and a few miles later stamped into Chile. I was happier knowing we were in a new country and hoped Chile would be easier on us than Argentina.

At the Chilean immigration office, an officer asked us to bring our bicycles inside, where he went through every pannier and threw away all our food. He informed us that we were not to enter Chile with any fruits, vegetables, or animal products of any kind. He dumped it into two garbage cans outside. I felt sick. We were left to climb fifty miles over the pass without food.

Fantastic.

The small town of Liucura wasn't too far away, and once there I waited outside a market while Ville went to buy more food. I picked the dirt from under my ratty fingernails and watched a hawk circling overhead. After loading our panniers with food, we camped in a vast field under a large pine tree. We awoke to black clouds that rained on us the entire day, with gusts of wind strong enough to blow us over. Twenty miles took us a good portion of the day as cars sprayed us with rocks and water. By the time we limped into the town of Icalma, soaking and freezing, we were ready to splurge on an expensive cabin instead of camping on the lake. Ville got a fire roaring in a pot-bellied stove, and I hung all our wet clothes to dry. The blood pulsed painfully back into my fingers while the storm raged outside. I'd never been happier and more grateful to be indoors.

There was a loud knock at the door. Ville opened it, and there was the owner of the cabin carrying an armload of wood for the stove.

"Is this weather normal for this time of year?" Ville asked him, as the rain pelted the windows outside.

"No! It's normally really hot right now," he responded.

Of course, it is.

As we rode away from the cabin early the following morning, a dusting of snow covered everything, and a chill hung in the air. Wispy fog hung in the branches of pine trees and our breath made clouds. Realizing the winds of Argentina might be preferable to freezing snow in Chile, we decided to head back to Argentina.

This time, at the Argentinean immigration office, a long-haired officer not only riffled through our frame bags but pulled everything out to inspect it: water bladder, tools, feathers, cord, butt cream, and my pee rag. To minimize littering toilet paper everywhere, I had carried a small, microbial rag in my frame bag, which I washed after each pee.

Now it was in the hands of the long-haired officer.

He turned it over, held it up, and sniffed it. Presumably searching for drugs.

Ville glanced sideways at me, a small smile creeping across his face. I looked directly at Ville, a big, proud smile on my face. Redemption.

27

Proceed with Caution

Once back in Argentina, we meandered along the Aluminé River, which cut through a deep rocky canyon. The weather was superb, and the scenery was spectacular. Most of the road was washboard-shit-gravel, but we took it slow, stopping every so often to jump in the river and cool off. We passed fishermen standing along the banks of the river with their lines adrift in the current. We exchanged waves. Every now and then, a car or truck would rocket by, kicking up rocks and dust. Most waved as they passed, although they hardly ever slowed down. Each reckless driver left us fuming.

We stopped in Aluminé to buy groceries on the way to Junín de los Andes, a beautiful little oasis of lush, green trees perched on the riverbank of the Chimehuin River. Exorbitantly overpriced, we paid thirty dollars to camp for a night after Ville haggled to get the price down.

San Martin de los Andes was rumored to be a chic town, but we refrained from getting our hopes up. Socialites wandered the streets, ducking in and out of shops with ridiculous names like Chill Spot, Casino Magic, By the Way, and GULP! It reminded me of a touristy ski town, but it was actually quite nice, nestled in the mountains on

the shore of a lake named Lago Lácar, which bordered Lanin National Park. It was home to an array of diverse wildlife and the Lanin
Volcano, but it was unaffordable, so we continued climbing south and
into the mountains.

After a long and treacherous climb high into the mountains that
overlooked Lácar Lake, we found a spot deep in the woods of head-
high scrub brush for a night of stealth camping. We found an area
large enough to fit our tent, but we would only be able to use one
door. Since I often got up to pee in the night, I took the door side.
With bellies full of a grocery-store meal we had eaten before leaving
town, we snuggled under our sleeping quilt and played a few hands of
cards before falling asleep.

I was jostled awake by Ville climbing over me on his way to relieve himself and then again on his way back in. I'm sure he tried to
scurry over me like a quiet, little mouse instead of executing a walrus
roll over me with a flipper slap to the face. Let's just say, he was not
very graceful. I shoved my earplugs deeper into my ears, pulled the
sleeping quilt over my shoulders, and fell back to sleep.

Moments later, he was climbing over me again. And then again.

As soon as he lay down, Ville was rolling back over me again on
his way out of the tent.

Somewhere, in the depths of my sleepy mind I wondered if something was wrong, but it hadn't been his first time getting up multiple
times to relieve himself or take dumps, so I just slept. I am not proud
of it, but like I said before, angry bear.

The sun was shining on the tent when I awoke and found Ville
asleep. I crept out of the tent, zipped the door and rain fly closed, and
stood up, shocked.

It looked like a murder scene.

There was vomit and diarrhea splattered in every direction. It was
all over the ground, in the bushes, and on the sides of trees. It was as
if he had sprayed it from a fire hose.

There were long, white sheets of toilet paper strewn across the ground and hanging from thorny bushes like Christmas decorations. And on top of that, it had dropped below freezing last night, so most of it was frozen. *How did he get it up in that bush? How did he get it on the side of the giant, fallen tree? How did he have that much liquid inside him?*

Damn.

I managed to take very slow, calculated steps around the mess, as if dodging landmines, and found a clean place to pee before returning to the tent to check on my patient.

When I returned, Ville was peeking out from under the rainfly, looking dazed and very confused.

"You okay there, buddy?" I said, trying not to laugh. "Looks like you're a little sick?"

"Oooooh," Ville moaned, "I feel like shit."

"I bet! Are you okay? What happened?"

"I think it was the chicken we ate from that grocery store," he replied.

"Whatever it was, it looks like you decorated the woods with it."

"I cut my hands pretty bad trying to hold onto those bushes," he said, lifting his hand, palm up, exposing multiple deep cuts over his palm and fingers. It looked painful. "For a while there it was coming out both ends, and I had to hang onto something to keep myself upright."

"Oh, no! I'm so sorry, babe." I squatted down next to him and wrapped my arms around his neck. "I'm really sorry. I didn't know you were sick." I felt horrible. And ashamed that I hadn't gotten up in the night to check on him.

He climbed out of the tent on unsteady legs and collected himself.

"You sit down on . . ." I looked around for a fallen log that Ville hadn't defecated on or covered in vomit. I saw none, and said, "You wait here, and I will go find you somewhere to sit." I walked very carefully around a few bushes and called for him. "Found a spot!"

Ville appeared from around the bush, still looking dizzy and pale, and sat on the stump of a tree with his hand on his stomach. I made my way back to the tent, packed up our stuff, broke down the tent, rolled it, and loaded everything onto our bikes, then returned to Ville.

"What do you want to do? Do you want to go back down to San Martin?" I asked. I dreaded the thought but knew it might be the only solution for Ville in his current condition.

"No way! We are *not* going back there," he said, indignantly, shaking his head.

"But, babe . . ."

"Nope. We will keep going." He marched toward the bikes.

"But . . ." It was obvious I wasn't going to talk any sense into him.

He opened his rear pannier, dug out the stove, pot, and oatmeal and began cooking, far from the crime scene. He needed to eat if we were going to keep pedaling. Once the water boiled, I added oatmeal, stirred until it became thick, covered it, and looked at him, "Okay, I know you don't want to go back down, but I really think you need to rest. At the very least hydrate."

"Let's just eat and see how I feel. Okay?" He downed a liter of water mixed with electrolytes and a bit of oatmeal, then we packed up and made our way back to the highway.

"Okay, let's keep going," Ville said, adamant.

I stared at him for a while, then asked, "Are you sure you want to keep climbing?"

"Yep."

"Do you want me to check the map and see how far—"

"Nope," he interrupted.

As stubborn as I was, vomiting and explosive diarrhea might have been enough to give me pause. He was obviously way more stubborn than I. So, we continued climbing.

We rode through a famously picturesque area called Ruta de los Siete Lagos (Route of Seven Lakes). We had planned to take our time, but Ville was sick and camping spots were unaffordable, so we pushed through it all and camped in the bushes before the start of the climb that would take us back over the Andes to Chile.

The next morning, we reached the Argentinean immigration office, and the officer who stamped our passports warned us that the pass had extreme weather conditions and recommended that we turn around. *And go where?* I wanted to ask him. We needed to get back to Chile so we could ride down the infamous Carretera Austral, and there wasn't an alternate route. The Carretera Austral was a coastal frontage road in Chile, roughly a thousand miles long, running north and south. It was famous for its spectacular scenery of remote Patagonian wilderness. It was a bucket list item, and we weren't keen to trade it for windy roads in Argentina. How bad could the pass be?

As we climbed toward Chile, it began to drizzle.

"Well, this isn't so bad," I yelled back at Ville as we hugged the narrow shoulder around hairpin turns. The road looked as if it had been paved directly on top of boulder fields; if I stuck my arm out I could touch the rocks as we passed.

We climbed higher. It began to pour. It took only a few minutes before we were soaked completely through our rain gear.

The rain turned into little snow flurries; our field of vision narrowed to three feet. I focused on the white line directly under my tire. *Just stay on the white line, just stay on the white line,* I repeated.

Sixteen miles later, we arrived at the Chilean immigration office, and the officer looked at us in shock when he realized we were riding bicycles in the storm. He shook his head, tsk tsked under his breath, stamped us in and told us to be careful.

How we made it down to the other side of the mountains alive was a miracle. When we arrived in Entre Lagos, Ville walked into the first motel we saw and I gave him that if-you-even-dare-to-haggle-and-piss-off-the-owner-of-this-place-I'll-kill-you look, and he walked back out with a set of motel keys. We peeled off wet clothes, took hot showers, and slipped into clean clothes. We ate a big pot of spaghetti and topped it off with some banana ice cream.

For the first time since the U.S., I drank unfiltered tap water. Not even an hour passed before my stomach lurched. I barely made it to the bathroom before covering it in vomit and diarrhea. I couldn't keep anything inside. I would barely lie down before my stomach rumbled and I ran for the bathroom. My saint of a husband not only got up to check on me, but he also held my hair out of my face when I threw up, made me chicken soup the next day, and paid for another night, even though we couldn't afford it, because he knew that I didn't have the strength to continue.

It was Christmas Eve, and spending the holiday dry and warm sounded like a better idea than being on our bikes in the cold rain, so that is what we did. We snuggled under warm blankets while the rain pounded on the roof and the wind threatened to take the walls down.

A couple of rain-filled, dreary days later, we climbed out of our tent to a clear, blue sunny sky. If we'd known it'd be our last hot, sunny day for the next two weeks, we would've appreciated it more. We were shocked at the view of snow-capped volcanoes that had previously been hidden by rain clouds.

After a hearty yet tasteless oatmeal breakfast, we continued south on V-69, a gravel road that hugged the east bank of the estuary and circumnavigated the Calbuco Volcano. We didn't care that the road became a roller coaster of steep ups and downs. We were busy enjoying the sun, the quiet wind, the pine forests, and the ability to see more than five feet in front of us. The road was mostly in the woods. We saw small villages comprising stuccoed houses on steep hillsides as well as fields and fish farms stocked with salmon.

When we reached the tiny village of Puelo we set up our cookstove on a picnic bench in the town square only to be sent scurrying under a church's awning with our hot stove and half-boiled pot of water because the rain gave little warning before coming down in torrents. At the first sign of a reprieve we continued west to the mouth of the estuary and the beginning of Highway 7, otherwise known as the Carretera Austral.

Within an hour, it began to sprinkle, the precursor to an oncoming storm, like warning shots fired off the bow of a ship before the onslaught of cannonball fire. We needed to find shelter fast.

Up ahead, a car was coming down a long driveway heading for the road.

"I am going to ask that farmer if we can camp in his barn," Ville called to me, as he pedaled faster to intersect the farmer before he exited the driveway.

I glanced over at the field and saw a weathered wooden barn surrounded by green pasture. When I caught up to Ville, he was already speaking with the farmer in his car.

". . . come, let me show you," I heard the farmer say to Ville, before turning his car around and heading back up his driveway toward the house.

"KG, let's go. He said we can camp."

When we reached the house, the farmer got out of his car, smiled, and said, "Come, this way." We followed with our bikes.

"Excuse me, amigo, is it alright if we sleep in that barn?" Ville asked politely, pointing to the barn.

"No. No, that's for the animals," the farmer replied in astonishment. "It's not hygienic."

Fearful that the farmer wouldn't give us a protected place to sleep, Ville pushed on, "Please, friend, we are fine with the barn."

The farmer looked over at me, "But . . ."

Ville continued unfazed, "My wife, she is fine in the barn. She grew up on a farm." He nodded emphatically. "Right, KG?" He looked at me, wide-eyed.

"Si, es okay," I said, nodding in agreement.

"Yes, yes, I know, but please let me show you to the shed. That barn is full of animals and feces. You cannot sleep there."

We followed the farmer past the barn full of animal feces up a hill to a small tool shed. Inside, it was clean with a concrete floor perfect for sleeping. We thanked him repeatedly before he returned to his car.

We set up our sleeping pads and quilt between the wall and shelves of farm equipment: ropes, bags of fertilizers, buckets of nails and screws, cans of gasoline, tools, wool blankets, and miscellaneous farm equipment. I walked behind the shed to pee. A couple of horses watched me as I squatted in the grass, the rain still falling in fat drops on my wet head. When I returned, Ville sat by the open door, looking out at the sheep and horses grazing in the pasture. I sat down next to him, kissing him on the cheek.

"Thanks for talking to the farmer and getting us this shed. This is perfect," I said, looking at him. "We will stay dry here."

"I was stressing that we wouldn't find a place with a cover," he replied.

"Did you happen to see the barn when we walked by it?"

"Yeah" he replied, sheepishly.

"I'm glad to know that you are more than happy to have your wife sleep in animal feces."

"Yes, yes, I know," he replied, kissing the tip of my nose. "Only the best for my wife."

"I appreciate that the farmer said, "'No, that's not hygienic,' and you insisted that I am not hygienic and love sleeping in animal feces."

"Hey, you can take the girl from the farm, but you can't take the farm out of the girl."

I shook my head and laughed.

We rode to Caleta Puelche, where the ferry docks after crossing the mouth of the Reloncaví Estuary. It is also where V-69 joins the Carretera Austral. Storm clouds were above, and the light drizzle had turned into a heavy rainfall.

The moment my tires hit the highway pavement, I exhaled deeply. After riding for days on sloppy, loose gravel, pavement feels effortless. We pedaled furiously through the rain for seven miles until we reached the next town, Contao, and sat under a sheltered bus stop to eat lunch. Ville pulled out a salami stick and a block of hard cheese, and I pulled out the remaining half of a bread round, and we made sandwiches. Every minute or so, a car would pass, spraying water. A young man with a backpack sat down in the seat next to us, smiled, and turned his attention up the road, watching for the bus.

A middle-aged woman carrying two large bags sat down on the other side of us.

"¡Hola!" She said, with smiling eyes.

"Hola ,señora," I responded, returning the smile.

She was quite chatty, asking where we were from, where we were going, where we lived, and so forth. When the bus pulled up, she turned and asked if we wanted to come to her house. "I will make you some hot cocoa," she said with a smile.

"Muchas gracias, señora, but we must keep going. We must catch the ferry today from Hornopirén. Pero, muchas gracias. Muy amable," Ville replied, putting his hand on his chest to show gratitude. It would be my birthday in a few days, and we hoped to reach Chaitén, a town large enough to have a hotel, where we might spend my birthday off bicycles.

We trudged on in the drizzle and rounded the next bend approaching a bunch of light-flashing machinery. A flagger stood with a sign that read, PARE. We pulled up behind a few cars stopped in front of us. One of the lanes ahead was roped off, and traffic was being diverted to a single lane that disappeared over a massive, steep hill. A deafening grader came down the hill toward us, leaving soft, loose dirt in its wake. The flagger turned around his sign so it read PROCEDER CON CUIDADO, and we proceeded to follow the cars.

Because of the mud and steepness, we were unable to ride at a speed that was any faster than we could walk. My heart pounded. I pedaled as hard as I could until my lungs burned. I needed a break. But I couldn't take one because cars were lined up behind us. There was no room for them to get around. The rain fell harder.

When we finally reached the end of the construction, my heart was pounding so hard I could barely catch my breath. We pulled over to let the drivers pass, leaning heavily on our handlebars gasping for air.

We trudged on.

Fifteen miles ticked by, and the pavement never reappeared. Nor did civilization. We were completely disoriented, deep in a forest, and stuck on a dirt road that had become mud in the heavy rain. Cars and trucks flew past, splattering us as they went. The hills grew increasingly steep until we had to dismount and push our bikes because the tires only spun out when we tried to pedal. I was completely soaked and freezing.

I hate this, I kept thinking. Over and over. *I hate this, I hate this, I hate this!*

The sun was almost gone, the wind was cold, and rain continued to fall in sheets.

More miles ticked by.

I'd no idea how much farther Hornopirén was, but I knew from the disappearing light in the sky that we'd missed the ferry.

We reached the summit; a long descent awaited us.

I kept pedaling until we came to the next long, slow uphill.

Miles ticked by.

I was exhausted, emotionally and physically drained.

"There is a market up there on the right; let's pull over and I can ask about a place for us to stay."

"Okay." I stopped outside the market and dismounted. I was still shaking. I couldn't remember the last time I was this wet and cold with clothes on. Ville dismounted; we leaned our bikes against the wall of the mini-mart. *No one was going to steal two bikes in this rain,* I thought. I was too cold to wait outside. I was going in with him.

A bell on the door jingled as Ville walked inside, holding the door open for me. I squinted at the bright lights. We stepped onto a large, flattened cardboard box on the floor, placed just inside the door to catch dripping water. I watched a cascade of water run off me onto the cardboard and then spill onto the floor. Ville stepped up to talk to the old man behind the counter.

The bell tinkled, and I stepped sideways as a man entered the store. He was middle-aged, as tall as I was, with a clean-shaven face, dark brown eyes, and light brown skin. I looked back down at the water dripping off my sleeves onto the floor. The man walked to the cooler, grabbed a drink, and walked to the counter. Ville, still in conversation with the cashier, stepped aside, allowed the man to pay, and then resumed the conversation. I overheard the man giving Ville directions to a hostel or hotel up the road. As the man turned to leave, he looked directly at me, his eyes panned down to my feet and back up, taking in how soaked I was, met my gaze, and chuckled. I was still shivering.

Then he said, in English, "What do you need?"

Without thinking, I said, "I don't know." I was in shock, my brain wouldn't work, and I couldn't think of anything to say. I needed absolutely everything and nothing that this man could possibly give us.

"Come with me," he said, opening the door and stepped outside. Ville was still talking with the cashier.

"Ville," I croaked.

"Okay . . . Okay . . . ¡Muchas gracias, señor!" Ville said, waving at the old man behind the counter as he followed me outside.

As I walked out the door, I leaned into Ville and whispered, "Ville, he asked us to come with him."

"What?" Ville leaned in closer to me.

The middle-aged man was standing there, just outside the door, umbrella over his head.

"Come with me," the man said to both of us this time.

We took our bikes from against the wall and followed him. He walked past two storefronts, slid open a large, solid metal gate and waved us inside. We followed him and found ourselves standing in a small, concrete courtyard, surrounded by buildings. The man walked to a large metal building across the courtyard, opened a padlock, and slid open another large, metal door.

"Come," he beckoned and stepped inside. We followed closely behind into a cavernous room, with floor-to-ceiling shelving, each one stacked high with lumber.

"Here? Can we put our bikes here?" Ville asked in English and then Spanish.

"Si. Si," he said, nodding emphatically.

We set our bikes against a shelf full of lumber.

"¡Gracias, gracias, amigo!" We both said, over and over. I pulled my jacket off, hung it on my handlebar, and watched the water puddle below Blue Bullet. Ville unstrapped and pulled the tent from the back rack of Rufio.

"Is it possible for us to camp here?" Ville asked, pointing to the concrete floor next to our bikes.

The man, whose name we learned was Aldo, laughed. "Come," he said again and stepped back outside. We followed him across the courtyard and into another building and a small empty room inside it, where we laid out our mattresses and sleeping quilt to bed down for the night. He hung our clothes to dry then made us hot tea. I was still in disbelief over the turn of events. He also showed us a bathroom. "Shower. Here. For you," he said in English.

Wow. A shower. I took the hottest, most incredible shower of my life.

The next morning, we dressed, packed up, and sat at the kitchen window watching the rain coming down in sheets, feeling conflicted and depressed at having to go out in it. Aldo walked in and asked us, practically begged us, to stay another day. It was too dangerous, he insisted. So, we stayed. I mean, he didn't have to twist my arm; the previous day had been complete and utter hell. Sure, we'd stay in his warm building, would be happy to, overjoyed to.

When Aldo found out the next day would be my birthday, he insisted we stay a third night and made a feast of pork ribs, potatoes, and sangria. And since the day after my birthday was New Year's Eve, he insisted we stay for that as well. We grilled a late-night asado and watched flares rocket into the air around town at midnight. Aldo had an affinity for televised singing competitions, so we watched hours of them on his cell phone before retreating to our room.

The next morning, we caught the ferry to the town of Caleta Gonzalo. We didn't make it six miles down the road before it was pouring again.

Owners of Patagonia and The North Face purchased large swaths of the land that the Carretera Austral passed through and vowed to protect it, turning it into a National Park. Those gravel roads went through wild, pristine pine forests.

A couple weeks prior to our arrival, there was a massive landslide that took out three sections of Highway 7, burying the town of Santa Lucia and killing eleven people. It was a horrible tragedy, and there was a solemness on the ferry when we passed where the town had once been. On that ferry we made three new friends. The first, a fat brown and white spaniel mix we called Twinkie, who made chase when we passed him riding to the terminal. While waiting for the ferry to load, Twinkie moseyed around looking for treats, then followed us right onto the ferry like a boss. For some reason, no one questioned him. As soon as he was on board he disappeared, probably to find snacks.

Latin ferries were noisy: video-game playing at max volume; screaming kids running amuck; loud arguments; and C-list movies playing on every TV, the volume so high it rattled the speakers. We met Canadians and fellow touring cyclists Roy and Lana and hit it off immediately. When the ferry arrived at Puerto Marin Balmaceda early the next morning, it took another four hours of being tossed about in a violent sea before it was safe enough to dock and disembark.

The remainder of the ride down Carretera Austral was tumultuous—more rain, more ferries, noisy campgrounds, coffee breaks, fields of wildflowers, swollen waterfalls, a peek-a-boo sun, hordes of hitchhikers, and stunning views. Roy and Lana had quit their jobs in their mid-forties, sold their house and most of their belongings, and were perusing their dreams. We were kindred spirits. We hadn't ridden with anyone since Camilo and PacMan, and it felt great. We told stupid jokes, laughed at ourselves, talked about the world and our shared commitment to lives of travel.

28

El Fin del Mundo

One of Ville's molars had been bothering him since Canada. He had attempted to fix it twice—first in Canada, then in Peru—but had not solved the problem. While riding around Lago Gral Carrera, Ville's tooth pain came back full force when he bit down on a cherry pit that lodged a broken piece of tooth farther into his gums. Scared he would have to go back to a dentist, he didn't tell me, bought a small bottle of whiskey at a gas station to dull the pain, and sipped it as we pedaled.

When we arrived in the town of Perito Moreno, Ville could no longer conceal his pain or drunkenness and admitted he needed to find a dentist. After inquiring at multiple mini-markets for a dentist, we were directed to what looked like a house in a less-than-desirable neighborhood.

"Maybe he takes patients through the back door," I said, trying to lighten the mood as we stood astride bikes outside.

"Not funny, KG."

"Alright," I conceded. "I am sure it will be fine."

Ville knocked on the door. No response. He knocked louder.

A man in a T-shirt and jeans answered. "Can I help you?" he asked, surprised to be bothered after hours. Ville explained his situation in a tone the man fortunately recognized as complete desperation.

"I'm closed now, but come on in. Come in," he said, motioning for us to follow him inside.

Ville followed him inside while I locked our bikes to the front porch. I planned to go in and sit where I could see them.

I walked into a small, fairly clean waiting room with a couple of chairs and sat down. Ville was already in a back room, the door ajar just enough to see him lying in a chair. The dentist pulled on a white lab coat but didn't bother to button it.

"Did you drink some alcohol?" I heard the dentist ask Ville. He was sitting over the top of him with Ville's mouth pried wide open.

"Yes, for the pain," he replied. *I mean, a couple can't ride from Alaska to Argentina sober, right doctor?* I wondered if this man was a licensed dentist. I scanned the walls for a framed license. No matter, too late now.

The dentist did his best to fix Ville's tooth. He pulled out the sliver of tooth jammed into his gum, cleaned, and filled the broken tooth. He hoped this would get him by until the end of the ride. I hoped it would get Ville back to somewhere that had dentists with framed licenses on the wall and closed storage-room doors, where I couldn't see tools scattered haphazardly about. I was grateful I didn't have to get a tooth fixed there.

Before we left the office, Ville paid the dentist twenty-five dollars for the treatment. I wasn't sure if I should be happy or concerned that it was so cheap. When we stepped outside, I said, "Did he use Duct tape?"

"Still not funny, KG." He had obviously sobered up in there.

By the time we left the dentist, it was too late to continue. On the way there we had seen a sign that read Mini Camping Raul and decided to backtrack. We knocked on the door of a house and a skinny, wiry man with long, brown dreads answered. It was Raul. After introductions, Raul showed us his tiny, fenced backyard and where to pitch our tent. We paid, took showers in the communal restrooms, and were invited into Raul's small house to eat.

Inside was a large kitchen and an aged black-and-white TV on a breakfast bar. There was a small bed on the floor in the back. Raul insisted on making egg sandwiches. When we were full he insisted on making a tray of pork ribs. Argentinians typically spoke fast, but this guy was on a whole new level. I understood about a tenth of what he said, and Ville only slightly more than I.

Ville asked about the Wi-Fi, pointing to the sign out front with the word Wi-Fi appearing directly underneath Mini Camping Raul.

"Ahhh . . . Sí, Sí," he mumbled, and waved at Ville to follow him. They walked down to the corner, where Raul put his fingers to his lips, insinuating they needed to be quiet, and pointed at the convenience store across the street and asked, "Do you get a signal?" while pointing at Ville's cell phone.

"Sí," Ville scrolled down and found the Wi-Fi signal on his cell phone.

"The password is NINO123," he said, smiling, and disappeared across the street to buy smokes while Ville caught up on emails.

"Tombola! Lottery! Shhhhh," Raul said when he got back. He bumbled about looking for a remote control and turned on the TV, which had a poor-quality picture. He flipped to a channel with a woman announcing lottery numbers and dug out a stack of lottery cards, laying them out one by one in front of himself, mumbling aimlessly the entire time.

I contained my laughter. I tried not to look at Ville.

Early the next morning, while cooking our breakfast oatmeal outside the tent, Raul walked up, mumbling spastically. We caught only bits and pieces of what he said: "Buenos dias, amigos . . . I need to leave town . . . I need to go visit my daughter . . . by bus . . . gone for a few days . . . you take care of my business and keep the money . . . here are the keys."

"No, no, no, Raul. We need to leave today. I am sorry, friend, but we are on a tight schedule and must leave today," Ville told him apologetically, stirring the oatmeal.

"Okay. Okay," he seemed to understand. We hugged him, thanked him for feeding us and letting us stay. He asked us to close the gate behind us when we left and then he was gone.

It felt like we had just met the real-life Tasmanian Devil.

On a long stretch of desolate road along Route 40, we saw a gas station ahead. The only building we had passed in eighty miles since Perito Moreno, there were at least fifteen cars parked out front, along with multiple motorcycles. The gas pumps outside were covered in stickers. The wooden sign above the door read Hotel Bajo Caracoles. The interior was decorated from floor to ceiling with kitschy clutter, reminiscent of an old, western film set, as tourists perused the aisles of ready-to-buy knickknacks. It was extremely crowded. We found a lone bar stool in front of a long counter with a snack bar and a barista. We sat next to a window and a group of boisterous travelers. We ordered two mediocre lattes and sipped on them slowly, dreading the return to the highway and its torrential winds. I had no idea biking in Argentina would be so hard. The fatigue and my backache were getting to me. I could tell it was gnawing at Ville as well.

A couple, traveling by motorcycle from somewhere in northern Argentina, were sitting on the stools next to us. They asked us how our ride was going. Normally happy to converse about our travels, I was too tired to engage and let Ville do the talking.

After we finished the lattes, there was nothing left to do but head back out into the wind. We unlocked the bikes, left the shelter of the building, and rode back onto the highway, where we were hit with gale-force winds as we headed forever south. The thought of just ten more minutes in this wind made my stomach knot with dread. It was complete hell. The side-wind was so fierce I could barely hold my front tire straight.

I thought, *How will I endure this? I hate the wind!! I want to scream into it. To punch it and kick it and stab it until it dies.*

A car flew by creating a vortex. That was close! I could barely stay on the white line, and there was hardly a shoulder to speak of. No room for error. I needed my mind to wander, or I would be there suffering in misery forever.

I visualized myself on a warm beach, sitting on a beach towel. I imagined the sand lumpy beneath the towel and the crashing of waves on the shore. The sun was warm on my face.

ZOOOOOOOOOOM! A large, white pickup flew by me, so close it startled me from my reverie. I felt my blood run cold. That was *really* close. That asshole almost killed me!

I had stared death in the face numerous times since we had started biking from Alaska. Why had it not scared me enough to stop riding?

If I were to give up and go home, death would still find me someday; better it found me doing something with passion, purpose, and love than merely dreaming of such things. I had no regrets. If I were to die out here, the one who would suffer most was Ville. God, what would happen to Ville? I shuddered at the thought. Or worse, what if he died and I lived? I would be completely crushed. After everything we had been through, I would be irreparably heartbroken. He was my everything. Tears welled in my eyes at the thought.

Between an allergic reaction that put me in the emergency room, followed by full-body hives for a month, a dengue fever–like virus that knocked me down for five weeks, migraines that often crippled me, and numerous tumbles from my bike, I should have been dead. People die every day doing far less. I knew I was stubborn, but I had no idea how stubborn and driven and resilient. I was also brave, confident, and fiery. Ville called me his Spicy Jalapeno or the Diplomat. He was always kinder, softer, sweeter, gentler, and calmer than me. Those were the traits I loved most about him, and he inspired me to improve.

ZOOOOOOOOM! A truck hauling a trailer zoomed past less than a foot away. The drivers in Argentina drove insanely fast, especially in the desert, where they could see long distances and there were fewer cars.

A fat, little armadillo zipped across the highway in front of me, its snout held high, little spiked ears flopping, and its armored tail stuck straight out like a carrot. We had seen at least a hundred of them skitter across the highway in front of us. I had no idea they were so fast. We also passed herds of unfenced llamas wandering in the desert and wild guanacos, an animal that looks like a llama but is more closely related to a camel.

We were beat up and exhausted by the time we reached El Calafate, the gateway for tourists to visit Los Glaciares National Park, home to the massive Perito Moreno Glacier. We had 635 miles left to reach Ushuaia. We were almost done with Argentina and the God-forsaken wind! I couldn't wait for it to be over, and yet I never wanted the adventure to end.

Now the wind was at our back, lifting us as we climbed a towering canyon wall, quite possibly the first time we hardly noticed a climb. Better late than never, I guess. We rode sixty miles rather painlessly and sheltered in a building that stored road-construction equipment. We were joined by four other cyclists, a couple of kittens, and a wiener dog named Miguelito.

Our good luck with tailwinds did not last when the road veered to the south and the wind hit us sideways. The pavement disappeared, becoming a washboarded gravel road, known locally as *ripio*, and we were forced to walk our bikes for miles at a time because our frame bags and panniers became sails, blowing us dangerously into traffic.

With few options for sheltered camping, we resorted to sleeping in everything from empty food stalls made of weathered plywood to bushes and even an abandoned hotel. When we were able to ride, Ville insisted on riding in front in a tight echelon to break the wind, giving me a generous reprieve from the insanity of it all. My shoulders ached constantly from hunching against the force of the winds. I couldn't imagine riding in this another mile, another hour, another day.

It wasn't that I wanted to quit. Quite the contrary. I wanted to keep going. Needed to keep going. Yes, it sounded crazy, even to me. But I had never loved anything more than living in a tent and riding on Blue Bullet with Ville. I could do this forever. I wanted to do this forever. I'd never been happier watching the world slowly glide by, my body in a constant state of sweating, climbing, always and forever climbing. I'd grown to love feasting on oatmeal, peeing on the ground, sleeping on an air mattress, washing my clothes in a sink, always having dirt under my fingernails, sleeping in sex motels, and talking with strangers.

I never wanted to go back to my life before this.

I would crawl to the end if I had to.

We stamped out of Argentina and into Chile for the last time. The desert was replaced with a wonderland of lush mountains. We came to a vivid blue lake and couldn't resist a swim. Cerro Tenerife Mountain and the Torres del Pine National Park rose steeply, providing a spectacular backdrop as we swam in the icy waters. Although we had chased summer since leaving Alaska, we found that summer in southern Patagonia was cold, with weather patterns that changed every fifteen minutes. We spent the night camped on a stage above rodeo grounds and dined on four-cheese pasta and sausages while watching the sunset. It made me happy. I knew I would recall this memory as the years passed.

On the first day out of Puerto Natales we witnessed a car plowing through a grassy field, swerving, and honking, the driver an enraged maniac heading straight for a herd of horses. The frantic horses began running, and the car followed chase. When the car roared past, we realized the auto cowboys were simply herding the horses in the comfort of a warm, dry car. I wondered if Chilean western movies featured auto cowboys who drove Toyota Hilux pickups to herd cattle?

With the winds at our backs, we were flying. I looked down at my speedometer and saw that I was going twenty-eight miles per hour. On our best of days, we averaged twelve miles per hour. I quit pedaling. Hours passed and the miles disappeared—twenty, thirty, forty miles. It was effortless. I pulled the earbud out of my ear, turned my head, and yelled back at Ville, "This is crazy, huh?!"

Silence.

"HEY, VILLE! THIS IS CRAZY, RIGHT?! LOOK HOW FAST WE ARE GOING!"

No response. I turned my head. Ville was not behind me.

Oh, shit. I stopped. The sound of the wind was deafening. With a tailwind, I had been riding in a quiet vortex. I waited. And waited.

Ten minutes passed. I didn't see Ville.

I began to panic. My heart beat faster. I began to shake. Where was he? The worst-case scenarios began to filter through my mind: he had a flat tire and was trying to fix it alone on the side of the road; he fell and was lying in a ditch somewhere, calling for me; or worse, he was hit by a car and seriously hurt! Oh, shit! Why didn't I check behind me sooner? How could I be so stupid!

I had to go back.

I turned back into the horrendous wind and began pedaling straight into it, moving now at five miles per hour.

I was never going to get to him in time.

The sight of Ville riding toward me felt like a punch to the gut. I began sobbing. I had ridden into the wind for over half an hour. Too many horrible things can go through the mind in that amount of time. I stopped the bike and waited for him to make it to me.

"KG! Why didn't you stop?" Ville yelled over the howling wind, just before reaching me. He was mad. I could hear it in his voice, see it in his furrowed brow.

"I'm sorry, Ville! I'm so sorry, I didn't know you stopped," I yelled into the wind.

"My brake locked up and my bike just stopped, so I had to stop and fix it and you just kept going until I couldn't see you anymore."

"Sorry," I said, crying. "I'm so sorry. I didn't see you stop."

He wrapped his arms around me, squeezing me tight, my cheek resting against his chest. I could feel his heart pounding in my ear. I thought I had lost him. All my worst fears had filled my mind and then, suddenly, there he was, pissed at me but alive. I had traded everything I owned to the universe to bring him back to me.

I thought Ville would see the worry on my face, feel the gratitude I felt for finding him in my hug, hear my apology, and forgive me for not looking back more often and stopping, but he didn't. We kept pedaling, his frustration lingered in the air between us. I tried to lighten the mood with a joke, then with a smile, and even a peace offering of my last cookie. None of it worked. It wasn't until that evening in an abandoned mobile home that Ville softened and we could laugh with each other again.

I hated it when he was mad at me. Luckily, he almost never was.

We finally reached the most populous southernmost city in the Americas, Punta Arenas, and the Strait of Magellan, a waterway considered the most important passage between the Atlantic and Pacific Oceans before the completion of the Panama Canal in 1914 and that separated South America and Tierra del Fuego, home to Ushuaia, the world's southernmost city.

We spent the night in an overpriced motel and early the next morning boarded a ferry across the Strait of Magellan to the town of Porvenir on Tierra del Fuego.

We had ridden our bikes from Alaska to the Strait of Magellan. Two hundred ninety-eight miles left to Ushuaia.

Ville and I returned to our bicycles and my underwear were gone! I had left them strapped to my pannier to dry after hand-washing them in a sink the night before. My panties were likely hanging from a semitruck's review mirror. I planned to retire them to a garbage can at the end of the ride, so it wasn't that I was sad or upset, but really? Geez.

A herd of touring cyclists streamed from the ferry as soon as we docked. Ville and I waited and rode away once the congestion cleared. For a couple of hours, we rode on the rolling hills that hugged the coastline of the strait. Although we had clear, blue skies, the wind was freezing and we were wearing everything we owned to stay warm, including our rain gear and gloves. By nightfall, we found a lone pine to set our tent behind, but still we froze.

We rode for ten miles the following morning before we reached an intersection where we exited onto a gravel road toward the Reserva Natural Pingüino Rey. One of the few places in the world with a viewing platform to watch a rookery of king penguins, the second-largest species of penguins, with markings similar to those of the emperor penguin. We timed our arrival perfectly, as the penguins were sunning themselves on the beach with black and gray molting babies in full view. It made the twenty-mile detour pushing through deep gravel worth it. On this bike ride, we encountered black bears, moose, macaws, alligators, musk ox, and now king penguins.

We returned to the intersection of the Y-71, where it became Highway 267, only to discover it was under heavy construction with a detour for cars but fortunately not for us; we rode around barricades and had freshly paved road all to ourselves. It was a touring cyclist's dream: tailwind, no cars, blue skies, and rolling grasslands. We laughed, cried, and hugged each other. It was beautiful. Eight miles shy of the Argentinean border, we asked to camp at an estancia (farm) and were given a small cabin with two small beds, a wood-fired cookstove, and a large stack of chopped wood. We cooked our pasta dinner on the stove with a clowder of meowing cats outside the door. We watched the farmer hauling a huge carcass across the yard. When we asked what it was, he replied "horse."

Once the sun was up, we ventured back onto the highway, stamped out of Chile (stocking up on five Sahne-Nuss chocolate bars with our remaining Chilean money) and into Argentina for the last time. Right after the Argentinean border we stopped at an ACA Gas Station/café and ate a plateful of fried meat for lunch before reaching the Atlantic Ocean and Highway 3. For three days, we rode through rolling grasslands with minimal trees, and then traffic became horrendous. The road turned south, the skies grew ominously dark and unloaded wet fury upon us. We pedaled furiously, making it to the town of Tolhuin by nightfall, where we stayed in a backroom at the La Union Bakery, a place known for its excellent baked goods and shelter.

Drenched, we stripped off our clothes and realized we had nothing else to put on, so we sat in the back of the bakery in our sleeping clothes, hung our wet things on chairs to dry and studied Blue Bullet and Rufio. They were battered. Duct tape and zip ties kept most of the parts from falling off. Battle wounds. We had our own share of battle wounds: my tail bone was still broken, and Ville still had scars from Peru.

We ate croissants and chocolate-filled pastries and then set off for Lake Escondido, where there were a couple of abandoned cabins in the woods along the shore. The trees obscured the view and the mountains grew taller. The showers drenched our clothing, but it didn't matter. We were almost done. Done with everything—the ride, the bikes, the rain, the wind, the pushing, always pushing. By late afternoon, we arrived at the lake.

This would be our final night in a little pink cabin with a tiny bed and a non-working toilet.

Only eighty-eight miles left to go.

We hardly slept. Not only because an Argentinean family was up partying until three in the morning but also because we were nervous and excited. We awoke before sunrise, ate our last bowl of oatmeal, packed up Blue Bullet and Rufio, pooped in the woods, and headed out into the beautiful day. On this last day of the Bike Adventure there was not a cloud in the sky and the sun was shining.

Almost immediately we encountered a long, slow climb over Paso Garibaldi but were too happy to care. The grasslands had long since fallen away and were replaced with mountains. We were getting closer, I could feel it, smell it, and hear it, with everything in my being. The miles ticked by on my odometer next to the dirty butt crack of the sumo wrestler, where I rested my hands. I looked down at the handlebars. It was home.

We rode past beautiful, pristine lakes and rivers, grassy meadows between groves of pine forests, continually climbing, until we reached the crest and began a long descent. The air was warmer, clearer, the sky bluer than I had ever seen it. The sun warmed my face. The forest was thick with fragrant pine trees dancing in the breeze like spectators lining the road and cheering us onward. We came around a corner, then another, and another until, suddenly, there it was, a wooden sign in front of us, with bold letters, proclaiming:

PARQUE NACIONAL
Tierra del Fuego
BAHIA LAPATAIA
Republica Argentine
Aqui finalize la Ruta Nac. No. 3
Buenos Aires 3.063 Km. Alaska 17.848 Km.

I buried my face in my hands, the tears falling through my fingers. I was laughing and crying. Ville's arms were around me, mine around him, Blue Bullet still under me. I'd never felt so proud in my life. We stood there for several minutes, hugging each other tightly, not wanting to let go. When we pulled away, we laughed as tears fell from our cheeks. It felt surreal, like an out-of-body experience.

All those days of rain, wind, sun, snow, hail, climbs, pain, sweat, camping, laughing, drowning, pushing, swearing, everything and all of it, flooded back to me at that moment. I pulled to the side of the road and stopped. Ville stopped next to me. We dismounted and hugged each other again.

And no one was there. No crowds. No applause. No high fives. Just us. Exactly how we had begun this adventure, twenty months beforehand, in Prudhoe Bay, just the two of us.

The date was February 16, 2017. Forty-two days later, on March 30, we would celebrate our ten-year anniversary, marking the day that two careless, fearless, irrational, and driven individuals met on a scuba-diving boat in Vietnam and decided to conquer the world together. What a memorable ten years it had been. I'd be forever grateful that I had someone I love so deeply to share this crazy life with. An equal, who is as passionate about seeing the world, making new friends, and being the positive change we both hoped to see in the world. It was a very special thing to find. Occasionally I would be asked, "How do you spend so much time together? Doesn't he drive you crazy? I could never do that with my spouse." And I would reply, "I don't want to know this life without him."

The woman I had been when I started in Alaska was not the woman I'd become. I hadn't been a cyclist, but I'd learned how to live on a bike. I'd been naive when it came to bike touring, but I'd learned to trust in Blue Bullet, Ville, others, and myself. I'd never lived by the mantra of "safety first," but I'd learned how to be vulnerable. I'd been independent and self-assured, but I'd learned how to ask for help without feeling shame. I had a deep understanding of my own world and my space in it until I'd realized I had so much more to learn. I had confidence in my own knowledge until I learned how to observe the world around me, listen, and learn. I had enjoyed the wilderness and returning to our five-bedroom house, but I became more at home in nature while sleeping in a two-person tent. I understood, in a way I never had before, the immense size of the world and the diversity within it. My life would never be the same because I was no longer the same.

A big group of tourists appeared to take pictures of the sign. One man turned toward us and said, "Congratulations! You made it!" He raised his right hand in the air, palm toward me, and we high-fived. Then he asked, "So, where did you start?"

"Alaska."

The man looked as shocked as if I had slapped him across the face. "What?!"

"Yeah, I know." I was already crying. I was at a loss for words. And, really, there was nothing I could say.

"Well, I'll be . . ." He trailed off. "Can I take your picture?"

"Sure."

We positioned ourselves astride our bikes in front of the sign, and many of the tourists took our picture. We handed the man our camera, and he took a picture for us. In that picture we are two seasoned cyclists, weathered and worn in faded yellow and orange rain jackets, cycling shorts, and biking shoes, beaming smiles across our faces—our excitement, determination, fearlessness, and gratitude apparent. Every small act of kindness had become a big act of greatness. And without them we would surely never have made it.

We dismounted, walked to the end of a wooden pier that hung out over the South Atlantic Ocean and the Beagle Channel and rested our bikes against the railing and looked out over the ocean. Back home, people were sitting at laptops, picking up their kids from school, and doing the daily grind. People were using any excuse to sneak outside for a smoke break or back to the coffee machine for a chat. Printers were jammed and the internet was down. I didn't have cell service or a care in the world. I was at el fin del mundo with my husband, and we had ridden our bicycles there from Alaska.

We walked our bikes down to the shore and walked in until the ice-cold water brushed our knees. I pulled my black talisman stone from my handlebar bag, rolled it over in my palm, felt how soft and smooth it was between my fingers. Then I reached into the water and pulled out a light-colored stone, setting it in my palm next to the black one. They were now a pair. One from the Arctic Ocean, carried for twenty months to find its mate in the Beagle Channel. End to end.

At the end of something so monumental, there should have been a parade. A large gathering of people screaming, cheering, posters flying, banners waving, horns blaring. A finish line to announce that we had reached the end. But there was nothing. Total quiet at the end of the world. Just Ville and me. The sun was shining, the thunderheads gathered overhead, the breeze was light, the gravel road disappeared into the Bay of Lapataia, and there were no more miles to ride.

"Well, Ville, how does it feel?" I asked.

"Surreal," he responded, as if in a daze. After a long pause, he looked out to sea. "I don't know what else to say."

"Yeah," I paused. "Well . . . what're we going to do tomorrow?"

"Let's buy a car."

I laughed, stepped close to him, took his cheeks into my palms, and kissed him hard on the lips. Then we hugged and we high-fived.

We had reached the end of the world.

Interview with Kristen Jokinen

What happened after you ended your ride?

After we completed the ride in Bahia Lapataia, we rode thirteen miles back to Ushuaia boxed our bikes, and flew to Buenos Aires, Argentina, for a few days. There we boarded a Princess Cruise ship (paid for by my grandparents) and sailed around Cape Horn to Los Angeles. On the ship, we gave two presentations about our adventure to approximately 1,200 passengers. From Los Angeles we took a train to Portland, Oregon, where my Mom and Dad picked us up and brought us home to Bend.

What was the return to Bend like?

A horrible adjustment. We knew what to expect from our return after the thru-hike of the Pacific Crest Trail, but this time was even harder. We had lived for two years in a tent together and were very happy. Being house rich, but not able to afford a continued life of travel, we had decided along the ride to sell our house in Bend. Upon our return, we had to dig in and finish the remodel we had started and were not in the mental place to do so after the ride. My parents were a huge help. I remember driving to the paint store a couple weeks after our return, sitting in traffic and becoming so overwhelmed I began to sob. The amount of stress we have become accustomed to in the developed world was overwhelming. I don't think Ville or I have ever adjusted back to our lives before the ride and we hope not to. We are committed to our life of travel, to inspire others to live the path that's true to themselves and enjoy this wild ride. Our favorite quote is by Hunter S. Thompson, "Life should not be a journey to the grave with the intention of arriving safely in a pretty and well preserved body, but rather to skid in broadside in a cloud of smoke, thoroughly used up, totally worn out, and loudly proclaiming 'Wow! What a ride!'"

What was your favorite country you traveled through?

Two favorites, for different reasons. We loved Mexico because of the people. Mexicans are proud of their culture and traditions. They are not striving to be different than who they are. Positive with a great sense of humor. Kindred spirits. And Peru for the scenery and simplicity of the lifestyle of the people. They live in the present.

Did you ever want to quit?

No, but we hoped nothing happened that would force us to quit. When I had a virus, we think possibly Dengue Fever, that was the closest we came to a forced end to the ride. I was still sick and out-of-shape climbing into the Andes so it took a lot of determination and drive to keep going, but it was better than quitting.

Would you do it again?

We don't want to ride from Alaska to Argentina again, but knowing the experiences we had on the adventure keeps us curious to continue this life of adventure.

Do you want to do any more bike adventures?

In 2019, we rode from Helsinki, Finland, to Split, Croatia, through Eastern Europe (roughly 2,000 miles). Then in winter 2021-22 we biked through Andalucia in Spain. While publishing this book we rode from top (Cape Reinga) to bottom (Bluff) of New Zealand. So yes, you could say we wanted to do more bike adventures.

How do you spend all day together?

I think that is the easiest part. I enjoy being with Ville. We don't take ourselves too seriously and we enjoy our sense of humor. It makes life fun. Also, when riding we had to ride in single file most of the time, so we were alone. We spent breaks, lunch and the end of the day together.

Were you ever scared?

Yes, when we were nearly mauled by a mother bear, that was terrifying. Also, when we were unsure what the intentions were of the guys watching the tractor in Michoacan. And when Ville was attacked by dogs, I feared for his life. When I fell, I thought I was seriously injured. But those moments passed, and the joyful moments outweighed the scary ones.

What inspired you to do this ride?

Ville and I had already hiked four-and-a-half-months on the Pacific Crest Trail, and in the Northern Cascades in southern Washington with fourteen days left to Canada one of us said, "We should try traveling by bicycle. I bet we could go a lot faster than walking." In most relationships, when one partner proposes "walking a trail for five months from Mexico to Canada" the other would most likely respond with a hard "No! Are you completely mad?" Partners keep one another in check to prevent the other from sailing off the cliff of sanity. However, that voice of reason doesn't exist in either Ville or me. We are committed to living the fullest life that is possible and are willing to do anything to achieve that. And so, when this idea was presented somewhere in the wilds of Washington, there was no guardrail and we sailed right off that cliff and into the great unknown called The Next Adventure – Riding bikes from the top of the world to the bottom.

What is something you learned from this adventure?

This world is full of kind people. Generally, we are all seeking the same things, health, happiness, and the best for our families. When given the opportunity we want to help each other. Also, you get what you give. Remember, a smile goes a long way. We also discovered that those who had less, gave more. Those who had more, had more to lose and became more guarded and paranoid.

If you could have done anything differently, what would it be?
Nothing. Being on a tight budget was a blessing because it forced us to rely on others. We met and interacted with so many people while camping in yards, farms, fire stations, rodeo grounds, etc. It was the best part of the journey.

What advice would you have for someone who dreams about embarking on an adventure?
No better time than now. Don't over plan. In fact, it's best to not make a plan. The best laid plans will always change. Plus, new opportunities you hadn't known existed will present themselves along the way and if your scheduled it's hard to deviate. Without a plan, the world is your oyster. The big picture can be overwhelming, so tackle things day-by-day. Want to hike the PCT? Start with a day hike. Or even take a walk around your block. Small successes will grow to big acts of greatness.

What makes you different than someone else? In a way that would bring you to do something like hike the PCT or ride from Alaska to Argentina?
When Ville and I were riding through Los Angeles, we met this man Roberto, who waved us into a diner and bought us lunch. He told us this story of his brother, who worked in a university lab. He was studying worms. They had made the environment perfect in a large terrarium. But there was this single worm, that continually tried to escape. He said, "You guys are that worm." And I think he is right. When things become too comfortable, we want to shake things up, try something new and challenge ourselves.

Do you have any permanent damage from the ride?

Probably. My tailbone wasn't fused by the end of the ride and I've had to continually work on it. I continue to get migraines because of the damage to my spine, but I would get them if I was sitting on a couch or out on an adventure so you can guess what I'd rather be doing.

Why is it important to share your story?

We believe that for all the kindness that has been shown to us and positive things that have happened to continue, they must be shared. We owe it to the people that have done so much for us. Also, we need to see the potential to know anything is possible. I wish someone had come to my high school and shown me all these things were possible, so I want to show it to others. I hope we inspire others to walk the path that is true to themselves. Especially in an era of cell phones, internet, social media, we want to inspire kids to get outside and get active. To see the world and make friends that are different than they are. In a time that feels so divided, we need to remember, "United we stand, divided we fall."

Have you always wanted to write a book?

Absolutely not! In fact, I had no intention of writing one. Ville and I began speaking in schools during our hike of the Pacific Crest Trail and continued even after the Alaska to Argentina bike ride. It was there that everyone wanted to know more of the story. When COVID grounded all of us, it gave me the opportunity to write the book. I wrote it from Buenos Aires, Argentina, Helsinki, Finland, Portland, Oregon, and New Zealand. I thought it would take a year and it took three. I planned to shelve it and head to New Zealand to bike. My goal was to inspire others, I hope it has done that for you.

Acknowledgments

We met a lot of people in two years and 18,215 miles. This book exists due to their kindness. I'm thankful to everyone on the road who shared a smile, a meal, laughter, music, tequila, or a safe place to sleep, and to everyone else who helped make the journey possible.

I am indebted for life to my companjera, Ville, for walking and riding behind me so we will always be together and for loving me just the way I am. Kiitos Ville.

I'm grateful for my dad and mom's unrelenting support, especially when it worried them to offer it; for Lisa, who loved me even when I made her play the wicked step-mother; and for Jordan hopping on a plane and showing up when it mattered.

Thank you to everyone who heard our presentation and asked me to write the rest of the story. I am especially grateful to my friend Alison Knight for your continuing encouragement and editing help; to Chuck Johnson for digging in; to Lee Montgomery for your literary expertise outshined only by your big heart and wanting to see this story published as badly as I did; to Scott Parker, copyeditor extraordinaire; to Diane Chonette, for your thoughtful and detailed design work; to Paul Evers for stunningly accurate maps; to MontsePDX for your unrelenting support and bringing the Latina force majeure; to Cheryl Strayed, for being my trial angel and kindred soul; and to Rhonda Hughes at Hawthorne Books, for your brilliant editing, taking a chance on me, and turning a good story into a great book.

Lastly, I am deeply grateful to all my friends all over the world. There are too many to name, but you know who you are, and I'm so fortunate to have you in my life.